Footwashing in John 13 and the Johannine Community

John Christopher Thomas

Journal for the Study of the New Testament
Supplement Series 61

for
Barbara, Paige and Lori

First published by JSOT Press 1991
Reprinted 1993

Copyright © 1991, 1993 Sheffield Academic Press

Published by JSOT Press
JSOT Press is an imprint of
Sheffield Academic Press Ltd
343 Fulwood Road
Sheffield S10 3BP
England

Typeset by Sheffield Academic Press
and
Printed on acid-free paper in Great Britain
by The Cromwell Press
Melksham, Wiltshire

British Library Cataloguing in Publication Data

Thomas, J.C.
    Footwashing in John 13 and the Johannine community.
    —(JSNT supplement series. ISSN 0143-5108; v. 61)
    I. Title II. Series
    232.95

ISBN 1-85075-308-3
ISBN 1-85075-710-0 Pbk

CONTENTS

JOURNAL FOR THE STUDY OF THE NEW TESTAMENT
SUPPLEMENT SERIES
61

Executive Editor
David Hill

JSOT Press
Sheffield

PREFACE

The idea for this study was conceived in ThM studies at Princeton Theological Seminary under the supervision of Dr Bruce M. Metzger. It developed in a variety of graduate seminars at the University of Virginia and came to completion as a doctoral dissertation at the University of Sheffield.

In a research project of this nature, one becomes indebted to a number of individuals for a variety of contributions. In my case, such indebtedness is all too real and I am quite happy for the opportunity to acknowledge publicly some of those debts.

The following institutions kindly opened their libraries to me in various parts of the world: Brown University, Cambridge University, Emory University, Princeton Theological Seminary, Tyndale House (Cambridge, England), University of Sheffield, University of Tennessee, University of Tübingen, University of Virginia, and Vanderbilt University. Special mention should be made of Barbara McCullough, Reference Librarian at the William Squires Library in Cleveland, Tennessee, who with great patience and precision secured many obscure items for me through inter-library loan.

Thanks are due to Dr Robin Killman White for her encouragement and special contributions. Appreciation is also expressed to a succession of secretaries who have typed various parts of this research. They include Donna Smith, Rebecca Simms, and Jewel Frazier. Special thanks are due to David Crick for assisting in the production of the final copy of this work.

Without financial support from a number of sources, this research would not have been possible. The generosity of my late grandfather, John D. Thomas, continues to be felt long after his death. A sabbatical leave granted by the Church of God School of Theology, as well as other constant supports, have made the completion of this study possible. The extreme generosity of my good friends, William and Peggy Bridges, eased many financial burdens.

This research was greatly enhanced by the superb supervision offered by Dr Andrew T. Lincoln. His warm hospitality, generous spirit, critical eye, inexhaustible energy, and perpetual willingness to argue out many points about footwashing not only served to stimulate my own thought about John 13, but have also taught me much about the interplay between literary and historical inquiries. It is difficult to imagine a better supervisor than Andrew, and I here acknowledge my heartfelt gratitude.

Members of the Woodward Avenue Church of God in Athens, Tennessee, and my colleagues and students at the Church of God School of Theology have offered a great deal of moral and spiritual support to me during the composition of this work. My parents, Wayne and Betty Fritts, have not only contributed generously to this and many other academic pursuits, but have provided a wide range of assistance to me and my family. Their contribution has been much more than even they realize and I appreciate their investment of time, energies, and finances.

I should also like to express my thanks to Dr David Hill for his acceptance of my work into the JSNT Supplement Series and to Professor D.J.A. Clines of Sheffield Academic Press for his detailed editing of the manuscript.

Finally, the greatest debt of gratitude is owed to my wife, Barbara, and my daughters, Paige and Lori, who have made enormous sacrifices so that this research could be brought to completion. The love, commitment, and devotion of my wife has sustained me through two nine-month separations owing to my doctoral studies. Her belief in me has been a constant source of encouragement. Such support is all the more extraordinary in that she has continued her own graduate training, has begun a successful teaching career, and has provided an excellent home for our family in the midst of the demands which my own research made necessary. I offer these words here as a small token of my love and gratitude to this remarkable woman. It is my sincere desire that my daughters, who have lived with this work all their lives and have endured numerous separations from daddy because of it, will one day understand the significance of their own contributions to this project. I fear that their hardships and sacrifices have been most severely felt and I offer my apologies for the disruption of their lives that has resulted. It is only fitting that this book be dedicated to those who have sacrificed the most for its completion: Barbara, Paige and Lori.

My hope is that this investigation might contribute in a small way to a better understanding of a passage that has so often been misunderstood, and that it might make necessary a reconsideration of the place of footwashing in the Fourth Gospel and the Johannine community.

John Christopher Thomas
Church of God School of Theology
Cleveland, Tennessee
May, 1991

ABBREVIATIONS

AJA	*American Journal of Archaeology*
Ang	*Angelos*
AsSeign	*Assemblées du Seigneur*
Bib	*Biblica*
BO	*Bibliotheca orientalis*
BSac	*Bibliotheca Sacra*
BZ	*Biblische Zeitschrift*
CBQ	*Catholic Biblical Quarterly*
DNTT	*New International Dictionary of New Testament Theology*
EstBib	*Estudios Bíblicos*
EvT	*Evangelische Theologie*
ExpTim	*The Expository Times*
HTR	*Harvard Theological Review*
Int	*Interpretation*
JBL	*Journal of Biblical Literature*
JSNT	*Journal for the Study of the New Testament*
MTZ	*Münchener theologische Zeitschrift*
Neot	*Neotestamentica*
NovT	*Novum Testamentum*
NTS	*New Testament Studies*
OTP	J.H. Charlesworth, *The Old Testament Pseudepigrapha*
RB	*Revue biblique*
RevQ	*Revue de Qumran*
RSPT	*Revue des sciences philosophiques et théologiques*
RSR	*Recherches de science religieuse*
TDNT	*Theological Dictionary of the New Testament*
TQ	*Theologische Quartalschrift*
TS	*Theological Studies*
ZNW	*Zeitschrift für die neutestamentliche Wissenschaft*

Chapter 1

INTRODUCTION

Among the canonical Gospels, only the Gospel according to John contains an account of Jesus washing the feet of the disciples (Jn 13.1-20). Although this unique passage has been the subject of intense study, there is as yet no scholarly consensus about its meaning. In fact, a variety of interpretations has been given to this pericope. A brief survey of scholarship documents this diversity.

A. *Prominent Interpretations of Footwashing*

The history of the interpretation of footwashing is the subject of two German monographs produced in the last quarter century by Georg Richter[1] and Wolfram Lohse,[2] identifying no less than 11 interpretations between them in the modern era alone.[3] It is difficult to offer an entirely consistent survey of the major views of footwashing because the complex issues in the pericope seldom allow interpreters to focus on a single aspect of the passage. Despite these obstacles, a survey of the major interpretations is beneficial, for it makes clear certain dominant themes and aspects of Jn 13.1-20. Of the eleven interpretations identified by Richter and Lohse, seven are most common:

1. *Footwashing as an Example of Humility*
Of the many interpretations given to this pericope, one of the most

---

1.   G. Richter, *Die Fusswaschung im Johannesevangelium* (Regensburg: Friedrich Pustet, 1967).
2.   W. Lohse, 'Die Fusswaschung (Joh 13.1-20): Eine Geschichte ihrer Deutung' (Dissertation, Friedrich-Alexander-Universität zu Erlangen–Nürnberg, 1967).
3.   While a history of interpretation is not the purpose of this section, much of the literature pertaining to Jn 13.1-20 published since 1967 is surveyed in what follows.

prominent is the view that in the footwashing episode Jesus offers a lesson in humility to his disciples. A variety of scholars view this aspect as the dominant one in Jn 13.1-20.[1] This understanding is rather natural, for footwashing itself was the work of slaves. The servant imagery is strengthened by the description of Jesus' actions, in particular the laying aside of his clothes and girding himself with a towel. The humble action of Jesus fits well with the instructions in vv. 13-17 which command the disciples to perform this task for one another. The servant motif is explicit in v. 16. In addition, Luke's account of the Last Supper, which includes a dispute about greatness (22.24-30), has been assessed by many commentators as providing independent evidence that the footwashing is a parabolic demonstration of humility. However, while most agree that humility is an important emphasis, it is often viewed as subordinate to other issues.

1.   Cf. the following works: F. Tillmann, *Das Johannesevangelium* (Bonn: Hanstein, 1931), pp. 246-53; A. Durand, *Evangile selon Saint Jean* (Paris: Beauchesne, 1927), pp. 360-62; M.J. Lagrange, *Evangile selon Saint Jean* (Paris: Gabalda 1936), pp. 348-59; P. Jouon, *L'Evangile de Notre Seigneur Jésus-Christ* (Paris: Gabalda, 1930), p. 544; J. Huby, *Le discours de Jésus après la cène suivi d'une étude sur la connaissance de foi dans saint Jean* (Paris: Beauchesne, 1951), pp. 140-41; E. Schick, *Das Evangelium nach Johannes* (Würzburg: Echterverlag, 1967), pp. 127-30; J. Michl, 'Der Sinn der Fusswaschung', *Bib* 40 (1959), pp. 697-708; G.-M. Behler, *Les paroles d'adieux du Seigneur* (Paris: Cerf, 1960), pp. 17-43; P. Benoit, 'Die eucharistischen Einsetzungsberichte und ihre Bedeutung', in *Exegese und Theologie: Gesammelte Aufsätze* (Düsseldorf: Patmos, 1965), p. 90; H. Windisch, *Johannes und die Synoptiker* (Leipzig: J.C. Hinrichs, 1926), p. 77; J.H. Bernard, *A Critical and Exegetical Commentary on the Gospel according to John* (Edinburgh: T. & T. Clark, 1928), II, p. 454-69; K. Bornhäuser, *Das Johannes evangelium eine Missionschrift für Israel* (Gütersloh: C. Bertelsmann, 1928), pp. 78-79; P. Fiebig, 'Die Fusswaschung', *Ang* 3 (1930), pp. 126-28; W.F. Howard, *Christianity according to St John* (London: Duckworth, 1958), pp. 137, 140, 179; R.A. Edwards, *The Gospel according to John: Its Criticism and Interpretation* (London: Eyre & Spottiswoode, 1954), pp. 103-104; W. Michaelis, *Die Sakramente im Johannesevangelium* (Bern: BEG, 1946), p. 32; W. Stählin, *Das johanneische Denken: Eine Einführung in die Eigenart des vierten Evangeliums* (Witten: Luther, 1954), pp. 32, 41; B.H. Streeter, *The Four Gospels: A Study of Origins* (London: Macmillan, 1961), p. 423. Cf. also C.K. Barrett, *The Gospel according to St. John* (Philadelphia: Westminster Press, 1978), p. 437; B. Zweifel, 'Jésus lave les pieds de ses disciples', Thesis, Lausanne University (1965), p. 158; and J. Owanga-Welo, 'The Function and Meaning of the Johannine Passion Narrative: a Structural Approach', Dissertation, Emory University (1980), p. 255.

2. *Footwashing as a Symbol of the Eucharist*

As unlikely as this identification may seem initially, several scholars have seen in the footwashing a reference to the eucharist.[1] One of the primary pieces of evidence that is claimed for this understanding is the pericope's context or setting. Since Jesus' actions in John take the place of the institution of the eucharist as recorded in the Synoptics, it is often assumed that the author of the Fourth Gospel is drawing attention to a connection between the two stories. It is further asserted that since John alludes to the eucharist through specific events in Jesus' life (for example, in the miracle at Cana and the bread of life discourse) it is natural to assume that the footwashing is also an allusion to the eucharist. The commands given by Jesus to continue the practice of footwashing are similar to the commands to repeat the eucharist (1 Cor. 11.23-26). More specifically, according to this interpretation, v. 10 states that the one who has been 'baptized' may continue to receive forgiveness of sin by participation in the eucharist.

3. *Footwashing as a Symbol of Baptism*

Footwashing is closely associated with water baptism in the minds of many scholars.[2] This interpretation is based on several points in Jn

---

1.   Cf. the following works: W. Bauer, *Das Johannesevangelium* (Tübingen: J.C.B. Mohr, 1912), p. 130; G.H.C. MacGregor, *The Gospel of John* (London: Harper, 1959), pp. 272-76 and 'The Eucharist in the Fourth Gospel', *NTS* 9 (1963), pp. 112-14; H. Strathmann, *Das Evangelium nach Johannes* (Göttingen: Vandenhoeck & Ruprecht, 1959), pp. 194-99; O. Cullmann, *Early Christian Worship* (trans. A.S. Todd and J.B. Torrance; London: SCM, 1953), pp. 107-10; W. Wilkens, *Die Entstehungsgeschichte des vierten Evangeliums* (Zöllikon: Evangelischer Verlag, 1958), p. 151; A.J.B. Higgins, *The Lord's Supper in the New Testament* (London: SCM, 1952), pp. 84-85; W. Grundmann, *Zeugnis und Gestalt des Johannesevangelium* (Stuttgart: Calwer Verlag, 1961), pp. 66-67; W.E. Moore, 'One Baptism', *NTS* 10 (1964), pp. 507-508; C.F.D. Moule, 'The Judgment Theme in the Sacraments', in *The Background of the New Testament and its Eschatology* (ed. W.D. Davies and D. Daube; Cambridge: Cambridge University Press, 1964), pp. 475-76; Zweifel, p. 159; Arthur Maynard, 'The Role of Peter in the Fourth Gospel', *NTS* 30 (1984), pp. 534-35; *idem*, 'The Function of Apparent Synonyms and Ambiguous Words in the Fourth Gospel', Dissertation, University of Southern California (1950), pp. 329-30; J. Goettmann, *Saint Jean* (Paris: Cerf, 1982), pp. 189-90; J.N. Suggit, 'John 13.1-30: The Mystery of the Incarnation and of the Eucharist', *Neot* 19 (1985), pp. 64-70.

2.   Cf. the following works: E. von Dobschütz, 'Zum Charakter des 4. Evan-

13.1-20. Most of the arguments offered in favor of this view stress the occurrence of λελουμένος in 13.10. Since the verb λούω conveys the idea of a complete bath, as in baptism, and since there is some evidence in the New Testament that λούω serves as a synonym for βαπτίζω, several interpreters take λελουμένος to be a direct reference to baptism. This interpretation of λελουμένος is not restricted to a single understanding of baptism, since baptism is assigned a variety of meanings by the different interpreters. Such an interpretation is strengthened by the emphatic language of Jesus in v. 8, where Peter is told that his part with Jesus will be forfeited if the washing is not administered, and the declaration in v. 10 that the disciples are clean as a result of the washing. Ordinarily, this view presupposes the omission of the variant εἰ μὴ τοὺς πόδας in v. 10. As a result, a direct correlation is then drawn between the footwashing and λελουμένος. Baptism imagery proves to be so appealing that a number of scholars find at least a secondary allusion to baptism in the pericope.

4. *Footwashing and the Forgiveness of Sin and/or Cleansing*

The idea that footwashing serves as a symbol of cleansing from sin is another interpretation of Jn 13.1-20 which has received a good deal of attention.[1] Many of the scholars who take this view distinguish be-

geliums', *ZNW* 28 (1929), p. 166; H. von Campenhausen, 'Zur Auslegung von Joh 13, 6-10', *ZNW* 33 (1934), pp. 259-71; C.T. Craig, 'Sacramental Interest in the Fourth Gospel', *JBL* 58 (1939), pp. 36-37; M. Werner, *The Formation of Christian Dogma* (trans. S.G.F. Brandon; London: A. & C. Black, 1957), pp. 180-81; F. Hauck, 'νίπτω', *TDNT*, IV (ed. G. Kittel and G. Friedrich; trans. G.W. Bromiley; Grand Rapids: Eerdmans, 1974), p. 947; R.H. Lightfoot, *St. John's Gospel* (Oxford: Oxford University Press, 1960), pp. 261-63; M.-E. Boismard, 'Le lavement des pieds' (Jn, XIII, 1-17)', *RB* 71 (1964), pp. 5-24; W.F. Howard, *The Fourth Gospel in Recent Criticism and Interpretation* (London: Epworth, 1955), p. 204; H. Windisch, *Taufe und Sünde im ältesten Christentum bis auf Origenes* (Tübingen: Mohr–Siebeck, 1908), pp. 275-77; Barrett, p. 436; and Brown, *The Gospel according to John* (Garden City, NY: Doubleday, 1966–70), II, pp. 566-68.

1.   Cf. the following works: E.W. Hengstenberg, *The Gospel of St John,* (Edinburgh: T. & T. Clark, 1865), II, pp. 146-50; F. Godet, *Commentary on the Gospel of John* (trans. T. Dwight; New York: Funk & Wagnalls, 1888), III, pp. 94-100; F. Spitta, *Das Johannes-Evangelium als Quelle der Geschichte Jesu* (Göttingen: Vandenhoeck & Ruprecht, 1910), pp. 285-96; J. Grill, *Untersuchungen über die Entstehung des vierten Evangeliums* (Tübingen: Mohr–Siebeck, 1923), II, pp. 140-41; T. Zahn, *Das Evangelium des Johannes* (Leipzig: Deichert, 1921),

tween baptism and footwashing, concluding that cleansing and/or forgiveness in addition to baptism was needed. Such explanations attribute to footwashing the removal of post-baptismal sin, the sins due to the frailty of the human condition, as well as errors committed daily by the disciples. Footwashing is also seen by some as a preparation for the reception of the eucharist. While cleansing and/or forgiveness is conveyed, the footwashing is but a symbol for the real cleansing agent, the blood of Christ. These interpretations are similar to one another in that they take v. 8 to signify the soteriological dimension of the footwashing. Also, the declaration that the disciples are clean (v. 10) is understood as documenting the efficacious nature of the footwashing.

5. *Footwashing as a Sacrament Separate from Baptism and Eucharist*
In addition to the interpretations which emphasize the relationship of footwashing to the eucharist and baptism, other sacramental possibilities have been advocated. For example, (a) footwashing is seen as a reference to the sacrament of penance which is instrumental in the removal of post-baptismal sin,[1] (b) footwashing has been identified as a new sacrament,[2] (c) as an ordination rite, the footwashing is said to have established the disciples as priests in Jesus' eschatological service. The footwashing prepares the disciples to serve at the Lord's table

pp. 522-35; E. Hirsch, *Das vierte Evangelium* (Tübingen: Mohr–Siebeck, 1936), pp. 330-37; A. Oepke, 'λούω', *TDNT*, IV, pp. 295-307; W. Koch, 'Zur Einsetzung des Busssakraments', *ThQ* 130 (1950), pp. 297-98; Barrett, p. 436; Zweifel, pp. 158-59; J.D.G. Dunn, 'The Washing of the Disciples' Feet in John 13.1-20', *ZNW* 61 (1970), pp. 247-52; Owanga-Welo, p. 255; H. Weiss, 'Footwashing in the Johannine Community', *NovT* 21 (1979), pp. 298-325; and G. Beasley-Murray, *John* (Waco: Word, 1987), p. 234.

1. Cf. the following works: B.W. Koch, p. 194; F. Mussner, 'Die Fusswaschung (Joh 13.1-17): Versuch einer Deutung', *Geist und Leben* 31 (1958), p. 28; A. Corell, *Consummatum est: Eschatology and Church in the Gospel of St John* (London: SPCK, 1958), p. 72; J. Sickenberger, *Leben Jesu nach den vier Evangelien: Kurzgefasste Erklärung* (Münster: Aschendorff, 1932), VI, pp. 66-69; and V. Warnach, *Agape: Die Liebe als Grundmotiv der neutestamentlichen Theologie* (Düsseldorf: Patmos, 1951), pp. 156-57.

2. B.W. Bacon, 'The Sacrament of Footwashing', *ExpTim* 43 (1931–32), pp. 218-21.

This symbol of preparation was a once and for all act done for the twelve.[1]

6. *Footwashing as Soteriological Sign*

The connection between footwashing and Jesus' death on the cross is such an important dimension of the pericope that many scholars emphasize that relationship.[2] Certain interpreters claim this theme to be the primary emphasis of the passage. The essential nature of the washing (v. 8), its cleansing effects, the centrality of the cross in John, the emphasis upon Jesus' love, and the pericope's setting at the

1.   E. Lohmeyer, 'Die Fusswaschung', *ZNW* 38 (1939), pp. 74-94.

2.   Cf. the following works: F.M. Braun, 'Le lavement des pieds et la réponse de Jésus à saint Pierre (Jean XIII, 4-10)', *RB* 44 (1935), pp. 22-33; E.C. Hoskyns, *The Fourth Gospel* (ed. F.M. Davey; London: Faber & Faber, 1956), pp. 436-42; R. Bultmann, *The Gospel of John* (trans. G.R. Beasley-Murray, Philadelphia: Westminster Press, 1971), pp. 461-79; P.H. Menoud, *L'Evangile de Jean d'après les recherches récentes* (Paris: Delachaux et Niestlé, 1943), pp. 47-50; K. Kundsin, 'Die Wiederkunft Jesu in den Abschiedsreden des Johannesevangeliums', *ZNW* 33 (1934), p. 211; E. Stauffer, *New Testament Theology* (trans. J. Marsh; London: SCM Press, 1955), p. 151; D. Mollat, *L'Evangile de Saint Jean* (Paris: Cerf, 1960), p. 149; R.V.G. Tasker, *The Gospel according to St John* (Grand Rapids: Eerdmans, 1965), pp. 154-56; J.C. Fenton, *The Passion according to John* (London: SPCK, 1961), p. 26; A.M. Hunter, *According to John* (London: SCM Press, 1968), pp. 87-88; V. Taylor, *Jesus and his Sacrifice* (London: Macmillan, 1959), pp. 221-25; F. Büchsel, *Das Evangelium nach Johannes* (Göttingen: Vandenhoeck & Ruprecht, 1946), p. 142; R.H. Strachan, *The Fourth Gospel* (London: SCM Press, 1960), pp. 266-67; W. Thüsing, *Die Erhöhung und Verherrlichung Jesu im Johannesevangelium* (Münster: Aschendorff, 1960), pp. 132-35, 235; H. van den Bussche, *L'Evangile du Verbe* (Brüssel: Pensée Catholique, 1961), II, p. 71; J.A.T. Robinson, 'The Significance of the Foot-Washing', in *Neotestamentica et Patristica* (Festgabe for Oscar Cullmann; ed. A.N. Wilder *et al.*; Leiden: E.J. Brill, 1962), pp. 144-47; A. Wikenhauser, *Das Evangelium nach Johannes* (Regensburg: Pustet, 1957), pp. 248-53; E. Schick, *Das Evangelium nach Johannes* (Würzburg: Echterverlag, 1956), p. 124; O.S. Brooks, 'The Johannine Eucharist: Another Interpretation', *JBL* 82 (1963), pp. 298-99; Barrett, p. 436; Zweifel, pp. 158-59; A. Feuillet, *Johannine Studies* (trans. T.E. Crane; New York: Alba House, 1965), p. 127; Richter, pp. 281-300; Brown, II, p. 562; R. Schnackenburg, *The Gospel according to St John* (trans. David Smith and G.A. Kon; New York: Crossroad, 1987), III, pp. 19-23; F.F. Segovia, 'John 13.1-20, The Footwashing in the Johannine Tradition', *ZNW* 73 (1982), pp. 31-51; E. Haenchen, *John* (trans. R. W. Funk; ed. R.W. Funk with U. Busse; Philadelphia: Fortress Press, 1984), II, pp. 108-109; and Beasley-Murray, p. 234.

beginning of the Book of Glory have all been claimed to support this identification. In this view the footwashing symbolizes the cleansing which takes place through the sacrificial death of Jesus.

7. *Footwashing as Polemic*

Despite the many interpretations which make some connection between footwashing and the sacraments or forgiveness of sin, the pericope has sometimes been interpreted as a polemic against baptism[1] or ritual purification.[2] The former conclusion is based upon the way in which footwashing appears to replace baptism in the pericope. Peter is told that footwashing is all important (v. 8) and that it cleanses (v. 10). The latter view is grounded in Peter's proposal that his hands and head be washed in addition to the feet. Jesus' response (v. 10) makes explicit that ritual washings of the kind Peter proposes are unnecessary; only the footwashing is needed.

8. *Conclusion*

In bringing this survey of the major interpretations of footwashing to a close, a concluding observation should be made. Though it is obvious that some of the views are mutually exclusive (e.g. footwashing as a symbol of baptism and footwashing as a polemic against baptism), most of these views are based upon themes found in the pericope. Despite the diverse emphases of various scholars, many of their basic insights are valid. A balanced understanding of the passage will do justice to any valid observations to be found in the preceding interpretations.

B. *Statement of Purpose and Method*

Many previous studies on Jn 13.1-20 have contributed to a better understanding of the pericope, but frequently they have not succeeded in holding together the individual elements of the footwashing passage, and further, some of these specific aspects have not received enough

---

1. J. Kreyenbühl, *Das Evangelium der Wahrheit* (Berlin: C.A. Schwetschke und Sohn, 1905), II, pp. 100-19.
2. A. Fridrichsen, 'Bemerkungen zur Fusswaschung', *ZNW* 38 (1939), pp. 94-96 and O. Betz, 'Die Proselytentaufe der Qumransekte und die Taufe im NT', *RevQ* 1 (1958), pp. 213-324.

attention. On some occasions the evidence has been reconstructed in an unsatisfactory fashion.

This study seeks to offer an interpretation of Jn 13.1-20 which addresses the pertinent critical issues of the pericope and which offers a new exegetical treatment based upon the incorporation of appropriate literary, philological, grammatical, and theological data. Two questions in particular provide the focus for this investigation. The first question centers upon literary and exegetical issues. What is the place and role of the footwashing pericope in the Fourth Gospel? The second question is historical in nature. What can be deduced about the actual meaning and function of footwashing in the Johannine community?

The method of this study is to re-examine each element of the footwashing pericope to ensure that no portion is ignored. Building upon these examinations, a literary and exegetical analysis is offered to account for the various and complex dimensions of Jn 13.1-20. Finally, the implications of this analysis for reconstructing part of the thought and practice of the Johannine community are explored.

Chapter 2

ESTABLISHMENT OF THE TEXT

Part of any literary analysis is the establishment of the text under examination. The text-critical problem of whether to include or omit the phrase εἰ μὴ τοὺς πόδας in 13.10 affects the interpretation of the entire passage and must be resolved at the outset. The United Bible Societies Greek New Testament identifies seven variants in this verse.

1. οὐκ ἔχει χρείαν εἰ μὴ τοὺς πόδας νίψασθαι BC* W Ψ arm Origen Augustine.

2. οὐ χρείαν ἔχει εἰ μὴ τοὺς πόδας νίψασθαι (K ἢ μή) L Π f¹³ 892 1071 1079 1216 1230 1546 1646 1⁵⁴⁷ syr^{h,pal}

3. οὐκ ἔχει χρείαν (or οὐ χρείαν ἔχει) εἰ μὴ τοὺς πόδας νίψασθαι it ^{a,b,e,f,ff21, q, p} vg^{cl,} cop^{sa,bo,ach2}

4. οὐ χρείαν ἔχει ἢ τοὺς πόδας νίψασθαι C³ E* Δ (A 1241 ἔχει χρείαν) f¹ 28 700 1009 1010 1195 (1242* omit ἢ) 1242^c 1344 1365 2148 2174 Byz Lect Cyril

5. οὐ χρείαν ἔχει εἰ μὴ τοὺς πόδας μόνον νίψασθαι (𝔓⁶⁶ οὐκ ἔχει χρείαν) Θ syr^{s,p} cop^{bom} geo (Chrysostom)

6. οὐκ ἔχει χρείαν νίψασθαι ℵ it^{aur,c} vg^{ww} Tertullian Origen

7. οὐ χρείαν ἔχει τὴν κεφαλὴν νίψασθαι εἰ μὴ τοὺς πόδας μόνον (see 13.9) D it^d

One thing is immediately obvious: the seven variants can be reduced to two basic readings. Readings 1, 2, 3, 4, 5 and 7 have essentially the same sense, while reading 6 offers a truly different meaning. The basic question then is whether εἰ μὴ τοὺς πόδας should be included or omitted. It is sometimes suggested that the diversity of readings which include the phrase εἰ μὴ τοὺς πόδας is a sign that the phrase is secondary. Barnabas Lindars notes:

The variants in other MSS betray uncertainty. The textual evidence thus
suggests that they are not original, but have been added in an attempt to
clarify the sense.[1]

However, such a view fails to appreciate the complexity of the evidence. On the one hand, despite their disagreements, each of the witnesses for readings 1, 2, 3, 4, 5 and 7 contains the words εἰ μὴ τοὺς πόδας. On the other hand, the kinds of variants attested in these witnesses are just the sorts of modification one might expect to appear if the phrase were original.

It is one of the basic rules of textual criticism that the shorter reading is to be preferred. In this case the shorter reading is variant 6, οὐκ ἔχει χρείαν νίψασθαι. The external evidence for this reading is relatively early and has good distribution. ℵ (fourth century) is an Alexandrian witness. Tertullian (third century), it^aur (seventh century), it^c (twelfth century) and vg^ww (fourth century) represent the Western family of witnesses. The Caesarean family is represented by Origen (third century). Even though the witnesses are early and widely distributed, the evidence as a whole is somewhat scanty.

Thus, a number of commentators have looked for internal support of the shorter reading. Several such considerations have been proposed for preferring the omission of εἰ μὴ τοὺς πόδας. Basically, they all are tied to the thesis that the footwashing prefigures the complete cleansing (v. 10) accomplished in Jesus' sacrificial death. This thesis is supported by a number of observations.

From the conviction that John must be speaking of only one washing several deductions are made. The stern language of v. 8b ('Εὰν μὴ νίψω σε, οὐκ ἔχεις μέρος μετ' ἐμοῦ) indicates that the footwashing is no trivial event. Several scholars argue that if λελουμένος refers to a previous washing and not to the footwashing, then the latter becomes trivial. Hoskyns and Davey conclude:

> If the longer reading be regarded as the original, the reference might be to the need of comparatively trivial washing, represented here by the washing of the feet only, after the complete purging of baptism. . . But the action of Jesus here is not even comparatively trivial.[2]

Dunn concurs: 'By referring to an earlier bathing the significance of

---

1. B. Lindars, *The Gospel of John* (London: Oliphants, 1972), p. 451.
2. Hoskyns and Davey, p. 439.

the footwashing is lost—as though there could be an earlier, more effective cleansing than that accomplished by Christ's redemptive action on the cross'.[1] Barrett suggests that even John's employment of the two verbs λούεσθαι and νίπτεσθαι as synonyms for cleansing points toward this interpretation. Consequently, the longer reading could owe its origin to nondiscerning scribes who saw a difference between the verbs.[2]

The suggestion that λελουμένος refers to the footwashing may be supported on form critical grounds as well. Bultmann labels the saying in v. 10 as a parabolic saying which would mean, 'Just as the man who has had a bath needs no further washing, but is completely clean. . . so too the man who has received fellowship with me through the footwashing, needs no further cleansing'.[3] Lindars agrees with this assessment and adds that v. 10 is not a direct reply to Peter's statement (v. 9).[4] This parabolic saying would suggest that the shorter reading is original.

Another rule of textual criticism states that the reading which best explains the origin of the other readings is probably original. Lohse follows this rule and concludes:

> One would do well to render a judgment according to internal probability and to ask which type of reading will explain the origin of the other. Here, together with external reasons, everything speaks against the long text. There is absolutely no reason why εἰ μὴ τοὺς πόδας should be missing. But it is easy to understand how so many different forms of an expanded v. 10 came about. One felt the short text presented a difficulty in thought and added an interpretive expansion to solve the difficulty.[5]

Most scholars who accept the shorter reading would suggest that the longer reading originated 'when the original meaning of the narrative was misunderstood'.[6] Brown offers the best summation of this view.

> The most plausible explanation is that a scribe, faced with the statement, 'The man who has bathed has no need to wash', and not recognizing that the bath was the footwashing, thought that he had to insert an exceptive

---

1. Dunn, p. 251. Cf. also Barrett, p. 441 and Bultmann, p. 470.
2. Barrett, pp. 441-42. Cf. also Lindars, p. 451.
3. Bultmann, p. 470
4. Lindars, p. 451.
5. Lohse, I, p. 8.
6. Hoskyns and Davey, p. 439.

phrase to show that Jesus did not mean to exclude the footwashing when
he said there was no need to wash.[1]

Therefore, in spite of its scanty external support, many scholars defend the shorter reading on the basis of internal considerations.[2]

Such arguments in favor of the shorter reading have some force, but they are not decisive. Rather than assuming that variations in the longer reading suffice to show its secondary character, it is necessary to explore these variations carefully before reaching a conclusion about the genuineness of εἰ μὴ τοὺς πόδας. For example, some witnesses (readings 2, 4, 5 and 7) have οὐ χρείαν ἔχει rather than οὐκ ἔχει χρείαν. However, this small difference in word order should not be overly valued. Several reasons can explain such a change. It may be that the words were transposed for the sake of euphony.[3] This is possible, but it is difficult to determine whether οὐ χρείαν ἔχει would really sound better than οὐκ ἔχει χρείαν. A better suggestion is that the change was made for the sake of emphasis.[4] By placing χρείαν in a more prominent position, a scribe may have wished to underscore its importance. (Then the negative οὐκ, which is appropriate before the vowel of ἔχει, changes form to οὐ, since it is now followed by the initial consonant of χρείαν.) The transposition may also be simply a transcriptional error of the mind, whereby the scribe saw οὐκ ἔχει χρείαν but inadvertently wrote οὐ χρείαν ἔχει. Whatever the actual explanation, only the verb and noun are transposed; the negative merely conforms to its following vowel or consonant. Bruce M. Metzger notes, 'Variations in the sequence of words is a common phenomenon...'[5] Since this same kind of alteration appears in a variety of places in the New Testament, it should not seem strange that it happens here as well.

That οὐκ is original is also supported by the fact that οὐ is found in

1.   Brown, *The Gospel according to John*, II, pp. 567-68.

2.   Cf. also R.V.G. Tasker, *The Gospel according to St John* (Grand Rapids: Eerdmans, 1960), pp. 157-58 and J. Marsh, *The Gospel of St John* (London: Penguin Books, 1968), pp. 489-90.

3.   B.M. Metzger, *A Textual Commentary on the Greek New Testament* (United Bible Societies, 1971), p. 240.

4.   This possibility was suggested by B.M. Metzger in conversation with the author.

5.   B.M. Metzger, *The Text of the New Testament* (New York: Oxford University Press, 1968), p. 193.

no Greek witness until the sixth century. It appears that D is the first
Greek manuscript to give this reading, joined by the third corrector
of C. It is natural that the rest of the witnesses supporting οὐ are Caesarean and Byzantine, for Caesarean witnesses generally preserve a
'distinctive mixture of Western readings and Alexandrian readings',[1]
and the Byzantine text is generally characterized by its lucidity and
completeness.

The other variations are relatively minor. μόνον has been inserted
between πόδας and νίψασθαι in a few witnesses. More than likely
this specification is due to 'the influence of the preceding verse'.[2] D
expands the verse by adding τὴν κεφαλήν and μόνον. Alterations of
this nature are not uncharacteristic of D. The substitution of ἥ for εἰ
μή might best be understood 'as though the evangelist had written
something like οὐκ ἄλλου τινὸς χρείαν ἔχει.'[3] This reading is found
almost exclusively in Caesarean and Byzantine texts. Since the differences among the attested longer readings are small and do not
significantly change the meaning of the phrase, it is legitimate to take
these together in support of εἰ μὴ τοὺς πόδας. With this in mind, the
major issue may now be considered.

The great preponderance of witnesses favor the inclusion of εἰ μὴ
τοὺς πόδας. This reading has the support of the Proto-Alexandrian
𝔓[66] (second/third century), B (fourth century) and cop[sa] (third century). Alexandrian witnesses include: C[*,3] (fifth century), W (fifth
century), and cop[bo] (fourth century). The Western support is strong
and early as well. The witnesses range from D (sixth century) to the
versions syr[s] (second/third century), it[a] (fourth century), it[b,c,d,e] (fifth
century). The Byzantine family is represented by A (fifth century) and
E[*] (sixth century). The Caesarean tradition includes: arm (fourth/fifth
century), geo (fifth century), Origen (third century), along with some
later witnesses. Thus, the support for the inclusion of εἰ μὴ τοὺς πόδας is strong, early, well-distributed and includes a number of different kinds of witnesses. If a decision were to be made on the basis of
external evidence alone, a verdict would have to be rendered in favor
of the longer reading.

However, several internal considerations must also be taken into ac-

---

1. Metzger, *The Text of the New Testament*, p. 215.
2. Metzger, *A Textual Commentary on the Greek New Testament*, p. 240.
3. *Ibid.*

count. Owanga-Welo argues that when 13.10 is identified as parabolic, it supports the longer reading. Against Bultmann, he cites a 'proverbial' phrase in Seneca (*Epistulae Morales*, 86.12) which mentions complete bathing and partial washing together.

> Friend, if you were wiser, you would know that Scipio did not bathe everyday. It is stated by those who have reported to us the old-time ways of Rome that the Romans washed only their arms and legs daily—because those were the members which gathered dirt in the daily toil—and bathed all over only once a week.[1]

This example, he says, demonstrates the proverbial character of v. 10 and supports the inclusion of εἰ μὴ τοὺς πόδας.[2] If the text cited by Owanga-Welo is not quite proverbial, it is nonetheless apparent that Seneca is describing the Roman practices by use of 'traditional materials'. Barrett's argument that λούω and νίπτω are used as synonyms is at best a guess and goes against philological evidence.[3] Also, the view that a previous washing (λελουμένος, v. 10) makes additional washing superfluous is not compelling.[4]

If, then, there are no sound reasons to reject the longer reading, it is necessary to explain the origin of the shorter reading. Two suggestions are quite plausible. The omission may be the result of 'the difficulty of reconciling εἰ μὴ τοὺς πόδας with the words ἀλλ' ἔστιν καθαρὸς ὅλος which follow'.[5] On the other hand, the omission may simply be the result of a mistake,[6] possibly homoioteleuton. If either of these suggestions is correct then all objections to the longer reading can be answered satisfactorily.

Finally, in terms of the internal coherence of the passage the longer reading makes better sense. As Robinson notes:

---

1. Cited according to the translation of R.M. Gummerie, *Seneca ad Lucilium Epistulae Morales* (London: William Heinemann, 1920), II, p. 317.
2. Owanga-Welo, p. 241. According to Owanga-Welo, since Bultmann assumes the shorter reading he is only partially correct in identifying v. 10 as parabolic.
3. The philological evidence will be fully discussed in Chapter 4 below.
4. Cullmann (p. 109) can argue on internal grounds for the inclusion of εἰ μὴ τοὺς πόδας. In his view, v. 10 refers to the continual cleansing of the eucharist.
5. Bernard, p. 462. Cf. also Metzger, *A Textual Commentary on the Greek New Testament*, p. 240.
6. Robinson, p. 146 n. 1. Cf. also Bernard, p. 462 and Metzger, *A Textual Commentary on the Greek New Testament*, p. 240.

If τοὺς πόδας alone were missing, it would make sense to say that 'he who has had a bath only needs to wash', but to say that 'he has no need to wash' cannot be squared with Jesus' insistence on the absolute necessity of the washing (v. 8).[1]

Consequently, on the basis of early and well distributed external support and convincing internal considerations the text which includes εἰ μὴ τοὺς πόδας may be accepted as original.[2]

On this longer reading the disciples (and through them the readers) are told that since they have bathed, they have no need to wash except the feet, that is, their bath needs only to be supplemented by footwashing.

1.   Robinson, p. 230.
2.   This is also in accord with the conclusions of F.F. Segovia (p. 44), who offers three reasons for favoring the longer reading: 'a. The external attestation is much superior; b. The reading can be satisfactorily explained in the context of the Gospel narrative; c. The shorter reading can be readily explained as an attempt to smooth out what could be construed as an irreconcilable clash with the following.' Other scholars who support the longer reading are J.N. Sanders, *A Commentary on the Gospel according to St John* (ed. B.A. Mastin; London: A. & C. Black, 1968), p. 308; L. Morris, *The Gospel according to John* (Grand Rapids: Eerdmans, 1971), p. 618; Haenchen, II, p. 108; F.F. Bruce, *The Gospel of John* (Grand Rapids: Eerdmans, 1983), pp. 282-83 and D.A. Carson, *The Gospel of John* (Grand Rapids: Eerdmans, 1990), pp. 464-66.

Chapter 3

FOOTWASHING IN THE JEWISH
AND GRAECO-ROMAN ENVIRONMENT

One contention of this study is that Jn 13.1-20 is correctly understood
only when one reads it in light of all the evidence of footwashing
practices in the ancient world. Yet, exegetes of John 13 have given
surprisingly little attention to Jewish and Graeco-Roman texts which
speak of footwashing.[1] The survey to be presented in this chapter is
distinct from previous studies in several ways. First, it is more comprehensive than those works which concentrate on John 13. Second,
the primary texts are cited with sufficient context provided for interpretation. Third, the results of this survey are brought to bear upon
the interpretation of footwashing in John 13. This chapter is concerned with identifying (a) the circumstances in which footwashing
occurs, (b) the motive and purpose which prompts the footwashing,
and (c) the individuals who normally perform or receive the act. With
such information as background, the Johannine pericope can be understood more fully.

1. The majority of commentators either assume the significance of footwashing
without documentation or supply one or two examples of its function. Even those
scholars who identify the importance of such an investigation do not follow through
with a comprehensive study. Hultgren ('The Johannine Footwashing (13.1-11) as
Symbol of Eschatological Hospitality', *NTS* 28 [1982], p. 541) laments, 'None (of
the previous studies on footwashing) is informed by a study of the general
significance of footwashing in the ancient world prior to exploring the question of
meaning within the Johannine context'. Yet his own survey is quite limited, particularly in Graeco-Roman parallels, and seldom gives citations of the examples. Lohse
(I, pp. 9-15) offers a more extensive collection of parallels but supplies few of the
primary texts. The major exception is the excellent article by B. Kötting,
'Fusswaschung', *Reallexikon für Antike und Christentum* (ed. T. Klauser; Stuttgart:
Hierseman, 1950–), VIII, pp. 743-59. However, Kötting does not give full citations
of the texts under discussion, nor does he make appropriate application of these
materials to John 13.

A. *Footwashing in the Old Testament and Early Judaism*[1]

There are at least three situations in which footwashing is observed: (1) cultic settings, (2) domestic settings for personal hygiene and comfort, and (3) domestic settings devoted to hospitality. Passages appropriate to each category are examined with special emphasis given to the identity of those who wash feet, those whose feet are washed, and the purpose of the footwashing. A final section is devoted to footwashing and servitude.

1. *Cultic Settings*

According to the Torah, the priests are required to wash their hands and feet before entering the holy place of the tabernacle to offer sacrifice upon the altar. Exod. 30.17-21 depicts Moses as receiving these commands:

> [17]Then the Lord said to Moses, [18]'Make a bronze basin, with its bronze stand, for washing. Place it between the Tent of Meeting and the altar, and put water in it. [19]Aaron and his sons are to wash their hands and feet with water from it. [20]Whenever they enter the Tent of Meeting, they shall wash with water so that they will not die. Also, when they approach the altar to minister by presenting an offering made to the Lord by fire, [21]they shall wash their hands and feet so that they will not die. This is to be a lasting ordinance for Aaron and his descendants for the generations to come'.[2]

Exod. 40.30-32 describes the carrying out of these instructions:

> [30]He placed the basin between the Tent of Meeting and the altar and put water in it for washing, [31]and Moses and Aaron and his sons used it to wash their hands and feet. [32]They washed whenever they entered the Tent of Meeting or approached the altar, as the Lord commanded Moses.[3]

Similar, although more elaborate, provisions for this washing are made in the Solomonic Temple. Both 1 Kgs 7.38 and 2 Chron. 4.6 mention ten lavers as well as 'the sea' (הים) in which the priests were to wash. Josephus (*Ant.* 8.87) confirms that a sea was available for the priests:

---

1.   The date of these materials ranges from early biblical texts to the earliest layer of mishnaic tradition.

2.   All biblical quotations in this chapter are taken from *The Holy Bible, New International Version* (Grand Rapids: Zondervan, 1978) unless designated otherwise.

3.   These verses, present in the Hebrew Text, are missing in the Septuagint.

> And having filled the sea with water, he set it apart for the priests to wash (νίπτειν) their hands and feet in when they entered the temple and were about to go up to the altar. . . [1]

This practice continues, at least in theory, until the time of Mishnah. *Yoma* (3.2-4, 6; 4.5; 7.3) documents that the High Priest is expected to wash his hands and feet on the Day of Atonement. In addition, a meal offering could be rendered invalid if offered by a priest who had not washed his hands and feet (cf. *Men.* 1.2).

The purpose of these repeatable washings is connected to one aspect of the consecration the priests were to undergo. Each priest's consecration included being bathed in water.[2] The precedent for this practice is found in Exod. 29.4, where Moses is instructed concerning the matter, and in Lev. 8.6, where the instructions are said to be carried out.

> Then Moses brought Aaron and his sons forward and washed (ἔλουσεν) them in water.

This action takes place at the entrance of the sanctuary to prepare the priests for entry. Such washing consecrates them for their sacred tasks.[3] As Keil and Delitzsch explain:

---

1.   Cited according to the translation of H.St J. Thackeray and R. Marcus, *Josephus: Jewish Antiquities* (Cambridge, MA: Harvard University Press, 1966), V, pp. 617-19.

2.   From all indications this bathing was a complete bath. Although רחץ is used to designate washing for parts of the body as well as complete baths, the context indicates that Lev. 8.6 implies the latter. Cf. F. Brown, S.R. Driver, and C.A. Briggs, *A Hebrew and English Lexicon of the Old Testament* (Oxford: Clarendon Press, 1976), p. 934. The LXX translators prefer this understanding in that ἔλουσεν is used to translate רחץ.

3.   *P. Oxy.* 840 appears to confirm this practice during the time of the ministry of Jesus or the early church. In this agraphon, a Pharisaic Chief Priest confronts Jesus and his disciples who have entered the outer court of the Temple. In defence of his own purity, the Pharisaic Chief Priest responds, 'I am clean. For I have bathed myself (ἐλουσάμην) in the pool of David and have gone down by one stair and come by the other and have put on white and clean clothes and only then have I come hither and viewed the holy utensils.' If, as J. Jeremias argues, this gospel fragment, which dates to about 400 CE, represents an authentic event from Jesus' life, this priestly practice is confirmed. If this is a wholly apocryphal story, at least a morsel of historical remembrance has been preserved in the description of priestly washing. Cf. J. Jeremias, *The Unknown Sayings of Jesus* (trans. R. Fuller; London: SPCK,

This cleansing from bodily uncleanness was a symbol of the putting away of the filth of sin; the washing of the body therefore was a symbol of spiritual cleansing, without which no one can draw near to God, and least of all those who were to perform the duties of reconciliation.[1]

It appears that the initiatory bath (Exod. 29.4) was thought to be valid for life since there is no evidence that it was to be repeated. In contrast, the hands and feet were washed regularly due to their constant exposure and possible contamination. Consequently, washings of the hands and feet are repeated acts of purification to prepare the priest for a variety of sacred activities.[2]

Philo (*Quaest. in Exod.* 1.2) bears witness to a similar idea. In a discussion of priestly preparation before the offer of a sacrifice, Philo mentions several aspects of preparing the soul and body. In a summary notation he observes:

according to the saying, one should not enter with unwashed feet on the pavement of the temple of God.[3]

Since the saying is in the context of a discussion of priestly duties it suggests the continuation of the practice as a part of cultic preparations for priests.

The purpose of these washings is bound up in obtaining cultic purity. Martin Noth observes:

The order for the High Priest and priests to wash themselves is made more emphatic by the observation that death will follow any performance of the priestly functions without cultic purity, as the 'holy' works destruc-

J. Jeremias, *The Unknown Sayings of Jesus* (trans. R. Fuller; London: SPCK, 1964), pp. 47-60.

1.   C.F. Keil and F. Delitzsch, *Commentary on the Old Testament in Ten Volumes: The Pentateuch* (trans. J. Martin; Grand Rapids: Eerdmans, 1975), I, p. 335. Cf. G.J. Wenham, *The Book of Leviticus* (Grand Rapids: Eerdmans, 1979), p. 139.

2.   It is also possible to view the washings as graphic depictions of the division between holy and profane. By removing the profane dirt and dust, the priests preserve the distinction between holy and secular domains. In this case, the dirt and dust is not so much the issue (since inside the tabernacle priests walk on dirt) as keeping elements in their respective spheres. Cf. M. Douglas, *Purity and Danger* (London: Routledge & Kegan Paul, 1966).

3.   Cited according to the translation of Ralph Marcus, *Philo: Questions and Answers on Exodus*, Supplement II (Cambridge, MA: Harvard University Press, 1970), p. 7.

tion on the 'unholy'. Here external bodily purity is thought to have a mysterious connection with cultic purity and is most probably a part of it.[1]

Bodily purity signifies that the priest is cultically acceptable to Yahweh. Philo (*Vit. Mos.* 2.138) understands these washings to symbolize ethical/moral realities:

> Washing the hands and feet is a symbol of a blameless life, of years of cleanliness employed in laudable actions, and in straight travelling, not on the rough road or more properly pathless waste of vice, but on the smooth high road through virtue's land. Let him, he means, who shall be purified with water, bethink him that the mirrors were the material of this vessel, to the end that he himself may behold his own mind as in a mirror; and, if some ugly spot appear of unreasoning passion, either of pleasure, uplifting and raising him to heights which nature forbids, or of its converse pain, making him shrink and pulling him down, or of fear, diverting and distorting the straight course to which his face was set, or of desire, pulling and dragging him perforce to what he has not got, then he may salve and heal the sore and hope to gain the beauty which is genuine and unalloyed. For beauty of body lies in wellproportioned parts, in a fine complexion and good condition of flesh, and short is the season of its bloom. But beauty of mind lies in harmony of creed, in consent of virtues.[2]

Without overestimating the value of Philo's statement, it appears that his understanding is representative of a particular contemporary attitude about the significance attached to the rite. In a mishnaic list of the kinds of things inappropriate for entry into the Temple, *Berakot* 9.5 includes entrance without washing the feet:

1. M. Noth, *Exodus* (trans. J.S. Bowden; Philadelphia: Westminster Press, 1962), p. 237. Cf. also J.P. Hyatt, *Exodus* (Grand Rapids: Eerdmans, 1980), p. 294.

2. Cited according to the translation of F.H. Colson, *Philo* (London: William Heinemann, 1966), VI, p. 517. Philo (*Spec. Leg.* 1.207) even sees significance for the worshipper in the washing of the feet of a sacrificial animal:

> By the washing of the feet is meant that his steps should no longer be on earth but tread the upper air. For the soul of the lover of God does in truth leap from earth to heaven and wing its way on high, eager to take its place in the ranks and share the ordered march of sun and moon and all-holy, all-harmonious host of the other stars, marshalled and led by God whose kingship none can dispute or usurp, the kingship by which everything is justly governed.

Cited according to the translation of F.A. Colson, *Philo* (London: William Heinemann, 1968), VII, p. 217.

G. One should not act silly while facing the Eastern Gate [of the Temple in Jerusalem] for it faces toward the Chamber of the Holy of Holies.

H. One should not enter the Temple Mount with his walking stick, his overshoes, his money bag, or with dust on his feet.

I. And one should not use [the Temple mount] for a shortcut.

J. And spitting [there likewise is forbidden, as is proven by an argument] *a minori ad majus* [if you may not use it for a shortcut, you obviously may not spit there].[1]

Although this law is not restricted to a discussion of the priests, as in the Philonic passage, it does suggest that footwashing had a significance for ritual purity from which other prohibitions (staff, sandal, and wallet) may have been deduced.[2]

2. *Domestic Settings for Personal Hygiene and Comfort*
The evidence for footwashing in domestic settings is divided into two sections, since footwashing for the purpose of hospitality ordinarily assumes a host or hostess offering water to the guest, whereas footwashing for the purpose of personal hygiene and comfort is usually secured by the individual him/herself.

Three Old Testament passages describe footwashing in domestic settings for personal hygiene and comfort: 2 Sam. 11.8-11; 19.24; and Cant. 5.3.

2 Samuel 11.6-13 describes David's attempts to divert responsibility for Bathsheba's pregnancy from himself to her husband Uriah. At David's request Bathsheba's husband is brought to the King. While in the royal presence Uriah is instructed, 'Go down to your house and wash your feet (καὶ νίψαι τοὺς πόδας σου)'. Exactly what David meant by 'wash your feet' is debated, with several explanations offered.

It has been suggested that 2 Sam. 11.8 must be understood within the context of regulations governing ritual purity for Holy War. One such alleged regulation is abstinence from cohabitation (cf. 1 Sam.

---

1. Cited according to the translation of J. Neusner, *The Mishnah: A New Translation* (New Haven: Yale University Press, 1988), p. 14.
2. On the other hand, if this law comes from either of the pre-70 groups which sought to extend purity to all areas of life, then it matters little whether *Ber.* 9.5 is specifically directed to priests or laity. The concern of both would be the same.

21.5; Deut. 23.10-15; Num. 31.16-24).[1] Two different proposals concerning the meaning of 'wash your feet' are derived from the premise of Holy War regulations. The more common of the two argues that 'wash your feet' is a 'euphemistic circumlocution in what amounts to a dispensation to Uriah to cohabit with his wife, since he would be free to stay long enough in town to purify himself'.[2] Therefore, to wash the feet would mean to cohabit with Bathsheba, and thereby, to lose his ritual purity for Holy War. However, James Swetnam argues that it is the act of footwashing itself which puts one into a state of ritual purity. According to Swetnam, David implicitly instructs Uriah, who is in a state of ritual purity for Holy War, to put himself out of the state by having sexual intercourse with Bathsheba. He is then to wash his feet to regain his previous status.[3] While certain Holy War regulations may have been in existence at this time, the evidence that footwashing must be understood in such a context is lacking. As for Swetnam's suggestion, it appears too conjectural to be plausible. Swetnam himself admits, 'This interpretation is speculative, for there is no clear proof elsewhere that the washing of the feet was a ceremony which initiated the ritual purity required by an Israelite warrior'.[4] Although few scholars find the Holy War context to be self-evident, the idea that footwashing is a euphemism for sexual intercourse does find advocates.[5] While certain Old Testament passages may refer to the feet in a euphemistic fashion (Judg. 3.25; 1 Sam. 24.3; Isa. 7.20; Ruth 3.7[?]), 'washing the feet' is not used euphemistically with the possible exception of this passage. Besides the etymological evidence, one must wonder whether David would speak so freely in light of the king's plan to conceal his own previous actions.

It is much more probable that David means no more than to go

---

1. Cf. G. von Rad, *Der heilige Krieg im Alten Israel* (Göttingen: Vandenhoeck & Ruprecht, 1958), p. 7.

2. U. Simon, 'The Poor Man's Ewe-Lamb. An Example of a Juridical Parable', *Bib* 48 (1967), p. 214. For a similar understanding, cf. J. Mauchline, *1 and 2 Samuel* (London: Oliphants, 1967), p. 249.

3. J. Swetnam, 'A Review of George Richter, *Die Fusswaschung im Johannesevangelium. Geschichte ihrer Deutung*', *Bib* 49 (1968), p. 441.

4. *Ibid.*

5. In addition to Simon and Mauchline, cf. P.K. McCarter, Jr, *2 Samuel* (Garden City, NY: Doubleday, 1984), p. 286.

home and make yourself comfortable.[1] Even though going to the comforts of home might imply a conjugal visit,[2] it appears to be reading too much into the command to wash the feet for it to be an instruction for Uriah to have sexual intercourse with Bathsheba. Again, it should be remembered that washing the feet was a comfort hard to come by in military service and would itself be a luxury compared to the sparsely furnished military camp. Of course, more than just footwashing might be implied, but at least washing the feet is designated.

An additional piece of information concerning footwashing for personal comfort and hygiene is found in 2 Sam. 19.24 (25). As David is returning to power, following the attempted coup by Absalom and his cohorts, Saul's grandson meets the king. David inquires as to why Mephibosheth did not join him earlier (cf. 2 Sam. 16.1-4). Mephibosheth is described in the following fashion:

> He had not taken care of his feet or trimmed his moustache or washed his clothes from the day the king left until the day he returned safely.

All these conditions are signs of mourning.[3] Mephibosheth's intention is to persuade David of his loyalty and of his genuine distress at the king's misfortune. The major issue for this inquiry is to understand what is meant by the phrase לא־עשה רגליו. In particular, how should עשה be understood? The LXX uses θεραπεύω to translate עשה. While in this context the idea of medical attention is not dominant, no doubt the translator chose this word due, in part, to Mephibosheth's infirmity. Most scholars interpret עשה in the sense of 'to wash the feet'.[4] The lone exception to this understanding is McCarter who opts to translate the phrase as 'trim the nails'.[5] Deuteronomy 21.12 is offered as supporting evidence. One of the procedures which an alien

---

1. For this view cf. H.P. Smith, *A Critical and Exegetical Commentary on the Books of Samuel* (Edinburgh: T. & T. Clark, 1899), p. 318; Keil and Delitzsch, *1 and 2 Samuel*, p. 384; and Brown, Driver, Briggs, p. 920.

2. While Hertzberg allows for this allusion, he seems to prefer 'make yourself comfortable' as the meaning of footwashing. H.W. Hertzberg, *1 and 2 Samuel* (trans. J.S. Bowden; Philadelphia: Westminster Press, 1964), p. 310.

3. P.R. Ackroyd, *The Second Book of Samuel* (Cambridge: Cambridge University Press, 1977), p. 181; and Hertzberg, p. 366.

4. Cf. Brown, Driver, Briggs, p. 749b; Ackroyd, p. 181; and Keil and Delitzsch, p. 447.

5. McCarter, p. 417.

must undergo to be accepted into Israel's midst is to 'trim the nails' (עשׂתה את־צפרניה). It is true that עשׂה is used in both verses; however, two points militate against this suggestion. First, while the feet may be implied in Deut. 21.12 they are not specifically mentioned, nor consequently emphasized. Second, and more importantly, these two passages represent two radically different contexts.

The trimming of the nails in Deuteronomy is given cultic significance by its placement in regulations for admission into Israel. The passage in 2 Samuel clearly deals with personal hygiene and comfort. While the phrase לא־עשׂה רגליו may mean not caring for the feet, this would in all probability include not washing the feet, even given the fact that Mephibosheth was crippled.

The final Old Testament passage clearly refers to footwashing for personal hygiene and comfort, Cant. 5.3. The beloved responds to her lover, who desires to enter:

> I have taken off my robe, must I put it on again? I have washed my feet, must I soil them again?

Despite the frequent use of double entendre in the Song, a fairly literal understanding of this verse is the best way to approach it. The beloved has already retired, which includes washing her feet.[1] This note is surely to be taken as a sign of comfort or personal hygiene. Any euphemistic connotation is secondary at best.[2]

In the first century CE footwashing came to be such an expected part of personal hygiene that to approach a task without adequate preparation could be described as acting 'with unwashed feet', i.e. impromptu. Defending Abraham's conduct in claiming Sarah as his sister, Philo (*Quaest. in Gen.* 4.60) warns:

> Wherefore anyone who says that this (was done) through levity of character with unwashed feet. . . is deserving of condemnation.[3]

---

1. Cf. C.D. Ginsburg, *The Song of Songs* (New York: Ktav, 1970), p. 165. Cf. also Keil and Delitzsch, *Song of Solomon*, p. 93.

2. This assessment appears to be in agreement with the positions of M.H. Pope, *The Song of Songs* (Garden City, NY: Doubleday, 1977), p. 515; G.L. Carr, *The Song of Solomon* (Downers Grove: InterVarsity, 1984), p. 133; and Lohse, II, p. 3 n. 12.

3. Cited according to the translation of R. Marcus, *Philo,* Supplement II (Cambridge, MA: Harvard University Press, 1971), p. 340.

In each passage examined in this inquiry, the feet are washed for reasons of personal hygiene and comfort. Ritual purity does not appear to be the primary emphasis nor do euphemistic understandings best explain the passages. Obviously, washing the feet is a comfort justified on its own merit. All the citations also seem to indicate that each individual washed his or her own feet.

3. *Footwashing in Domestic Settings for the Purpose of Hospitality*

By far the most frequent references to footwashing occur in contexts of hospitality, with much of the evidence being found in Genesis. Each citation refers to footwashing as an expected form of hospitality. Genesis 18 contains the story of Abram's encounter with the messengers from God who bring word that Sarah will conceive and give birth to a son. In greeting these men Abram says, 'Let a little water be brought, and then you may all wash your feet and rest under this tree'. Footwashing is obviously an act of hospitality, especially in light of its context, i.e., the other hospitable gestures.[1] Yet, while the purpose is rather easy to discern, it is unclear who actually washes the feet, the messenger or Abraham's servants. If the Hebrew text were relied upon solely, it would appear that these messengers washed their own feet. In the phrase רחצו רגליכם, רחץ is in the imperative. Since the form is second person plural, it seems that after water is brought these messengers could refresh themselves by washing their tired, dusty feet. However, the LXX implies that someone else will wash the feet of the messengers. The LXX renders Gen. 18.4 in the following manner: λημφθήτω δὴ ὕδωρ καὶ νιψάτωσαν τοὺς πόδας ὑμῶν, καὶ καταψύξατε ὑπὸ τὸ δένδρον. The only command these individuals are given is to rest under the tree. The other two verbs imply that those actions will be done for them. Of particular importance is the way in which רחצו is translated. Instead of the expected second person plural, the imperative occurs in the third person plural νιψάτωσαν, with the meaning 'let them wash your feet'. This rendering clearly implies that Abram's servants (who also bring the water) are to wash the feet of the guests.

The next text of importance for this inquiry (19.2) continues the story line of the messengers. After leaving Abram they journey to

1. Cf. especially the remarks of C. Westermann, *Genesis 12–36: A Commentary* (trans. J.J. Scullion; Minneapolis: Augsburg, 1985), p. 278.

Sodom. Upon their arrival they wait at the city gate, where Lot invites them to his home.

> 'My lords', he said, 'please turn aside to your servant's house. You can wash your feet and spend the night and then go on your way early in the morning.'

As in 18.4, the invitation to wash the feet is in the context of hospitality. Once again, the offer of water to wash the feet, which are tired and dusty from travel, is portrayed as a very natural suggestion. Both 18.4 and 19.2 contain the same Hebrew phrase רגליכם ורחצו. However, on this occasion the LXX renders it as καὶ νίψασθε τοὺς πόδας ὑμῶν, indicating that the two messengers are to wash their own feet. Why the LXX translates the same form of רחץ in two different ways is hard to determine, unless it be that the translators supposed that since Abraham had servants, while Lot did not, they would be employed in such a task. At any rate, the messengers appear to wash their own feet in 19.2.

Footwashing is mentioned in another Genesis passage, 24.32, as a hospitable act. Abram sends his servant, Eleazar, to bring back a wife for Isaac. Laban, the brother of the prospective bride, offers Eleazar and his associates water to wash their feet and fodder for their camels. The Hebrew text is again ambiguous as to who washes the feet. The infinitive construct, רגליו לרחץ, could simply mean that the guests are to wash their own feet or that someone else would do the washing for them. However, the LXX makes clear that the guests are to wash their own feet: ὕδωρ νίψασθαι τοῖς ποσὶν αὐτοῦ καὶ τοῖς ποσὶν τῶν ἀνδρῶν τῶν μετ' αὐτοῦ.

A final passage in Genesis is relevant to this inquiry. In 43.24 Joseph's brothers are given water to wash their feet and are given fodder for their donkeys. Not only is this offer an act of hospitality, but it appears that the footwashing is in some way related to the fact that they soon eat with Joseph. Again the Hebrew text and the LXX seem to disagree about who washes the feet. The clause רגליהם וירחצו states that they (the brothers) washed their own feet. Since in the previous clause, יתן־מים, the verb is third person singular, the shift to third person plural, וירחצו, makes this conclusion fairly obvious. However, the LXX renders the verse in a different fashion. Instead of the brothers washing their feet, the LXX implies that Joseph's steward performs this task, καὶ ἤνεγκεν ὕδωρ νίψαι τοὺς πόδας αὐτῶν. By using the aorist active infinitive the translators imply that the steward washes the feet. Otherwise, one would expect the middle voice, as in 24.32.

Among the many difficult stories recorded in Judges, the narrative devoted to the Levite and his concubine is one of the most troublesome. Tucked away almost incidentally is a reference to footwashing. An old man from Ephraim invites the Levite and his companions to his home for the evening. The text records (19.21), 'After they had washed their feet, they had something to eat and drink'. Several aspects of this verse are noteworthy. Similarly to a number of other passages, as part of the act of hospitality, water is provided by a host for footwashing. In addition, the footwashing immediately precedes a meal. Finally, both the Hebrew text and the LXX agree about who washes the feet: the guests themselves. The same Hebrew phrase is used as in Gen. 43.24, whereas the LXX renders it on this occasion as καὶ [αὐτοὶ]¹ ἐνίψαντο τοὺς πόδας αὐτῶν. Instead of the aorist middle infinitive the translators chose the aorist middle indicative.

Another Old Testament passage which includes a reference to footwashing is found in 1 Samuel. Chapter 25 relates the intriguing account of David, Nabal, and Abigail. After Abigail's husband dies, David sends his servants to bring her to him as his wife. Abigail greets them by bowing her face to the ground and saying, 'Here is your maidservant, ready to serve you and wash the feet of my master's servants'. While the offer of footwashing is a hospitable gesture, the emphasis is upon the fact that Abigail is ready to serve David's servants. Both the Hebrew text and the LXX underscore the idea that Abigail is placing herself in the position of a servant (אמתך and ἡ δούλη respectively). As Smith observes, 'She is willing to be the lowest of his servants, a maid to wash the feet of his slaves'.[2]

The idea of the host or hostess personally washing the feet of guests continues in later Jewish literature. Closer to the time of the Fourth Gospel's composition is evidence from the Testament of Abraham.[3]

---

1. This pronoun appears in Sinaiticus but not in Alexandrinus.
2. Smith, p. 228.
3. It appears that the most probable date for the *Testament of Abraham* is c. 100 CE. Cf. the discussions in *The Apocryphal Old Testament* (ed. H.F.D. Sparks; Oxford: Clarendon Press, 1984), pp. 394-95 and J.H. Charlesworth, *The Old Testament Pseudepigrapha* (Garden City, NY: Doubleday, 1983), I, pp. 874-75.

This document purports to be an account of Abraham's preparation for death. To accomplish such a task God dispatches Michael, the angel, to inform Abraham of his impending death so that he might make the appropriate arrangements. Having praised Abraham for his hospitality (1.1-2), the text goes on to relate how he meets Michael and they travel to Abraham's home. When they arrive, Abraham instructs his son (3.6-9):

> 'Issac, my child, draw water from the well and bring it to me in the vessel so that we may wash this stranger's feet; for he is tired, having come to us from a long journey.' And so Isaac ran to the well and drew water into the vessel and brought it to them. Then Abraham went forward and washed the feet of the Commander-in-Chief Michael. Abraham's heart was moved and he wept over the stranger.[1]

Immediately after this reception Abraham and Michael recline and eat. This story not only shows that footwashing is an act of hospitality, but it also indicates that Abraham is willing to serve the angelic messenger by washing his feet. This is similar to Abigail's response, but the account differs from Gen. 18.4 where it appears that either the messengers or Abram's servants perform the task of washing the feet.[2] A final significant point is that the footwashing immediately precedes a meal.

Other evidence from this general period is found in the story of Joseph and Aseneth.[3] A description of Joseph being received

---

1.   Cited according to the translation of E.P. Sanders, 'Testament of Abraham', in *OTP*, I, p. 882.

2.   Recension B of the *Testament of Abraham* relates that story in a somewhat different fashion:

> As he came into the house, Abraham said to his servants, 'Arise and go out to the flock and bring three lambs and slaughter (them) quickly and prepare (them), so that we may eat and drink, because this day is (a day of) good cheer'. And the servants brought the lambs, and Abraham called his son Isaac and said to him, 'Isaac, my child, arise and put water into the vessel, so that we may wash the feet of this stranger'. And he brought (it) as he was commanded. And Abraham said, 'I have an insight (into) what will come to pass, that in this bowl I shall not again wash the feet of a man who is entertained as a guest with us'. When Isaac heard his father saying these things, he wept and said to him, 'My father, what is this that you say, "It is my last time to wash a stranger's feet"?' (Sanders, pp. 896-97).

3.   In all probability this document should be dated somewhere between the first

in Pentephres' house is given in 7.1:

> And Joseph entered the house of Pentephres and sat upon the throne. And they washed his feet and set a table before him by itself, because Joseph never ate with the Egyptians, for this was an abomination to him.[1]

Again, footwashing is a hospitable gesture, and it immediately precedes a meal.[2]

Later in the story (13.15), while Aseneth is making a confession of sin and praying, she asks God for Joseph's safety and the opportunity to serve as his slave, which includes washing his feet:

> Lord, I commit him to you,
>> because I love him beyond my (own) soul.
> Preserve him in the wisdom of your grace.
> And you, Lord, commit me to him
>> for a maidservant and slave.
> And I will make his bed
>> and wash his feet
>> and wait for him
>> and be a slave for him and serve him forever (and) ever.[3]

Aseneth's prayer equates the washing of another's feet with a sign of service. If, indeed, 7.1 implies that servants washed Joseph's feet on that occasion, the point can hardly be missed here. It is also evident that this desire comes from her love for Joseph.

In ch. 20 Aseneth receives Joseph into her father's house for a special banquet which Joseph is to attend. From the context it is obvious that Joseph and Aseneth are to be married. 20.1-5 describes what precedes the meal:

---

century BCE and the second century CE . Cf. Sparks (pp. 496-97) and Charlesworth (*OTP*, II, pp. 187-88).

1. Cited according to the translation of C. Burchard in *OTP*, II, p. 210.

2. There is some textual uncertainty concerning the reading 'they washed his feet'. Certain witnesses support 'he washed his feet'. The former should be accepted for at least two reasons. On the one hand, the better witnesses support 'they washed his feet'. On the other hand, this reading coheres with the characteristics of the book. For if the original reading should be 'he washed his feet', this is the only place in the document where Joseph must perform this task on his own behalf. In all likelihood Pentephres' servants wash Joseph's feet.

3. *OTP*, II, p. 224.

And Aseneth said to Joseph, 'Come, my Lord, and enter our house, because I have prepared our house and made a great dinner'. And she grasped his right hand and led him into her house and seated him on Pentephres' her father's throne. And she brought water to wash his feet. And Joseph said, 'Let one of the virgins come and wash my feet'. And Aseneth said to him, 'No my Lord, because you are my lord from now on, and I (am) your maidservant. And why do you say this (that) another virgin (is) to wash your feet? For your feet are my feet, and your hands are my hands, and your soul my soul, and your feet another (woman) will never wash'. And she urged him and washed his feet. And Joseph looked at her hands, and they were like hands of life, and her fingers fine like (the) fingers of a fast writing scribe. And after this Joseph grasped her right hand and kissed it, and Aseneth kissed his head and sat at his right (hand).[1]

In sending away her servant girls, Aseneth exhibits her deep love and concern for Joseph. In sum, footwashing, in this context, is offered as a sign of hospitality before a banquet by the hostess herself.

4. *Footwashing and Servitude*
A final group of texts makes clear that footwashing is to be associated with servitude. In addition to the evidence about Abigail and Aseneth, another example is found in two different Psalms. In both songs, the context is one of military battle and future conquest. Both Ps. 60.8 (10) and Ps. 108.9 (10) record:

> Moab is my washbasin,
>> upon Edom I toss my sandal;
>> over Philistia I shout in triumph.

The lines about Moab and Edom are of special interest. Moab is described as a washbasin (סיר רחצי.) Edward Neufeld observes, 'The reference to a 'wash pot' or 'basin'... in connection with 'casting off the sandal' clearly indicates their common use for the purpose of washing feet'.[2] It is clear from the reference that Moab '... is to be so reduced that he becomes the wash basin which is carried by a slave to pour water over his master's hands or feet'.[3] Clearly, the footbasin

---

1.   *OTP*, II, p. 234.

2.   E. Neufeld, 'Hygiene Conditions in Ancient Israel (Iron Age)', *Biblical Archaeologist Reader* (ed. E.F. Campbell, Jr and D.N. Freedman; Sheffield: Almond Press, 1983), IV, p. 158.

3.   C.A. Briggs and E.G. Briggs, *The Book of Psalms* (Edinburgh: T. & T.

and, by extension, footwashing itself are associated with servitude.[1]

It may be that the reference to the sandal being tossed upon Edom is no more than a traditional sign of ownership.[2] However, there is good reason to believe that a symbol of footwashing is present. Derek Kidner notes, '. . . the picture is of a man returning home and flinging his shoes to a slave or into a corner'.[3] Briggs's observations relate this verse to footwashing in a more explicit fashion:

> Edom, the troublesome neighbor of Judah, on the southeast, was also so reduced as to become another slave to whom the master kicks off the sandals when he would have them removed to wash his feet.[4]

At the very least, one can safely assume a connection between the sandal and servitude.

In hyperbolic language[5] Ps. 58.10 (11) uses footwashing imagery to express the vindication of the righteous over evil foes.

> The righteous will be glad when they are avenged,
>   when they bathe their feet in the blood of the wicked.

In this picture of vengeance the very life's blood of the wicked will be used to wash the feet of the righteous. Not only is there the idea of the free-flowing blood of the wicked, but also the issue of subjugation. The wicked will certainly be defeated.[6]

Clark, 1907), II, p. 60. Cf. also Keil and Delitzsch, *Psalms*, p. 199.

1.   Several examples of footbaths are extant from the archaeological excavations in central Samaria. Most of the footbaths, which come from about the eighth century BCE, are round with a support in the center on which the foot could rest. Cf. J.W. Crowfoot, G.M. Crowfoot, and K.M. Kenyon, *The Objects from Samaria* (London: Palestine Exploration Fund, 1957), pp. 185-87 fig. 29, and plate XVII 16.

2.   Cf. Keil–Delitzsch, p. 199; A.A. Anderson, *Psalms* (London: Oliphants, 1975), I, p. 445; and J.H. Eaton, *Psalms* (London: SCM Press, 1967), p. 156.

3.   D. Kidner, *Psalms 1–72* (Downers Grove, IL: IVP, 1978), p. 218.

4.   Briggs, p. 60.

5.   Anderson, I, p. 434.

6.   There are several texts which extend this idea of the subjugation of the enemies of the righteous that use the imagery of the feet to convey its message. Both Isaiah (49.23) and the War Rule (12 and 19) describe a time when foreign kings and queens will not only bow before Zion but '. . . will lick the dust of their feet'. It is difficult to determine whether the imagery here has in mind a most graphic form of footwashing (the foreign kings and queens will lick clean the feet of Zion) or whether licking the dust of the feet is simply a way of emphasizing the humbling of these foreign leaders (until their faces are in the dust at their conquerors' feet).

5. *Summary*

In ancient Jewish society footwashing functions in a variety of ways. From requirements for priestly admission into the tabernacle and temple to personal comfort and hospitality, the practice of footwashing is commonplace. Several concluding observations may contribute to a better understanding of the footwashing episode recorded in John 13.

First, footwashing prepared one for a variety of things in Jewish antiquity. Footwashing was so common that the lack of adequate preparation could be expressed by the phrase 'with unwashed feet'. Second, references to footwashing for the purpose of hospitality are very frequent and this function is quite significant for John 13. Ordinarily, this usage entails the offer of a meal. In certain situations footwashing is specifically portrayed as preparation for the meal. Third, footwashing is generally the responsibility of servants. A host or hostess offers the hospitable act, but it is ordinarily carried out by slaves, even though the guest may sometimes wash his or her own feet. There is so much an identification of servants and footwashing that the footbasin comes to function figuratively as a sign of servitude. Those who receive footwashing are always the social superiors of those who render the service. Fourth, in cases of deep love or extreme devotion a host or loved one might wash the feet of another. Due to its humble nature, the performance of such an act demonstrates tremendous affection, servitude, or both.

B. *Footwashing in the Graeco-Roman World*

The evidence for footwashing is divided into four sections in this part of the inquiry: (1) ritual settings, (2) domestic settings for personal hygiene and comfort, (3) domestic settings devoted to hospitality: (a) footwashing as a gesture of welcome or greeting, and (b) in preparation for a banquet, and finally, (4) settings which identify those who perform this task.

1. *Footwashing and Ritual Settings*

General washings of a ritual nature in Graeco-Roman life are too numerous to elaborate in the present study, for ritual purity required various kinds of washings.[1] Footwashing, on the other hand, appears infrequently, with little evidence in support of the practice.

Near the end of Homer's *Odyssey* (22.454-80), Telemachus together with the neatherd and the swineherd, slays Melanthius and a number of women. Following the murders, Homer recounts:

> Therefore, they washed their hands and feet, and went into the house of Odysseus, and the work was done.[2]

This first step of purification is followed by a request from Odysseus for sulphur and fire to purge the hall completely. In this text the feet are washed along with the hands to purify the killers.

Other evidence of footwashing for ritual purposes is related to entrance into holy sites. Both Homer (*Iliad* 16.235) and Strabo (*Geography* 7.328) imply that footwashing normally precedes entrance into a sacred place, whether oracle or temple. In a prayer to Zeus, Achilles describes the Selli, Zeus' interpreters (who dwell in the neighborhood of the temple of Dodona), as 'men with unwashed feet that couch on the ground'.[3] In describing the Selli in this fashion Achilles is drawing attention to the fact that their behavior is different from what is customary among prophetic figures. Strabo (7.328) explains that Homer's phrase should be taken to mean the Selli were barbarians. The implication of Strabo's explanation is that the behavior of the Selli is so unusual that it must owe its origin to foreign influences. During Strabo's time it can be deduced that among the Greeks most individuals washed their feet before entering a holy place.

Fabius Pictor (*De Iure Sacerdotis* 16), a Roman historian in the third century BCE, preserves testimony that at some point certain Roman priests participated in ritual footwashing:

---

1. Examples of such rites are found in: Homer, *Iliad* 6.265; *Odyssey* 2.60-61; Hesiod, *Works and Days* 724-25; Juvenal, *Satires* 6.520-31; Theophrastus, *Characters* 16; Pausanias, *Description of Greece: Phocis, Ozolian Locri* 34.8; *Elius* 13.3.

2. Cited according to the translation of A.T. Murray, *Homer: The Odyssey* (London: William Heinemann, 1919), II, p. 371.

3. Cited according to the translation of A.T. Murray, *Homer: The Iliad* (Cambridge, MA: Harvard University Press, 1946), II, p. 181.

> He (or she) has to present water for hands and feet; in the left hand he has
> to hold the wash basin, in his right hand a vessel with water.[1]

Unfortunately, this fragment is unrelated to other instructions so that neither the cult nor the occasion are identifiable.

Pliny (*Natural History* 24.102) notes that a certain selago plant should be gathered in a state of purity with bare feet that have just been washed:

> Like this sabine herb is the plant called selago. It is gathered without iron
> with the right hand, thrust under the tunic through the left arm hole, as
> though the gatherer were thieving. He should be clad in white, and have
> bare feet washed clean; before gathering he should make a sacrificial
> offering of bread and wine. The plant is carried in a new napkin. The
> Druids of Gaul have recorded that it should be kept on the person to ward
> off fatalities, and that smoke of it is good for all diseases of the eyes.[2]

Obviously, the plant is considered to have such powers that ritual purity is required in its gathering.

2. *Footwashing and Hygiene*

Several pieces of evidence document the common usage of footwashing for hygienic purposes. Lucian (*Demonax* 4) demonstrates the frequency of domestic footwashing in describing Demonax's decision to study philosophy:

> You must not conceive, however, that he rushed into these matters with
> unwashed feet, as the saying goes.[3]

It appears that footwashing was so common in domestic contexts for hygienic purposes that it gave rise to a traditional saying which described the commencement of a course of action without due preparation as rushing into matters with unwashed feet.

Juvenal (*Satires* 3.271-77), a Latin satirist from the early second century CE, describes the hazards of walking about the streets of

1. H. Peter, *Historicorum Romanorum Reliquiae* (Stuttgart: B.G. Teubner, 1967), I, p. 116.

2. Cited according to the translation of W.H.S. Jones, *Pliny: Natural History* (Cambridge, MA: Harvard University Press, 1956), VII, p. 75.

3. Cited according to the translation of A.M. Harmon, *Lucian: Demonax* (London: William Heinemann, 1913), p. 145.

Rome at night in a way that implies that footwashing is a normal part of hygiene:

> See how pots strike and dent the sturdy pavement. There's death from every window where you move. You'd be a fool to venture out to dine, oblivious of what goes on above, without having penned that dotted line of your last testament. You can but hope they spill a chamber pot (*pelvis*).[1]

This humorous note indicates that much worse accidents can occur than being drenched with water thrown out of a foot basin from above. The expected nature of such an event argues for the commonness of footwashing in the home.

The clearest affirmation that footwashing was commonplace in personal hygiene comes from Apuleius (*Apology* 8). After being ridiculed for advocating the use of tooth powder for oral hygiene, Apuleius seeks to defend its use by suggesting it to be as essential as footwashing:

> I should be obliged, therefore, if my critic Aemilianus would answer me whether he is ever in the habit of washing the feet, or, if he admits that he is in the habit of so doing, whether he is prepared to argue that a man should pay more attention to the cleanliness of his feet than that of his teeth.[2]

The intent of the comparison is the identification of a common hygienic practice with which oral cleanliness might be compared. Footwashing is seen as an expected custom in this passage.

Additional documentation of footwashing for hygienic purposes is to be found in the form of a Cryptic terracotta of a nude woman washing her feet in a foot basin.[3] The frequency with which texts re-

---

1. Cited according to the translation of J. Mazzaro, *Juvenal: Satires* (Ann Arbor, MI: University of Michigan Press, 1965), p. 45.

2. Cited according to the translation of H.E. Butler, *The Apology and Florida of Apuleius of Madaura* (Oxford: Clarendon Press, 1909), p. 29.

3. K. Sudhoff, *Aus dem antiken Badewesen. Medizinisch-kulturgeschichtliche Studien an Vasenbildern* (Berlin: Allgemeine Medizinische Verlagsanstalt, 1910), pp. 4-5. A related scene, which appears on a painted vase, is that of a man washing his feet before a journey (Sudhoff, p. 17). Another painted vase depicts a servant girl tying her sandals after having washed her feet (Sudhoff, p. 20). A painted vase contains scenes of women washing at a large vase. One of them is using a sponge on her feet (Sudhoff, pp. 35, 40). Still another scene is preserved on a drawing where

fer to tripods used for footwashing, and the archaeological discovery of foot basins also support the practice of footwashing for hygienic purposes.[1]

3. *Footwashing and Hospitality*

a. *Welcome.* One of the functions of footwashing in contexts of hospitality is as a sign of welcome. The classic example of such a custom is found in Homer (*Odyssey* 19.308-19). Without being recognized, Odysseus comes into the home of Penelope and predicts that Odysseus will return to this home:

> Then wise Penelope answered him: 'Ah, stranger, I would that this word of thine might be fulfilled. Then shouldest thou straightway know of kindness and many a gift from me, so that one who met thee would call thee blessed. Yet in my heart I forebode it thus, even as it shall be. Neither shall Odysseus any more come home, nor shalt thou obtain a convoy hence, since there are not now in the house such masters as Odysseus was among men—as sure as ever such a man there was—to send reverend strangers on their way, and to welcome them. But still my maidens, wash the stranger's feet and prepare his bed—bedstead and cloaks and bright coverlets—that in warmth and comfort he may come to the golden Dawn.[2]

In this context the welcome of a guest is explicitly connected with washing the person's feet. This episode is depicted in a number of works of art. A marble relief, housed in the national museum in Athens, portrays Odysseus sitting while his feet are washed by a servant.[3] Penelope stands with her back turned as Odysseus holds the mouth of the servant girl closed. No doubt he keeps her from revealing his identity to Penelope.

A *skyphos* from Chios depicts still another welcome by footwashing. Supported by a walking stick, Odysseus has his left foot washed by a servant as he enters the home of Eumaios, who appears in the background.[4] That Odysseus is still carrying his belongings

one woman is washing her hair in a large vase while another prepares to wash her feet in the vase (Sudhoff, p. 41).

1.   Cf. Pindar, *Isthmian Odes* 1.18-21 and M.J. Miline, 'A Greek Footbath in the Metropolitan Museum of Art', *AJA* 48 (1944), pp. 26-63.

2.   Cited according to the translation of Murray, *Homer: The Odyssey*, II, p. 251.

3.   Sudhoff, p. 7. For other examples cf. Kötting, pp. 746-48.

4.   *Ibid.*, p. 9.

implies that he has just arrived.

Athenaeus (*Deipnosophists* 13.583-84) records an episode which demonstrates that this practice continues in the third century CE. He describes a young woman, Gnathaena, who is madly in love with a comic poet, Diphilus.

> Once in a dramatic contest it happened that he (Diphilus) was shamefully defeated and 'lifted' out of the theater, yet none the less he went to visit Gnathaena. As Diphilus bade her wash his feet Gnathaena asked, 'Why need I, indeed? Haven't you come to me on your head?'[1]

The point of interest for the present inquiry is that even after Diphilus suffers a humiliating defeat, he still expects his feet to be washed when he arrives at Gnathaena's home.

b. *Banquet.* By far the best documented and most frequent accounts of footwashing are to be found in contexts where the washing precedes a meal or banquet. The evidence for this practice is both explicit and implicit in nature.

Herodotus (2.172) records the story of Amasis who became king of Egypt. One episode in particular depicts Amasis's cunning ability:

> Apries being thus deposed, Amasis became king; he was of a town called Siuph in the province of Sais. Now at first he was condemned and held in but little regard by the Egyptians, as having been but a common man and of no high family, but presently he won them to him by being cunning and not arrogant. He had among his countless treasures a golden footbath, in which he and all those who feasted with him were ever wont to wash their feet. This he broke in pieces and made thereof a god's image, which he set in the most fitting place in the city; and the Egyptians came ever and anon to this image and held it in great reverence. When Amasis knew what the townsmen did, he called the Egyptians together and told them that the image had been made out of the footbath; once (said he) his subjects had washed their feet in it and put it to yet viler uses; now they greatly revered it. 'So now' (quoth he to them) 'it has fared with me as with the footbath; once I was a common man, now I am your king; it is your duty to honor me and hold me in regard.'[2]

One issue of relevance to the present study is that the golden foot bath

---

1. Cited according to the translation of C.B. Gulick, *Athenaeus: The Deipnosophists* (London: William Heinemann, 1937), VI, p. 147.

2. Cited according to the translation of A.D. Godley, *Herodotus* (Cambridge, MA: Harvard University Press, 1964), I, pp. 485-87.

was used for banquet guests to wash their feet. This text clearly indicates that footwashing was a regular part of the king's feasts. It should also be observed that footwashing and degradation are closely associated in this text.

An extraordinary footwashing is described by Plutarch (*Phocion* 1.20.2). The account relates how Phocion's son, Phocus, competed in the Pan-Athenian games and was victorious. As a result, a number of banquet invitations were extended to Phocus, who had a proclivity for wine and irregular behavior:

> But Phocion declined the other invitations and granted the coveted honor to one host only. And when he (Phocion) went to the banquet and saw the general magnificence of the preparations, and particularly the footbasins of spiced wine that were brought to the guests as they entered, he called his son and said: 'Phocus, do not let thy companion ruin thy victory'.[1]

Not only does Plutarch document the place of footwashing at a banquet, but he also demonstrates that the footwashing itself could be made more luxurious depending upon the stature of the guest. In this case, water is replaced by spiced wine.

On a painted vase, a scene depicts Procrustes and a 'guest' reclining on a bed. Under the bed is a foot basin.[2] Despite Procrustes' inhumane treatment of strangers, the foot basin gives the appearance of hospitality.

Athenaeus (*Deipnosophists* 9.408-409) makes numerous references to washing the hands before a banquet but says little in an explicit fashion about the feet. However, at the end of this discussion he notes:

> They used to call the dirty water (ἀπόνιμμα) from the hands and feet ἀπόνιπτρον.[3]

Without ever describing footwashing, Athenaeus here implies that washing the feet did take place before the meal.

An elegant reception is recounted (*Satyricon* 31) by Petronius, a Latin writer of the mid-first century CE:

---

1. Cited according to the translation of B. Perrin, *Plutarch's Lives* (New York: G.P. Putnam's Sons, 1919), VIII, pp. 189-91.

2. Cf. Sudhoff, p. 25.

3. Cited according to the translation of C.B. Gulick, *Athenaeus: The Deipnosophists* (London: William Heinemann, 1969), IV, p. 357.

> At last then we sat down, and boys from Alexandria poured water cooled with snow over our hands. Others followed and knelt down at our feet, and proceeded with great skill to pare our hangnails. Even this unpleasant duty did not silence them, but they kept singing at their work.[1]

As in the banquet described by Plutarch, the host spares no effort in providing his guests with the most gracious pleasures available. Even though the feet are not mentioned as being washed, the note about their hangnails being removed implies that the footwashing has already taken place. Petronius gives primary attention to the excessive gesture of hospitality offered.

In some evidence it appears that removing the shoes before a banquet intimates that footwashing follows. Plato (*Symposium* 213 B) describes the arrival of Alcibiades at the home of Agathon, where Socrates is already at the table:

> Then Agathon said to the servants, 'Take off Alcibiades' shoes, so that he can recline here with us two'.[2]

Alcibiades then joins the two at the table. The removal of the shoes possibly entails the washing of the feet.

Martial, a Latin epigrammatist of the first century CE, uses a similar expression in describing the strategy whereby a certain Ligurinus secures an audience for the reading of his literary works (*Epigrams* 3.50):

> This, no other, is your reason for inviting me to dine, that you may recite your verses, Ligurinus. I have put off my shoes; at once a huge volume is brought along with the lettuce and the fish sauce. A second is read through while the first course stands waiting; there is a third, and the dessert does not yet appear; and you recite a fourth, and finally a fifth book. Sickening is a boar if you serve it to me so often. If you don't consign your accursed poems to the mackerel, in future, Ligurinus, you shall dine at home alone.[3]

In this text the unfolding of the meal is described in careful detail. The shoes are unquestionably removed at the moment the guests

---

1.   Cited according to the translation of M. Heseltine, *Petronius: Satyricon* (London: William Heinemann, 1930), p. 47.

2.   Cited according to the translation of W.R.M. Lamb, *Plato: Lysis, Symposium, Gorgias* (London: William Heinemann, 1925), p. 211.

3.   Cited according to the translation of W.C.A. Ker, *Martial: Epigrams* (London: William Heinemann, 1930), I, pp. 193-94.

arrive. Again, the washing of the feet may be implied in the comment about the removal of the shoes.

Removal of the shoes at a banquet is also documented by artistic works. An Alexandrian relief of the third century BCE portrays Dionysus's arrival at a home. His host welcomes him to recline at the table while a servant removes Dionysus's sandals.[1] Similarly, a dining room wall painting from a house in Pompeii depicts a banquet in progress. An arriving guest is greeted with a cup of wine offered by one servant and the removal of his shoes is accomplished by another servant.[2]

4. *Footwashing and Service*

Of special importance in understanding the meaning of Jn 13.1-20 is an identification of those normally required to wash another's feet. Without doubt, this task was generally the duty of slaves or servants. Many pieces of evidence cited previously in the study have anticipated this fact. The following additional evidence indicates the status of those who wash the feet of others.

Homer (*Odyssey* 19.308) indicates that servant girls welcome Odysseus into the home of Penelope (cf. section 3.a. above). The marble relief which depicts this scene portrays Odysseus's feet being washed by a servant. The skyphos from Chios shows the wandering Odysseus leaning on a walking stick while a servant washes his left foot. Plato (*Symposium* 213 B), Petronius (*Satyricon* 31), an Alexandrian relief of Dionysus, and the wall painting from Pompeii (all discussed above) imply that servants are instrumental in the process of welcoming a guest by footwashing.

In Homer's story Odysseus insists that none but an old servant woman be allowed to wash his feet:

> Nor shall any woman touch my foot of all those who are serving-women in the hall, unless there is some old, true-hearted dame who has suffered in her heart as many woes as I; such a one I would not grudge to touch my feet (*Odyssey* 19.344-48).[3]

---

1. Cf. J. Godwin, *Mystery Religions in the Ancient World* (San Francisco: Harper & Row, 1981), p. 139.
2. Cf. M. Grant, *The Art and Life of Pompeii and Herculaneum* (New York: Newsweek, 1979), p. 107.
3. Murray, *Homer: Odyssey*, II, p. 253.

Penelope intercedes and offers Eurycleia for this task:

> She shall wash thy feet, weak with age though she be. Come now, wise Eurycleia, arise and wash the feet of the one of like age with thy master (*Odyssey* 19.356-58).[1]

Eurycleia responds:

> Therefore will I wash thy feet, both for Penelope's own sake and for thine (*Odyssey* 19.376-77).[2]

Homer continues the narrative:

> So he spoke and the old dame took the shining cauldron with water where-from she was about to wash his feet, and poured in cold water in plenty, and then added thereto warm. . . So he (Odysseus) spoke, and the old woman went forth through the hall to bring water for his feet, for all the first was spilled. And when she had washed him, and anointed him richly with oil, Odysseus again drew his chair nearer to the fire to warm himself, and hid his scar with his rags (*Odyssey* 19.386-89, 503-507).[3]

In describing the fall of Miletus to the Persians, Herodotus (6.19) documents that footwashing could be used as a synonym for slavery. He cites a Delphic utterance and explains it as being fulfilled:

> In that day, Miletus, thou planner of works that are evil,
> Thou for a banquet shall serve a guerdon rich shall be the spoiler;
> Many the long-locked gallants whose feet shall be washed by thy women.
> Woe for my Didyman shrine! No more shall its ministers tend it.
>
> All this now came upon the Milesians; for the most part of their men were slain by the longhaired Persians, and their women and children were accounted as slaves. . .[4]

Not only is the reference to the Milesian women washing the feet of the Persians an obvious sign of subjugation, but Herodotus refers to the women as slaves. The involuntary nature of the service and the forced slavery of the women indicate a concrete connection between between slavery and footwashing.

Catullus, a Latin poet of the first century BCE, also associates foot-

---

1. Murray, *Homer: Odyssey*, II, p. 255.
2. *Ibid.*
3. *Ibid.*, pp. 263-65.
4. Cited according to the translation of A.D. Godley, *Herodotus* (Cambridge, MA: Harvard University Press, 1963), III, pp. 165-67.

washing with slavery. He describes the anguish of Ariadna over abandonment by Theseus in this manner (64.158-63):

> If thou hadst no mind to wed with me for dread of the harsh bidding of thy stern father, yet thou couldst have led me into thy dwellings to serve thee as a slave with labour of love, laving thy white feet with liquid water, or with purple coverlet spreading thy bed.[1]

Ariadna so loves Theseus that given the choice between being abandoned by him or being his slave, she would prefer slavery. Again, the act of footwashing is used as a symbol of slavery.

A significant text is found in Plutarch's *Pompey* (73.6-7), which describes Pompey's defeat by Caesar and the former's subsequent humiliation and flight in retreat. Pompey, who is described as being totally at the mercy of others, boards a ship with two associates, Lentul and Favonius:

> Now, when it was time for supper and the master of the ship had made such provision for them as he could, Favonius, seeing that Pompey, for lack of servants, was beginning to take off his shoes, ran to him and took off his shoes for him, and helped him to anoint himself. And from that time on he continued to give Pompey such ministry and service as slaves give their masters, even down to the washing of his feet and the preparation of his meals. . . [2]

The text is quite clear in identifying footwashing and slavery. Also important here is the possible equation between 'removing the shoes' and 'washing the feet'.

Another text in Plutarch (*Theseus* 11) makes explicit the derogatory nature of being compelled to wash another's feet. In this section Plutarch tells how and why Theseus killed Sciron:

> Sciron robbed the passers by, according to the prevalent traditions; but as some say, he would insolently and wantonly thrust out his feet to strangers and bid them wash them, and then, while they were washing them, kick them off into the sea.[3]

1.   Cited according to the translation of F.W. Cornish, *The Poems of Gaius Valerius Catullus* (Cambridge, MA: Harvard University Press, 1912), p. 109.

2.   Cited according to the translation of B. Perrin, *Plutarch's Lives* (London: William Heinemann, 1917), I, p. 309.

3.   Cited according to the translation of B. Perrin, *Plutarch's Lives* (New York: Macmillan, 1914), I, p. 21.

Here Plutarch emphasizes the indignity of this forced footwashing by stressing that these victims were strangers. When Sciron tried to inflict these injuries upon Theseus, Sciron was thrown off the cliffs.

The story of Sciron and Theseus inspired a number of artistic renderings. One painted vase shows Sciron with his foot in a foot basin gesturing to a young traveler to wash his feet.[1] Several other painted vases portray Theseus in various stages of dispensing with Sciron. These include Theseus attacking Sciron with the footbasin,[2] as well as Theseus throwing Sciron, over the footbasin, into the sea.[3]

Petronius (*Satyricon* 70.8) records an extravagant footwashing:

> I am ashamed to tell you what followed: in defiance of all convention, some longhaired boys brought ointment in a silver basin (pelve), and anointed our feet as we lay, after winding little garlands around our feet and ankles.[4]

As in the other reference in Petronius (*Satyricon* 31), the preparations are quite elegant.

The lowly nature of the service of washing the feet is made graphically clear by Epictetus, a Stoic philosopher of the first century CE. In a discussion about undue arrogance, Epictetus demonstrates that everyone must perform certain unpleasant tasks (*Discourses* 1.19):

> All men pay respect to me. Well, I also pay respect to my platter, and I wash it and wipe it; and for the sake of my oil flask, I drive a peg into the wall. Well then, are these things superior to me? No, but they supply some of my wants and for this reason I take care of them. Well, do I not attend to my ass? Do I not wash his feet? Do I not clean him?[5]

Several passages in Athenaeus (*Deipnosophists* 9.408-11) assign the task of washing the hands and feet of banquet guests to servants.[6]

---

1.   Cf. Sudhoff, p. 12.
2.   Cf. *ibid.*, p. 13.
3.   Cf. *ibid.*, pp. 14-15.
4.   Cited according to the translation of M. Heseltine, *Petronius* (London: William Heinemann, 1925), p. 135.
5.   Cited according to the translation of G. Long, *The Discourses of Epictetus* (New York: A.L. Burt, 1897), p. 65.
6.   In Athenaeus's *Deipnosophists* 13.583-84, the discussion about Gnathaena's refusal to wash the feet of the poet Diphilus may offer a small piece of relevant information. Gnathaena refuses to wash Diphilus's feet because he has been humiliated in defeat and comes running to her. It may be that due to his disastrous

A final piece of evidence that footwashing is the responsibility of servants is found on a painted vase. Here a young nude woman is emptying water from a foot basin.[1]

In Greek literature it is extremely rare for a non-slave to wash someone else's feet. These occasions ordinarily call for special comment by the author(s).

Aristophanes, a Greek poet of the fifth to fourth century BCE, describes such a practice in recounting the boasts of a father returning home from work (*Wasps* 605-11):

> But the nicest and pleasantest part of it all is this, which I'd wholly forgotten to say. 'Tis when with my fee in my wallet I come, returning home at the close of the day. O then what a welcome I get for its sake; my daughter, the darling, is foremost of all, And she washes my feet and anoints them with care, And above them she stoops, and a kiss lets fall, Till at last by the pretty Papas of her tongue she angles withal my three-obol away.[2]

Without doubt the actions of the daughter are unusual, since there is little evidence that children washed their parents' feet. On this occasion, it appears that the true motivation for the footwashing is greed, since her 'loving' ministrations are actually calculated to result in the acquisition of the three-obol piece. Despite the stigma attached to footwashing, the motive of the daughter overrides societal norms.

The Loeb *Greek Anthology* contains an epigram that shows a rather more genuine tie between footwashing and devotion (*Palatine*

attempt to win the dramatic contest and his subsequent undignified flight, Gnathaena may not feel that she is subordinate to Diphilus. Consequently, it is not necessary for her to now wash his feet. If this interpretation is correct, the text speaks to the issue of footwashing and servitude from a different perspective. Since Gnathaena is no longer subordinate, she is no longer required to wash Diphilus's feet. On the other hand, the point may be that Diphilus came 'on his head', hence his feet did not get dirty. Several other passages in Athenaeus (*Deipnosophists* 9.408-11) assign the task of washing the hands and feet of banquet guests to servants.

1.   Cf. Sudhoff, p. 24. There is some question as to the woman's identity and that of the one for whom she empties the basin. Sudhoff calls the woman a *Dämchen* (woman of ill-repute?). Kötting refers to her in a discussion of servitude. Whether she is emptying the footbasin for herself or another, the task is a difficult one for her. Sudhoff emphasizes the effort which she must put forth to manage the job. The main point here is that this woman must perform this menial task because of her position in society.

2.   Cited according to the translation of B.B. Rogers, *Aeschylus, Sophocles, Euripides, and Aristophanes* (Chicago: Encyclopedia Britannica, 1952), p. 515.

Anthology 12.68). Meleager, the first-century BCE Greek epi-grammatist describes the emotions of a person about to be separated from a loved one by death:

> I wish not Charidemus to be mine; for the fair boy looks to Zeus, as if al-ready serving the god with nectar. I wish it not. . . I am content if only the boy, as he mounts to Olympus, take from earth my tears to wash his feet in memory of my love; and could he but give me one sweet, melting glance and let our lips just meet as I snatch one kiss! Let Zeus have all the rest, as is right; but yet, if he were willing, perchance I, too, should taste ambrosia.[1]

The extreme of devotion to someone can be exemplified in washing the feet with tears. Love is clearly the motive.

Finally, Plutarch (*Moralia, Bravery of Women* 12.249d) describes the exceptional conduct of a group of young women on the island of Ceos, stating that they went so far as to wash the feet of one another's parents and brothers:

> It was a custom for the maidens of Ceos to go in a company to the public shrines and spend the day together, and their suitors watched their sports and dances. At evening they went by turns to each one's home and waited upon (διηκονοῦντο) one another's parents and brothers even to washing their feet.[2]

This episode confirms that footwashing was considered a servile task; it also shows that, despite the unseemly connotations, certain young women could voluntarily wash the feet of those whom they honored.

5. *Summary*

Footwashing was a widespread practice in the Graeco-Roman world. It appears in a variety of contexts, from ritual purification to personal comfort. Several aspects of this survey are important for a proper un-derstanding of Jesus' actions in John 13.

First, footwashing was a sign of preparation in Graeco-Roman antiquity. It was so commonplace that to approach a task without

---

1. Cited according to the translation of W.R. Paton, *The Greek Anthology* (Cambridge, MA: Harvard University Press, 1963), IV, pp. 313-15.
2. Cited according to the translation of F.C. Babbitt, *Plutarch's Moralia* (Cambridge, MA: Harvard University Press, 1968), III, pp. 509-11.

adequate preparation could be described in a traditional saying as acting 'with unwashed feet'.

Second, descriptions of footwashing most frequently occur in banquet settings. In these situations a host provides water (in some cases spiced wine or ointments) for the use of the guests. Such practice was commonplace and appears to be presumed. Most texts place the washing at the time the guests arrive.

Third, slaves usually perform this task. Not only do servants draw the water, wash the feet, and dispose of the water, but it appears that a slave could not refuse to render this service, no matter how old he or she might be. Consequently, footwashing could be used as a synonym for slavery. To wash another's feet symbolized the subjugation of one person to another. Therefore, those who received footwashing from another were social superiors of those who performed the task.

Fourth, on rare occasions an individual might perform this chore without obligation as an act of love and honor. In these exceptional situations love is often the motivation for such service.

Each of these conclusions is of significance for understanding John 13.

C. *Footwashing in the New Testament*

In addition to footwashing in John 13, the motif of footwashing occurs several times in the New Testament. Two passages in the gospels relate how Jesus had his feet washed by a woman's tears and dried with her hair.

In Luke 7.36-50, a sinful woman enters the home of a Pharisee and anoints Jesus' feet:

> [36]Now one of the Pharisees invited Jesus to have dinner with him, so he went to the Pharisee's house and reclined at the table. [37]When a woman who had lived a sinful life in that town learned that Jesus was eating at the Pharisee's house, she brought an alabaster jar of perfume, [38]and as she stood behind him at his feet weeping, she began to wet his feet with her tears. Then she wiped them with her hair, kissed them and poured perfume on them. [39]When the Pharisee who had invited him saw this, he said to himself, 'If this man were a prophet, he would know who is touching him and what kind of woman she is—that she is a sinner'. [40]Jesus answered him, 'Simon, I have something to tell you'. 'Tell me, teacher', he said. [41]'Two men owed money to a certain moneylender. One owed him five hundred denarii, and the other fifty. [42]Neither of them had

the money to pay him back, so he canceled the debts of both. Now which of them will love him more?' [43]Simon replied, 'I suppose the one who had the bigger debt canceled'. 'You have judged correctly, Jesus said. [44]Then he turned toward the woman and said Simon, 'Do you see this woman? I came into your house. You did not give me any water for my feet, but she wet my feet with her tears and wiped them with her hair.[45]You did not give me a kiss, but this woman, from the time I entered, has not stopped kissing my feet. [46]You did not put oil on my head, but she has poured perfume on my feet. [47]Therefore, I tell you, her many sins have been forgiven—for she loved much. But he who has been forgiven little loves little'. [48]Then Jesus said to her, 'Your sins are forgiven'. [49]The other guests began to say among themselves, 'Who is this who even forgives sins?' [50]Jesus said to the woman, 'Your faith has saved you; go in peace'.

There are a number of similarities between this text and others considered in this chapter. First, v. 44 confirms that footwashing was regarded as a normal part of hospitality in that Jesus reminds his host that no water was offered for washing the feet. Second, the subordinate role of the woman who performs the washing and anointing is made clear by the frequent mention of her sinful status (vv. 37, 39, 47-49). In fact, Simon thinks that her sinful status disqualifies her as one fit to touch Jesus' feet. Third, although she is subordinate in role, nothing requires the woman to wash the feet of Jesus except love (v. 47). Her use of perfume instead of water also suggests love as the motive for the action.

In addition to the account found in Jn 13.1-20, the Fourth Gospel contains yet another pericope in which footwashing is described.[1] Jn 12.1-8 describes the anointing of Jesus' feet by Mary, Lazarus's sister:

[1]Six days before the Passover, Jesus arrived at Bethany, where Lazarus lived, whom Jesus had raised from the dead. [2]Here a dinner was given in Jesus' honor. Martha served, while Lazarus was among those reclining at the table with him. [3]Then Mary took about a pint of pure nard, an expensive perfume; she poured it on Jesus' feet and wiped his feet with her hair. And the house was filled with the fragrance of the perfume. [4]But one of his disciples, Judas Iscariot, who was later to betray him, objected, [5]'Why wasn't this perfume sold and the money given to the poor? It was worth a year's wages'. [6]He did not say this because he cared about the

---

1.   Mt. 26.6-13 and Mk 14.3-9 show a number of similarities to Jn 12.1-8. However, since they do not explicitly mention footwashing they will not be considered in this survey.

poor but because he was a thief; as keeper of the money bag, he used to help himself to what was put into it. [7]'Leave her alone', Jesus replied. 'It was meant that she should save this perfume for the day of my burial. [8]You will always have the poor among you, but you will not always have me'.

This passage contains some features typical in accounts of footwashing. First, the washing takes place in the context of a meal. Second— as in certain banquet contexts—the washing/anointing is done with an extravagant substance, an expensive perfume costing one year's wages. However, a third aspect of this passage is not part of the other footwashing materials surveyed. Jesus defends this elaborate anointing as justified because it is preparation for his burial. Therefore, Jn 12.7 adds a new dimension which may relate to the significance of Jesus' own actions in John 13.

Finally, one passage in the Pastorals (1 Tim. 5.9, 10) mentions footwashing:

[9]No widow may be put on the list of widows unless she is over sixty, has been faithful to her husband, [10]and is well-known for her good deeds, such as bringing up children, showing hospitality, washing the feet of the saints, helping those in trouble and devoting herself to all kinds of good deeds.

For several reasons it is difficult to discern the significance of footwashing in this passage. 1 Tim. 5.9, 10 will be discussed more fully in Chapter 5, but for now it should be noted that, of all the materials surveyed, this text is the only one which places footwashing within a list of duties and responsibilities. While one might conclude that these widows are expected to wash the feet of others due to the generally subordinate position of women in antiquity, these women appear to have a role of prominence in the community.

D. *Implications for John 13.1-20*

Some of the most important implications of this survey of footwashing texts for the interpretation of Jn 13.1-20 are listed here. Chapter 4 will explore the other relevant data.

1. A finding of this survey which has extremely important implications for an examination of John 13 is the close connection that exists between footwashing and preparation. In the vast majority of texts and

artistic representations consulted, footwashing serves to prepare one for a specific task, experience, or relationship. Specifically, footwashing can prepare one for religious duties, or for sharing a meal, a bed, or an intimate relationship. In point of fact, the idiomatic use of 'with unwashed feet' comes to mean 'without adequate preparation'. The emphasis on preparation is immensely significant in Jn 13.1-20, for the whole of John 13–17 is devoted to Jesus' preparation of the disciples for his departure and for their subsequent role and function. Standing first in this strategic section of the Johannine narrative, the footwashing account serves to emphasize in a very powerful fashion the disciples' need for adequate preparation and Jesus' personal agency in the preparatory process. This aspect of footwashing's significance not only clarifies the meaning of Jesus' action but also deserves to be taken into account when grappling with Jesus' instructions that the disciples should wash one another's feet.

2. The servant motif is clearly a prominent dimension of Jn 13.1-20. Since servants perform this task in the majority of cases, Jesus implicitly assumes the role of the servant in washing the feet of the disciples. But in order that this aspect is not missed, Jesus' actions themselves draw attention to the function of the slave. Jesus removes his clothes and girds himself with a towel, attire that is reminiscent of the dress of servants depicted in Roman works of art. John also describes the taking of the basin and the drawing of water, actions that were assigned specifically to slaves according to the evidence from antiquity. Therefore, whatever else may be in view in Jn 13.1-20, Jesus' identification with the servant's role is prominent.

3. The motivation for the action is explicitly described as love (v. 1). On the one hand, this statement coheres well with the sparse evidence that on rare occasions an individual might freely take on this chore as an act of love or devotion. On the other hand, Jesus' action is unparalleled in ancient evidence, for no other person of superior status is described as voluntarily washing the feet of a subordinate. The unique aspect of Jesus' action emphasizes that the footwashing was motivated by love.

4. Peter's initial response to Jesus' action is also clarified through the preceding survey. Since footwashing most frequently took place in

banquet settings or functioned as a sign of hospitality, Peter's protest is natural. He interprets Jesus' actions as an offer of hospitality. Peter rejects Jesus' offer because it violates so many standards of status and, as a result, threatens to prove humiliating to Peter personally. Such misunderstanding is recognized as a typical feature of the Fourth Gospel.

5. Jesus makes clear that his washing of the disciples' feet is no mere gesture of hospitality, but an act which cleanses them and ensures their membership (μέρος) with Jesus. Since footwashing figures as a part of cultic cleansing, its use as a sign of cleansing and purification by Jesus is neither inexplicable nor completely unexpected.

6. Given the burial interpretation ascribed to the footwashing described in Jn 12.1-8, it is possible that Jesus' actions are to be regarded as having reference to his death. The reader is thus prepared beforehand for the way in which footwashing prefigures the cross in John 13.

7. The text from 1 Timothy indicates that footwashing was practiced by widows in some early Christian churches, which raises the question of whether Jn 13.14 is to be understood literally.

Chapter 4

LITERARY AND EXEGETICAL ANALYSIS

A. *General Introduction*

The purpose of this chapter is to examine the text of Jn 13.1-20 on its own terms. In order to do this, two distinct but complementary aspects of literary inquiry are utilized.

The first major division of the chapter is devoted to literary contextualization. Three issues in particular are explored. (1) The literary structure of the Fourth Gospel is examined, giving special emphasis to the major literary divisions evident in the work. (2) Growing out of this inquiry is a study of the section which provides the immediate context of the footwashing pericope, namely, the farewell materials. (3) This leads to an investigation of the relationship between Jesus and his disciples in the preceding narrative of chs. 1–12.

The second major section of this chapter is given to a detailed literary-exegetical analysis of 13.1-20. The verse by verse format allows for extended discussions on particular literary themes and concepts at various points in the analysis.

The chapter ends withe two sections: the first summarizes the results of the analysis, and the second articulates the implications which these results have for the questions about the literary unity of Jn 13.1-20.

B. *Literary Contextualization*

1. *John 13.1-20 and the Literary Structure of the Fourth Gospel*
a. *John 13.1-20 and the 'Book of Glory'*
Although a number of views concerning the literary structure of John have been advocated,[1] for a variety of reasons the majority of scholars

---

1. For an extensive survey of the scholarly views on the literary structure of the Fourth Gospel, cf. G. Mlakuzhyil, *The Christocentric Literary Structure of the*

identify a major division in John's Gospel between chs. 12 and 13.[1] Perhaps the most important evidence for such a division of the text is the content and audience of each part. The first part of the Gospel portrays Jesus' interactions with the public, and the events tend to serve as signs. The second portion is preoccupied with 'the hour' and with Jesus' relationship with those closest to him. These two sections have been titled 'The Book of Signs' and 'The Book of Glory', respectively.[2] Brown describes the differences between the books in the following manner:

> First during the public ministry, as described in the Book of Signs, Jesus' words and deeds were addressed to a wide audience, provoking a crisis of faith—some believed and some refused to believe. The Book of Glory, however, is addressed to a restricted audience of those who believed. Second, the signs of the First Book anticipated what Jesus would do for men once He was glorified. The Second Book describes the glorification, i.e., 'the hour' of passion, crucifixion, resurrection, and ascension wherein Jesus is lifted up to the Father to enjoy again the glory that he had with the Father before the world existed (xvii 5).[3]

Other evidence for this division of the book is found in the final section of ch. 12. Jn 12.37-43 is a retrospective summation of Jesus' public ministry, which is now at a close. In particular, there is an emphasis on the unbelief of the majority of the Jewish people and the half-hearted belief by some of the leaders who would not confess their faith because of intimidation by the Pharisees. This unbelief on the part of the Jews is given a theological explanation on the basis of Isa. 6.10. Schnackenburg suggests that 12.37-43 functions as an epilogue

---

Fourth Gospel (Rome: Editrice Pontifico Istituto Biblico, 1987), p. 137-68.

   1.   This conviction is graphically exhibited in the physical format of Brown's two-volume commentary on the Gospel of John. Chapters 1–12 are treated in volume one, and volume two is devoted to chs. 13–21. Bultmann (p. 48) and Schnackenburg (II, p. 411) are other major commentators who share this position.

   2.   Brown, *The Gospel according to John*, I, pp. cxxxviii-cxxxviv and II, p. 541.

   3.   *Ibid.*, II, p. 541. Bultmann's position (p. 111) is compatible with Brown's. 'It is easy to discern the basic structure of the gospel: chs. 3–12 portray the revelation of the δόξα to the world. . . while in chs. 13–17 (or alternatively–20) is portrayed the revelation of the δόξα to the believers'.

to the first major division, balancing the epilogue to the entire book found in 20.30.[1]

Not only does John provide a summary about Jewish unbelief, but he also includes a compressed form of Jesus' public teaching in his final public discourse, which immediately follows the previous epilogue. This concluding discourse sums up 'the main points of all the revelatory discourse in the first main section, and it even takes up the message of the prologue'.[2] The final public discourse in itself suggests an ending of sorts, but when joined to the previous summation it carries even more weight as a conclusion.[3]

John combines these summary statements with the arrival of Jesus' hour in 13.1 to produce a rather obvious new beginning.[4] Brown describes 13.1 as the introduction to the entire book of glory,[5] and

1.　Schnackenburg, II, p. 411.

2.　*Ibid.*, p. 425.

3.　Mlakuzhyil (pp. 89-90) gives similar reasons for seeing a major division between 12 and 13. However, he sees 11–12 as a bridge section which serves to bring the first major division (2–12) to a close, while introducing the second major section of John's Gospel.

4.　Owanga-Welo offers a dissenting viewpoint based upon a structural analysis of the passion narrative. By using spatial and temporal indicators in the text, he argues that the passion narrative begins at 11.55 (cf. p. 123). Of primary importance to Owanga-Welo's view is the introduction of the nearness of Passover in 11.55. He suggests that since the rest of the passion narrative is concerned with the approach and arrival of Passover, the last portion of the Gospel begins at this point. Temporal indicators notwithstanding, one of the primary weaknesses of Owanga-Welo's view is that he does not come to terms with the summary statements which appear in the text. For example, after noting (p. 153) that 12.37-43 'represents an attempt by the narrator to interpret and explain what has been reported up to this point', little else is said. This mode of interpretation implies that if temporal and spatial indicators are absent, a passage does not serve as a major break (or division) in the text. J.L. Staley *The Print's First Kiss* (Atlanta: Scholars Press, 1988), pp. 66-70, also has a differing view. On the basis of a rhetorical reading of the Fourth Gospel, Staley defines the literary structure of John by means of the four ministry tours recorded therein (1.19–3.36; 4.1–6.71; 7.1–10.42; and 11.1–21.25). Yet, Staley acknowledges (p. 107) the pivotal nature of John 13. 'The first major division in the second half of the gospel (11.1–21.25) occurs at chapter 13. The section is universally recognized as the place in the story where Jesus turns toward his disciples and starts to reveal himself to them more openly through extended, private discourses.'

5.　Brown, *The Gospel according to John*, II, p. 560.

Schnackenburg observes, 'Even seen only from the outside there is nowhere else in the gospel such a strongly marked new beginning as the one at 13.1'.[1] From this point in the Fourth Gospel, there is little doubt that the passion narrative is underway.

What are the implications of such a division for an understanding of the footwashing pericope? First, because it stands at the beginning of the second portion of the gospel, footwashing takes on great importance. This location indicates that a close tie exists between the passion and the footwashing, for the latter is narrated in the shadow of 'the hour'.

The change in narrative audience is also significant for the meaning of footwashing. For the most part the 'Book of Signs' recounts Jesus' public ministry. However, despite those who respond in faith to Jesus and his message, most of the Jews either do not believe or have inadequate belief. The footwashing is clearly offered within the context of belief. Standing at the very beginning of the 'Book of Glory', it graphically introduces the idea of the passion and does so in a way which communicates the benefits of the passion to those who have responded in faith: the disciples.

b. *John 13.1-20 and the Farewell Materials*
If inclusion in the Book of Glory suggests that the context of Jn 13.1-20 is one of belief, the location of the pericope within the farewell materials makes this context of belief certain. John 13–17 describes the time which Jesus and his disciples spend together in private just before his arrest and departure. Obviously, the relation of the footwashing pericope to the farewell materials is significant for its interpretation.

There are well-known and numerous questions about the composition history of the farewell discourses. Many interpreters reconstruct their versions of the composition history of John 13–17, assign the various discourses to different hands, and explain each discourse on the basis of its assigned *Sitz im Leben*.[2] Although such endeavors

1.   Schnackenburg, III, p. 1.
2.   For representatives of this approach cf. Bultmann, pp. 455-631; J. Painter, 'The Farewell Discourses and the History of Johannine Christianity', *NTS* 27 (1980–81), pp. 525-43; and F.F. Segovia, *Love Relationships in the Johannine Tradition* (Chico, CA: Scholars Press, 1982).

contribute much, the question of the nature and purpose of the farewell discourses as a unit often receives inadequate attention. Thus it becomes important at this point to identify the purpose of the farewell discourse in the Johannine narrative and to survey the dominant themes of chs. 13–17. Both these inquiries should bring additional illumination to the footwashing pericope.

(1) *The Nature and Purpose of John 13–17.* The question concerning the purpose of the farewell materials may very well be tied to the literary genre of John 13–17. These chapters bear a number of similarities to farewell discourses found in a variety of contexts, particularly in the Old Testament, the literature of early Judaism, and other portions of the New Testament. Although not every characteristic is found in each text, it remains true that several aspects of the farewell discourses occur frequently enough to allow the contours of the genre to be discerned.[1]

Ordinarily, farewell discourses include several of the following elements.

1. A pious individual receives knowledge that death is imminent.
2. This revelation leads to a summons of his descendants, followers, or family.
3. The speaker reveals that he will soon depart.
4. This information leads variously to sorrow, anguish, and fear on the part of those in attendance.
5. Reference is often made to the history of the speaker or to his nation's history.
6. In many cases the figure gives a supreme and definitive teaching.
7. This teaching sometimes includes admonitions to love one another and to maintain unity with each other.
8. Promises and blessings are given concerning the future, as well as

---

1.   One of the more complete assessments of farewell discourses generally is that by J. Munck, 'Discours d'adieu dans le Nouveau Testament et dans la littérature biblique', in *Aux sources de la tradition chrétienne* (ed. O. Cullmann and P.H. Menoud; Neuchâtel: Delachaux et Niestlé, 1950), pp. 155-70. Cf. also the table of farewell discourses recorded by Stauffer, *New Testament Theology*, pp. 344-47.

9.   warnings about disobedience, false teaching, persecution, and the like.
10. A challenge is sometimes given by the speaker to follow or imitate his example.
11. On occasion, the farewell discourse concludes with a prayer.

Many of these elements are readily discernible in John 13–17.[1] Such similarity between John 13–17 and farewell discourses generally, when added to the mounting interest in Jesus' hour throughout the Gospel and the dramatic emphasis of 13.1, makes it likely that the readers of the Fourth Gospel would appreciate the strong emphasis the author places upon the departure and death of Jesus.

Yet, for all its similarities to the genre, John 13–17 is not simply one among many farewell discourses. Brown notes that

> in the Last Discourse Jesus speaks to 'his own' (xiii 1) for whom he is willing to lay down his life, so intense is his love (xv 13). The Jesus who speaks here transcends time and space; he is a Jesus who is already on his way to the Father, and his concern is that he shall not abandon those who believe in him but must remain in the world (xiv 18, xvii 11). Although he speaks at the Last Supper, he is really speaking from heaven; although those who hear him are his disciples, his words are directed to Christians of all times. The Last Discourse is Jesus' last testament: it is meant to be read after he has left the earth. Yet it is not like other last testaments, which are the recorded words of men who are dead and can speak no more;. . . (these words have) been transformed in the light of the resurrection and through the coming of the Paraclete into a living discourse delivered, not by a dead man, but by one who has life (vi 57), to all readers of the Gospel.[2]

Through the farewell discourses the author is preparing the reader for Jesus' departure and death. Whereas in the Book of Signs the explanation of a sign's significance comes after the act, here it may be said that the explanation precedes the event (death–resurrection), functioning as a means to prepare the reader for the climax of the story. The post-resurrection perspective of the author makes such an inversion possible.[3]

---

1.   For a comparison of the Johannine farewell discourses with those found in the Old Testament and the literature of early Judaism, cf. Brown, *The Gospel according to John*, II, pp. 597-601.
2.   *Ibid.*, pp. 581-82.
3.   *Ibid.*, p. 581.

The primary purpose of the Johannine farewell materials 'is above all to provide a basis for the disciples' (and all believers') continuing community with Jesus, in spite of the imminent separation, and to strengthen the future Christian community in its believing existence'.[1] The context of belief (the Book of Glory) and the context of 'his own' (the farewell materials) indicate that Jesus prepares the disciples for his imminent departure by building upon their present belief and assuring them about their future (continued) relationship and mission.

(2) *Structure and Dominant Themes of John 13–17.* The identification of the major themes of John 13–17 is in many ways bound to the issue of the structure of these chapters. However, because of lingering questions about the literary unity of the farewell discourses, there is as yet no consensus concerning the literary structure.[2] Segovia asserts, 'Nowadays hardly any exegete would vigorously maintain that Jn 13.31–18.1 constitutes a literary unity as it stands'.[3] Convinced of the composite nature of the section, many exegetes believe that the most appropriate way to interpret chs. 13–17 is to examine each individual discourse according to its redactional Sitz im Leben.

The obstacles to treating 13–17 as a literary unit are indeed formidable (the most notable example being the major break in sequence between 14.31 and 18.1 caused by 15.1–17.26). Yet despite the many problems, scholars continue to find signs of literary coherence and congruence in these chapters.[4] Such signs are evidence that the composition of these chapters was not without design and reflection. Therefore, it is legitimate to attempt to reconsider the structure of chs. 13–17, as they now stand, as a coherent unit.

---

1.   Schnackenburg, III, p. 4.
2.   For an overview of the scholarly debate about the composition of the Johannine farewell discourses, cf. Segovia, *Love Relationships in the Johannine Tradition,* pp. 82-97; Brown, *The Gospel according to John,* II, pp. 582-97; Schnackenburg, III, pp. 89-93; and J. Ph. Kaefer, 'Les discourses d'adieu en Jean 13.31–17.26: rédaction et théologie', *NovT* 26 (1984), pp. 253-82.
3.   Segovia, *Love Relationships in the Johannine Tradition,* p. 82.
4.   Notable are the thematic parallels between 13.31–14.31 and 16.4b-33 (cf. Brown, *The Gospel according to John,* II, pp. 588-97), the claims for the literary unity of 15.1–16.1 (cf. Schnackenburg, III, pp. 91-93), and the common themes of 13 and 17 (cf. Brown, *The Gospel according to John,* II, p. 745).

Part 1: 'Preparation through Cleansing and Prediction of Betrayal' (13.1-30).[1] It is quite appropriate for the initial portion of the farewell materials to be devoted to the footwashing. As observed in Chapter 3, the practice of footwashing always conveyed the idea of preparation. Since preparation for departure is one of the primary reasons for a farewell discourse, John's use of the footwashing story at this particular juncture underscores the transition in his narrative from the Book of Signs to the Book of Glory.

Of the many themes that might be identified in the footwashing pericope, perhaps the most dominant one is that of cleansing. For not only does Jesus declare the disciples to be clean after the footwashing (v. 10), but it also appears that this cleansing was necessary for the disciples to have μέρος with him (v. 8). The combination of the farewell genre, the general association of footwashing with preparation, and the position of this pericope within the Book of Glory serve to emphasize the importance of this cleansing.

Another major theme in 13.1-30 is the prediction of Jesus' betrayal and denial. Although the readers of the Fourth Gospel know quite well that Jesus will be betrayed by Judas (in the immediate context cf. 13.2, 11 and 18), the disciples are stunned by this revelation (cf. v. 22) and find themselves confused about who is going to betray Jesus (cf. v. 28).

Part 2: 'The First Farewell Discourse' (13.31–14.31). The main theme of departure and return is introduced in 13.31-38, for here Jesus begins to inform the disciples of his departure and predicts Peter's threefold denial. The major emphasis in ch. 14 is Jesus' offer of comfort and his promise to provide certain resources for the disciples during his absence. Primarily, this provision takes shape in (1) the promise of a future dwelling place in the Father's house, (2) the assurance that Jesus is going to the Father to intercede on their behalf with him, (3) the promise that the disciples will work greater works than Jesus and will receive what they request from the Father for his

---

1. Several items, which will be discussed later, support the decision to take 13.1-30 as part of the farewell materials. Of special significance is v. 1 which (a) describes the arrival of Jesus' hour, (b) mentions his complete love for the disciples, and (c) emphasizes Jesus' knowledge of his imminent departure and return to the Father. Each of these issues is not only important in the Book of Glory, but in the farewell discourses as well.

glory, and (4) the promise to send another paraclete who will be with the disciples, to teach them, and to remind them of Jesus' words.

The promised provisions serve to encourage the disciples not to be troubled or to abandon their faith. Jesus promises certain provisions to ensure their spiritual well-being.

Part 3: 'The Second Farewell Discourse' (15.1–16.3). Part 3a: 'The True Vine' (15.1-17). This section confirms the disciples' union/ solidarity with Jesus and challenges them to continue in that unity. The metaphor of the vine graphically conveys the importance of spiritual intimacy between Jesus and his disciples. Their present belief and status as believers are confirmed several times in the passage (15.3, 5, 15, and 16). Such affirmation from Jesus in the farewell discourse would serve to encourage and comfort the disciples who have just recently learned of his impending betrayal and departure. Yet, much of the pericope consists of admonitions to the effect that the disciples must maintain their relationship with and in Jesus or risk being 'cut off' and 'cast out'. To ensure unity with Jesus, the disciples are directed to remain in him by keeping his commands, most particularly, that of loving one another. Through these actions, a close bond is promised to continue between the Father, Jesus, and the disciples.

Part 3b: 'The World's Hatred' (15.18–16.4a). Again the unity between Jesus and the disciples is stressed in this section of the farewell discourse, although this time from a negative perspective. Here the solidarity is emphasized by pointing to the similarity of the treatment which Jesus and the disciples receive at the hands of a hating world. So close is the identity between the Father, Jesus, and the disciples, that to hate one necessarily entails hatred of the others. However, instead of becoming discouraged, the disciples are called to reflect upon the implications of such vile treatment. For even this negative experience gives testimony of the disciples' knowledge of and life in Jesus. Yet for all of this, the disciples are not to experience persecution passively. The Paraclete will aid them in bearing witness even in conditions of extreme duress. This divine aid, coupled with Jesus' warning that such treatment will surely come, helps to alleviate feelings of abandonment. Persecution confirms the disciples' solidarity with Jesus.

Part 3c: 'The Work of the Spirit' (16.4b-33). The departure and return of Jesus are at the heart of this section. Again the disciples are promised resources with which they may confront the future. Although it is similar to 13.31–14.31, this section gives more attention to provision for the believers as they encounter the world. (1) The Paraclete is reintroduced in order to present his role of proving the world guilty as well as that of providing additional guidance for the believers. (2) Although Jesus' departure will result in deep sorrow for his followers, the suffering will be transformed into joy, as with a woman in labor whose pain turns to joy at delivery. In part, this joy is the result of the disciples' direct access to the Father through Jesus' name. (3) In addition, the disciples are encouraged by the fact that Jesus has overcome the world. They will share in this victory. Ironically, these promises are given with the knowledge that soon many of the disciples will desert Jesus.

Part 4: 'Preparation through Jesus' Prayer' (17.1-26). The final part of the farewell materials differs in genre from that which precedes it. John 17 is a prayer which Jesus offers on behalf of his disciples. In addition to the thematic affinities between them, John 17 and 13 are similar in that the prayer, like the footwashing, is an action which takes place in the presence (and attention) of the disciples. In other words, the prayer is not only directed to the Father, but also functions as an instrument by which Jesus gives final preparation to the disciples for his departure.[1] (1) Verses 1-8 reflect upon the glorification of Jesus and the disciples' role in that glorification. (2) Verses 9-19 are devoted to petitions concerning the disciples' future safety and welfare. Special emphasis is given to their place in the world following Jesus' departure. (3) Verses 20-26 are more universal in scope and include petitions for all those who come to faith through the testimony of his disciples. Glory, love, protection, and unity are the major themes in the prayer.

From this survey, it is easy to appreciate the fashion in which each section of John 13–17 functions as part of the disciples' preparation. Not only do those passages traditionally identified as farewell discourses (14.1–16.33) bear out this observation, but the discourses find themselves enclosed by two significant actions on Jesus' part (the footwashing and his prayer), which have a similar emphasis.[2] Given its prominent position in chs. 13–17, its associations with preparation, and its cleansing significance, the footwashing pericope may be seen to play an integral part in this portion of the Johannine narrative.

1. Cf. Behler, p. 210.
2. Cf. Behler (p. 17), who comes to a similar conclusion.

2. *The Disciples in John 1–12*

Due to the obvious prominence of the disciples in chs. 13–17, a brief overview of their role in John 1–12 is provided to suggest an appropriate context for reading 13.1-20.

Unlike what has occurred in Markan studies, where the scholarly debate about discipleship has been intense, little attention has been devoted to discipleship in the Fourth Gospel.[1] Of the few available studies only the more recent attempts have sought to discern the literary significance of the disciples in John.[2] In this survey, the primary objectives are to discern the literary role of the disciples in the Fourth Gospel, assessing the way in which this group is utilized in the development of the Johannine plot.

Although they do not take part in every episode, the disciples appear frequently throughout the gospel in very strategic locations. Schnackenburg rightly observes:

> In those passages in which the disciples figure, they are not simply mentioned in passing, (but). . . they are introduced into these Johannine texts quite deliberately. They participate with Jesus in the activity in question and are actively involved in the event.[3]

In particular, attention needs to be paid to the disciples' function in the Fourth Gospel's plot. Culpepper has suggested that the Johannine plot is repeated over and over again in different stories in the gospel. He notes:

1.   Some of the earlier works include: A. Schulz, *Nachfolgen und Nachahmen* (Munich: Kösel, 1962), pp. 137-44, 161-76; R. Moreno Jimenez, 'El discípulo de Jesucristo, según el evangelio de S. Juan', *EstBíb* 30 (1971), pp. 269-311; and M. de Jonge, *Jesus: Stranger from Heaven and Son of God* (ed. and trans. J.E. Steely; Missoula, MT: Scholars Press, 1977), pp. 1-27.

2.   Cf. Schnackenburg, III, pp. 205-209; R.A. Culpepper, *Anatomy of the Fourth Gospel* (Philadelphia: Fortress Press, 1983), pp. 115-25; and F.F. Segovia, 'Discipleship in the Fourth Gospel', *Discipleship in the New Testament* (ed. F.F. Segovia; Philadelphia: Fortress Press, 1985), pp. 76-102. Segovia's contribution is both helpful and frustrating. After promising an analysis of the way in which the disciples function in the development of the Fourth Gospel, Segovia limits his study to John's original sequence and content. As a result, he omits from consideration Jn 21, 15–17; 13.34-35, and 13.1b-3, 12-20, and reverses the order of chs. 5 and 6. Unfortunately, this otherwise excellent study disregards one of the basic tenets of more recent literary analysis, the attempt to interpret the text as it now stands.

3.   Schnackenburg, III, p. 206.

Plot development in John, then, is a matter of how Jesus' identity comes to be recognized and how it fails to be recognized. Not only is Jesus' identity progressively revealed by the repetitive signs and discourses and the progressive enhancement of metaphysical and symbolic images, but each episode has essentially the same plot as the story as a whole. Will Nicodemus, the Samaritan woman, or the lame man recognize Jesus and thereby receive eternal life? The story is repeated over and over. No one can miss it. Individual episodes can almost convey the message of the whole; at least they suggest or recall it for those who know the story.[1]

If Culpepper is correct, any time the disciples are introduced into the narrative, their presence serves to teach the reader something about belief. Schnackenburg exhibits agreement with this same basic premise by noting, 'Whenever the disciples are mentioned by the evangelist, it is their faith that is the important issue'.[2] The following survey seeks to highlight the way in which the disciples' own faith is chronicled as well as the way in which they serve as examples by which to judge the response of other characters in the narrative.

From very near the narrative's start the disciples are present. The first two disciples, Andrew and an unnamed disciple (perhaps Philip), come from the circle of the Baptist's followers. In fact, their initial interest in Jesus comes as the direct result of John's testimony about Jesus. In words filled with deeper meaning, Jesus responds to the duo's inquiries with 'Come and see'. Andrew quickly finds his brother, Simon, and informs him that the Messiah has been found. Simon's short initial encounter with Jesus results in a new name, Cephas.

Philip (the earlier unnamed disciple?), a resident of the same town as Andrew and Simon, also brings someone to Jesus. The discussion about Jesus, in part, revolves around the possibility of 'anything good' coming from Nazareth. Philip's response to Nathaniel echoes Jesus' own words, 'Come and see'. Jesus' encounter with Nathaniel is no less revealing than his introduction to Simon. Not only has Jesus seen Nathaniel before they meet, but he is also aware of Nathaniel's spiritual integrity. Jesus calls him 'a true Israelite'. Nathaniel's response is to heap several significant titles upon Jesus: rabbi, Son of God, and King of Israel. These two passages end with a prediction that the new disciples will see even greater things.

Two issues stand out as most important in these stories. First, the

1.   Culpepper, pp. 88-89.
2.   Schnackenburg, III, p. 206.

disciples respond to Jesus with unbridled belief. Although explicit statements about faith come later (2.11), the titles given to Jesus by these individuals are lofty and give clear evidence of their decision to identify themselves with Jesus. There can be little doubt that the narrator intends the readers to see in these disciples the first fulfillment of the prologue's affirmation that those who receive the Logos are given the authority to become children of God (1.12).

Second, these stories also demonstrate the legitimacy of faith which results from the acceptance of another's testimony about Jesus. Since each of these first disciples has come to Jesus via someone's witness,[1] the reader comes to view such a route to belief as an appropriate means to faith.

The high expectations of the readers evoked by 1.50-51 are not disappointed in the following chapter, for ch. 2 provides additional shape and color to the disciples as well as glimpses into the complexities of discipleship and belief as they are presented in the Fourth Gospel. While at first glance it appears that the disciples play only a minor role in the two major stories narrated in John 2 (cf. vv. 2, 11, 12, 22), upon closer inspection it becomes clear that in some ways, both major events in this chapter transpire for the express benefit of the disciples. Although the disciples are at first given only passing mention in the beginning of the narrative of the wedding in Cana, v. 11 leaves no doubt that the purpose of this first sign was to produce faith in the disciples. Verse 12 testifies to a close relationship between Jesus and the disciples and to their developing belief in him.

In the pericope devoted to the cleansing of the temple, the role of the disciples is given attention only at the end of the story. Here, the readers are informed that it was only after the resurrection that Jesus' quotation of scripture (v. 17) and his prophetic utterance (v. 19) came to the memory of the disciples.

Verse 22, where it is said that the disciples remembered his words after Jesus' death, broadens the readers' scope immensely. Not only do the readers now have the advantage of the prologue's christological backdrop for the story of Jesus, but the introduction of a post-resurrectional perspective supplies a more well defined foreground.

---

1.   If Philip is not to be identified with the unnamed disciple in 1.37-39, then he is the only person whom Jesus personally calls in these opening verses. Even then, the majority of disciples come to faith by means of another's testimony.

Through the description of the disciples, the readers are being informed about adequate faith. That is to say, the post-resurrection frame of reference suggests that *complete* understanding is impossible before the resurrection. In some ways, such an enlargement of the narrative field of vision works to enhance the evaluation of the progress the disciples make in the narrative, despite their apparent failures.

This event is followed by a description of many who believed (ἐπίστευσαν) in Jesus' name due to the signs he performed, but to whom Jesus would not entrust (ἐπίστευεν) himself. Though the disciples are not mentioned in vv. 23-25, these verses serve to enhance the quality of the disciples' faith. Here for the first time, the readers encounter believers who apparently do not have adequate or genuine faith. These 'believers' are not believed by Jesus. The disciples serve as a sharp contrast to those of inadequate faith.

Other references to the disciples in the first portion of the Fourth Gospel primarily serve to affirm their role as workers with Jesus and to define more clearly their mission. Not only are they present as Jesus baptizes (3.22), but they themselves baptize (4.2). The most revealing passage comes in 4.31-38. Set in the context of the Samaritan encounter, these verses form an interlude of sorts. This passage is noteworthy in part because for the first time the disciples themselves misunderstand Jesus' words. Since they have just returned from town on a mission to purchase food, the disciples make rather literal assumptions concerning Jesus' talk about 'food'. In point of fact, Jesus is speaking about the sustenance derived from working in the harvest (of his Father). Such misunderstanding on the disciples' part will become more prominent as the narrative unfolds.

Before leaving this passage a further point should be made concerning the disciples and misunderstanding. It is possible to construe this literary device as a means by which the disciples are denigrated. On this view, their inability to comprehend Jesus is a sign that their own faith is inadequate. However, such a view is unwarranted and misses the overall image of the disciples. For not only has John been very careful to present them as distinct from the world and from other believers in the narrative, but he also always counterbalances their misunderstanding. Segovia notes:

> practically every instance in which lack of understanding is found gives way directly to further action or teaching on Jesus' part. Such action or

teaching serves to place the pronouncement or event in question in its proper perspective.[1]

Since the disciples' misunderstanding is not allowed to go unchallenged by Jesus, the readers' perception of the disciples in their misunderstanding is more sympathetic than antagonistic. The disciples have limited understanding, not inadequate faith.

In the section of the Fourth Gospel which chronicles the escalation of hostilities toward Jesus (chs. 5–10), for the most part the disciples are noticeably absent. Most of the exceptions are in 6.1-15, 16-21, and 9.1-7, where the theme of misunderstanding (followed by Jesus' counterbalancing) continues.[2] Perhaps the most important appearance of the disciples is found in 6.60-71. After Jesus' scandalous words about 'eating his flesh' and 'drinking his blood' many of his disciples leave and follow him no longer. In this climactic episode, the response of the disciples, here called the Twelve, is all important. 'Yet in the midst of this sustained and mounting opposition, the circle of disciples continue to follow him and to reaffirm their earlier belief in him.'[3] In line both with their general portrayal throughout and with the frequent counterbalancing offered by Jesus, this pericope clearly presents the disciples as casting their lot with Jesus and possessing adequate, if limited, faith.

In chs. 11 and 12 both the disciples' misunderstanding and their steadfast resolve in following Jesus continue. Although misunderstanding much of what Jesus says about Lazarus, Thomas voices the disciples' dedication in v. 16, 'Let us also go, that we may die with him'. By the end of ch. 11 the Jewish hostility towards Jesus is at an extremely high level. Yet, in spite of the desire on the part of the Jewish authorities to arrest Jesus (and his followers?), the disciples continue to display their loyalty to him by following him to Ephraim (11.54).

As the Book of Signs draws to a close, the disciples witness Jesus' preparation for burial through Mary's extravagant footwashing (12.8) and witness his triumphal entry into Jerusalem (12.12-19). They also encounter Greeks who seek Jesus (12.20-6). Both a post-resurrectional understanding of scripture (12.16) and the now familiar feature of counterbalancing the disciples' misunderstanding (12.24-26) appear in

1. Segovia, 'Discipleship in the Fourth Gospel', p. 85.
2. These passages also confirm the disciples' share in Jesus' ministry.
3. Segovia, 'Discipleship in the Fourth Gospel', p. 85.

this chapter. The disciples, still loyal and continuing in belief, are about to enter their most intense period with Jesus in John 13–17.

What may be concluded from this overview of the disciples in John 1–12? First and foremost, the disciples, as here depicted, really do believe in Jesus. In contrast to secret believers, potential believers hindered by fear of the Jews, and former believers scandalized by Jesus' words, the disciples unequivocally cast their lot with Jesus. If anyone fulfills the promise of the Prologue (1.12), it is this group. Second, throughout the first twelve chapters the disciples have struggled with misunderstanding. Yet, as Culpepper notes, 'the lack of understanding does not pose any threat to their discipleship'.[1] For Jesus always addresses their misunderstanding through additional teaching or explanation. Third, the disciples' belief requires a process of further understanding and perception.[2] They are recorded as having believed as early in the text as 2.11 and they have confirmed their continued belief later in 6.68-69 (cf. also 11.16). But, as the farewell materials will make clear, it is essential for them to continue in their belief. Fourth, the disciples are in need of additional instruction and preparation, especially as it relates to Jesus' departure and return. If Jesus is to depart, as indicated by the post-resurrection observations in the text, the disciples need revelation about how to maintain their relationship with him and how to function during his absence. Finally, the future mission and role of the disciples is anticipated both by their participation in Jesus' ministry and by his direct teaching on the subject (cf. 4.31-38). The emphasis upon the faith which comes by means of testimony also suggests their future vocation. However, fuller clarification must await the Book of Glory. In it the farewell materials are designed to provide precisely the further instruction and preparation which the believing disciples require at this stage of the narrative.

C. *Literary and Exegetical Analysis*

One of the basic assumptions of this study is that the text, as it now stands, makes sense. Two primary reasons may be offered as justification for this premise. On the one hand, despite signs of redactional activity in the text, there is as yet no consensus regarding the

---

1. Culpepper, p. 118.
2. Segovia, 'Discipleship in the Fourth Gospel', p. 92.

history of the Fourth Gospel's composition. Even the most careful redactional reconstructions are highly speculative and hypothetical in nature.

On the other hand, the existence of the text in its final form suggests that it was regarded by author(s) and readers alike as comprehensible and interpretable. In other words, the text as it stands must have made sense to some group at a particular point in history. Probability on this point is surely greater than can be claimed for the hypothetical proposals about earlier versions. The remarks of de Jonge express this sentiment well:

> the possibility of development in thought and ways of expression cannot be excluded and a long literary process with different stages of redaction may lie behind the present Gospel. Yet the first task of an exegete should be to interpret the documents as they lie before him [/her]; even if in some cases the present text cannot be explained without some knowledge of its history one can never be content with simply describing that history and restrict oneself to the 'original' meaning and function of the constituent parts.[1]

Further discussion of this issue will be provided at the conclusion of the analysis, but before that point, attention will be focused more fully upon the text of 13.1-20 as it now stands. Here the emphasis is upon listening to the text in order to discover the story as communicated from the implied author to the implied reader. Therefore, primary attention is given to the text itself and its narrative world. However, as the historical survey in chapter three indicates, certain information not contained in the text may be valuable for the interpretation of that text. Consequently, this literary and exegetical analysis also makes use of insights gained from historical, philological, and exegetical studies. Such extra-textual information is used only to facilitate the reading process, not to superimpose hypothetical interpretive theories upon the text. The desire is to expose the thought of the text itself, not to bury it.[2]

1. De Jonge, pp. vii-viii.
2. It is acknowledged that this procedure differs from that of some rhetorical critics. Staley's comments (p. 35) offer a more extreme position concerning the implied reader:

> While the implied author knows the text forward and backward, the implied reader has knowledge of what has been read up to the given moment. Although

The footwashing pericope is strategically located in the Fourth Gospel. Standing at the beginning of the second portion of the work, it indicates a close tie between the passion and the footwashing, for the latter is described in the shadow of 'the hour'. As the first event in the Book of Glory (chs. 13–21), the episode holds great significance and comes at a time when Jesus' attention is focused upon those who believe in him. Therefore, the footwashing is offered within the context of belief. The disciples, as depicted in John 1–12, possess a correct belief in Jesus,[1] but such belief must be strengthened, since at times they do not understand (4.32-33; 11.7-16; 14.4-14). The context of belief is also underscored by the location of this pericope within the farewell materials. Generally, farewell discourses prepare followers for the death of the leader. In John 13–17, Jesus seeks to prepare his disciples for his own departure. The preparation consists of two actions and discourses (cf. section B.1.b(2) above, present chapter). The footwashing pericope stands first, due in part to the general associations in antiquity between footwashing and preparation of one kind or another.

Structurally, Jn 13.1-20 is easily divisible into three distinct parts. The pericope includes a narrative introduction (vv. 1-5), a dialogue (vv. 6-11), and a discourse (vv. 12-20). This basic structure is found in a number of other places in the Fourth Gospel (e.g. 3.1-21, 22-36; 4.1-26; 5.1-47; 6).[2] Each part of the passage is integral to the move-

the implied reader has a perfect knowledge and memory of what has been read, it is nevertheless limited by its temporal status. An implied reader must also gain all its knowledge of the story from the narrative medium itself, even if the general outline of the story is known in a culture, as is most likely the case with the first readers of the Fourth Gospel.

While such a methodology offers a much needed balance to the many all-too-subjective 'historical' reconstructions of the text, its exclusion of all extra-textual information risks producing an artificial reading of another kind. For it is evident that the implied author assumes the implied readers know Greek, have a basic vocabulary, and stand in a place of familiarity with a variety of customs and characters. Cautious reflection of the implied readers' assumptions concerning extra-textual information can facilitate, rather than prevent, a balanced reading.

1.   Cf. the above discussion in section B.2. of the present chapter.
2.   Mlakuzhyil observes (p. 117):

Many of the episodes in the Fourth Gospel have the dramatic sequence of action–dialogue–discourse, that is, often an episode begins with an action of Jesus

ment of the action and makes its own contribution to the progression
of the story.

1. *The Narrative Introduction (vv. 1-5)*

A variety of temporal indicators, characters, themes, actions, and
other elements indispensable to the story as a whole are provided in
the narrative introduction. Culpepper calls Jn 13.1-6 the most majestic
introduction of a scene in the Fourth Gospel and he notes that it illustrates a stereoscopic perspective:

> First, it does the required: it sets the time, the place, and the characters in-
> volved in the ensuing action. Beyond that, it sets the footwashing and the
> farewell discourse in the context of Jesus' awareness of his origin and his
> destiny. That which has been explained to the reader by the narration and
> shown by the action and dialogue of the narrative is now said to be self-
> conscious in Jesus. He had come from the Father, and he was going to be
> exalted and glorified. The hour had come for him to go from this world to
> the Father.[1]

Special mention should be made of John's use of narrative time,
particularly as it relates to this pericope. Whereas the first half of the
gospel (chs. 1–12) covers a period of roughly two years (excluding
the prologue), John 13–21 covers a two-week period with chs. 13–19

---

which sparks off a dialogue between him and another character, which in turn,
ends in a discourse by Jesus. . . the episodes may be said to follow the pattern
of narrative–dialogue–discourse.

1. Culpepper, p. 33. Staley (p. 108 n. 62) argues that in this narrative
introduction the author summarizes the entire meta-historical plot of the book in
reverse order: That is, Jesus

Knowing [v. 1: internal focalization]
(E) that his hour had come to depart from this world to the Father, [this is the
most recent plot element to be resolved, 12.23](D) having loved his own who
were in the world, he loved them to the end [the first time the implied reader
learns of Jesus' love for other people is 11.3, 5, 36]. (C) The devil, having put
into the heart of Judas, the son of Simon Iscariot to betray him [external
focalization; the first time the implied reader learns of Judas the betrayer is 6.71],
knowing [v. 3; internal focalization again] (B) that the Father had given all
things into his hands [the first time the implied reader explicitly learns of Jesus'
authority is 3.35] (A) and that he had come from God and was going to God'
[the first time the implied reader learns where Jesus is from and where he is to
return is 1.1-18].

devoted to a description of a single twenty-four hour period. As Culpepper observes, 'The "speed" of the narrative reduces steadily, therefore, until it virtually grinds to a halt at the climatic day'.[1] The temporal deliberativeness is another means by which the reader's attention is focused upon the importance of the ensuing events.

a. *Verse 1.* Since John has closed the first half of his work with a very definite epilogue (12.37-50), it is quite natural that he should commence the second portion with an introductory statement. Verse 1 functions in this fashion[2] and contains several themes which are prominent in the passion narrative: the Passover, Jesus' hour, his return to the Father, his love for his own, and his foreknowledge. The first phrase (πρὸ δὲ τῆς ἑορτῆς τοῦ πάσχα) at once places the event at a particular time (before the Passover Feast) and advances the Johannine interest in the Passover Feast (cf. 2.13, 23; 6.4; 11.55; 12.1; 18.28, 39; 19.14, 31). In the light of the countdown to the Passover (11.55; 12.1), and in the light of the description of his death on the day of preparation for the Passover (19.31), mention of the Passover propels the death of Jesus into view and ties what follows to it. Closely associated with this idea is the acknowledgement that Jesus' hour has come. The ὥρα, which is one of the main temporal indicators, is loaded with theological content. In the Fourth Gospel nothing is thrust upon Jesus without the Father's approval, and the ὥρα 'is God's appointed hour before whose coming no one can take any decisive steps against Jesus. Fundamentally, it is. . . the hour of divine salvation history'.[3] It is the time which God has fixed and Jesus fulfills by going to

---

1. Culpepper, p. 72.
2. Cf. Brown, *The Gospel according to John*, II, p. 562; Lightfoot, p. 260; Sanders and Mastin, p. 304; and Tasker, p. 153. For a similar assessment on vv. 1-3, cf. W.K. Grossouw, 'A Note on John XIII 1-3', *NovT* 8 (1966), p. 129 and F. Manns, 'Le lavement de pieds. Essai sur la structure et la signification de Jean 13', *RSR* 55 (1981), p. 152. On the other hand, F.F. Segovia ('John 13.1-20. The Footwashing in the Johannine Tradition', *ZNW* 73 [1982], p. 40) believes v. 1 to be 'a definite part of the introduction to the specific narrative of the washing of the feet'. In all likelihood, the verse introduces both the Book of Glory and the footwashing pericope.
3. J. Schneider, 'ἔρχομαι', *TDNT* (ed. G. Kittel; trans. G. Bromiley; Grand Rapids: Eerdmans, 1964), II, p. 673.

his death on the cross.[1] As with other episodes in John, Jesus is not taken by surprise on this occasion but knows what is to come (cf. 2.24-25; 4.16-18; 6.5, 6, 70-71; 10.17-18; 11.1-5, 23; 12.30; 13.19-30, 38; 14.29; 16.4; 18.4; 19.28-30; 21.18-19). Throughout the Fourth Gospel 'the hour' (ἡ ὥρα) is used to describe Jesus' mission in terms of incompleteness or completeness (cf. 2.4; 8.20; 12.23; 17.1).[2]

While the first part of the Gospel tends toward 'the hour' (cf. 2.4; 7.30; 8.20), the second part explains its theological meaning and its soteriological and chronological context (cf. 13.1; 17.1; 19.27).[3]

In particular, the arrival of the hour signifies Jesus' departure from this world and return to the Father. This idea, mentioned occasionally before ch. 13, appears frequently after 13.1 (cf. 13.33–14.4, 28-31; 16.5-11, 16, 28; 17.11-13; 20.17). The ἵνα clause calls to mind Jesus' origin and mission. In addition, the arrival of the hour brings into clear focus Jesus' love for his own. The term ἀγαπάω is used (in John) to denote the love which Jesus has for the disciples (13.1, 34; 14.21; 15.9, 12; cf. 11.5), the love of the disciples for one another (13.34; 15.12, 17), and especially the love Jesus has for the Father (14.31).[4] The concentration of ἀγαπάω terminology in the farewell materials serves to define the intimate dynamics of these chapers. In 13.1, this deep-seated love primarily refers to Jesus' supreme act on the cross,[5] which is foreshadowed in the footwashing.[6] Such love is directed toward his own,[7] and this love is εἰς τέλος. It is possible to

---

1. Cf. G. Delling, 'ὥρα', *TDNT*, IX, p. 678. According to H.C. Hahn, 'Time', *DNTT* (ed. C. Brown; Grand Rapids: Zondervan, 1978), III, p. 849, a similar idea of time is present in other portions of the Fourth Gospel:

For the glory of God to shine out, Jesus must wait for the right hour, the *kairos*. This is true of Jesus' miraculous actions (cf. Jn 2.4) as it is of his suffering (cf. Jn 7.30; 8.20; 13.1).

2. ὁ καιρὸς ὁ ἐμός (7.6) and ὁ ἐμὸς καιρός (7.8) seem to serve the same function as ἡ ὥρα.
3. Mlakuzhyil, p. 165.
4. G. Stahlin, 'ἱλέω', *TDNT*, IX, p. 134. Cf. also Bultmann, 'γινώσκω', *TDNT*, I, p. 711. Zweifel (p. 80) notes the increased frequency of this theme in the farewell discourse.
5. Schnackenburg, III, p. 16.
6. *Ibid.*; Haenchen, II, p. 106.
7. Barrett, quoting Bultmann, suggests that the use of τοὺς ἰδίους instead of

take εἰς τέλος temporally as 'to the end (of his life)' or quantitatively as 'fully', 'wholly', or 'completely'.[1] However, more than likely John here intends εἰς τέλος to have a double meaning,[2] 'for Jesus loved his own until the end of his life and he loved them completely', as his death indicates.[3]

b. *Verses 2-4.* Several interesting issues arise in v. 2. Almost nonchalantly, John makes mention of the fact that Jesus and his disciples were at a meal.[4] However, mention of the meal is important for the progression of the narrative. In addition to providing the needed backdrop to the footwashing, it also prepares for the quotation of Ps. 41.9 in v. 18. Yet such observations do not exhaust the significance of δεῖπνον here. The reader knows of another meal which took place earlier in the narrative (12.1-8). On this occasion an extraordinary event occurred. Mary, Lazarus's sister, anointed the feet of Jesus with costly ointment and dried his feet with her hair. Responding to Judas's challenge concerning the propriety of such an extravagant anointing, Jesus made clear that this 'washing' had been done in preparation for his burial. Therefore, when δεῖπνον is read in 13.2, the reader, recalling the earlier account (cf. 12.2), is mentally prepared for the footwashing as well as its association with death.[5]

μαθηταί emphasizes that these are 'representatives of all those who believe' (*The Gospel According to St John*, p. 438).

1. An idea preferred by Blass, Debrunner, Funk, p. 207 (3); G. Delling, 'τέλος', *TDNT*, VIII, p. 56; R. Schippers, 'Goal', *DNTT*, I, p. 64; P. Beeckman, *L'Evangile selon Saint Jean* (Paris: Peyaert-Bruges, 1951), p. 290; Behler, p. 24; and Tasker, p. 154.

2. Cf. Brown, *The Gospel according to John*, II, p. 550; Bruce, p. 278; Lindars, p. 448; Morris, p. 614 n. 8; E. Stauffer, 'εἰς', *TDNT*, II, p. 427. Barrett suggests that εἰς τέλος has a double meaning which combines the idea of the end of Jesus' life and the eschatological end (*The Gospel according to St John*, p. 438).

3. It may be more than coincidence that at his death Jesus cries, Τετέλεσται (19.30).

4. The point is made in such a casual fashion that Michaels concludes, 'it is unlikely. . . that the narrator attaches any particular significance to the supper itself (any more than to the "dinner" at Bethany. . . mentioned in 12.2)' (J.R. Michaels, *John* [New York: Harper & Row, 1984], p. 223).

5. For the relationship between Jn 12.1-8 and 13.1-20 cf. E. Schüssler Fiorenza, *In Memory of Her* (New York: Crossroad, 1983), pp. 330-31 and J.R. Michaels, 'John 12.1-22', *Int* 43 (1989), pp. 287-91.

In all likelihood the actual readers of the Fourth Gospel would understand the meal to be the traditional Last Supper, for knowledge of the institution of the Eucharist was basic and widespread by the last part of the first century CE (1 Cor. 11.23-26; Mk 14.22-25; Mt. 26.26-30; Lk. 22.15-20; Jn 6.26-51; Did. 9, 10, 14).[1] John 6.51-59 also suggests that the implied readers were also acquainted with the eucharist, and would thus understand the meal to be the traditional Last Supper. Because of the mention of the meal the reader expects a significant event, perhaps even words of institution. Thereby, this reference prepares one for what follows.

It is during the meal[2] that the following events take place. This notation, 'during supper', in itself calls attention to the peculiarity of Jesus' action. The historical survey in Chapter 3 notes that water for washing the feet was provided before the meal, not during (or after) the meal.[3] Clearly, the Evangelist is underscoring the importance of the footwashing by its unusual placement, with Jesus interrupting the

---

1. Such knowledge of the eucharist on the actual readers' part is probable, whether they know the Synoptic tradition or not. However, it is not beyond the bounds of reason to suspect that these readers have a general knowledge of the story line found in the Synoptic tradition. This judgment is based on the way John seems to build upon a knowledge of events from the life of Jesus, as described in the Synoptics. For example, the Fourth Gospel introduces John the Baptist as a witness (1.6, p. 19-20). He is not described as a baptizer nor is the content of his preaching disclosed, yet 1.26 (ἀπεκρίθη αὐτοῖς ὁ Ἰωάννης λέγων, Ἐγὼ βαπτίζω ἐν ὕδατι· μέσος ὑμῶν ἔστηκεν ὃν ὑμεῖς οὐκ οἴδατε) is introduced with no explanation. The Fourth Gospel nowhere records Jesus' baptism by the Baptist; however, vv. 32-33 describe the descent of the Spirit upon Jesus. For similar views on the relationship of John and the Synoptics, cf. the following works: L. Goppelt, *Theology of the New Testament* (ed. J. Roloff; trans. J. Alsup; Grand Rapids: Eerdmans, 1981), I, pp. 16-17; B. de Solages, *Jean et les Synoptiques* (Leiden: E.J. Brill, 1979); and D.M. Smith, 'John and the Synoptics', *NTS* 26 (1979–80), pp. 425-44.

2. Despite some strong support for δείπνου γενομένου ('when supper had ended') δείπνου γινομένου is preferred as the original reading. This judgment is based upon (1) slightly better external evidence (א* B W it[d] syr[pal] arm) and (2) internal coherence, for it is obvious from the context (v. 26) that the meal continues after the footwashing episode is complete. Cf. Metzger, *A Textual Commentary on the Greek New Testament*, p. 239. However, either reading demonstrates the point that Jesus washes the disciples' feet at an unusual time.

3. Cf. Behler, p. 26.

meal to perform it.[1] The remainder of v. 2 is devoted to the role that both the Devil and Judas play in the betrayal.

In the Fourth Gospel there is no uncertainty concerning Judas' destiny and subsequent action. Every time he appears in the narrative Judas is quickly designated as the betrayer. However, despite his obvious function as antagonist and the consistently negative portrait, his character in the narrative proves to be a little more complex. A survey of the relevant passages demonstrates the rationale for this assessment.

The reader is first informed of Jesus' betrayal in 6.64. This information is passed on by the (omniscient) narrator to inform the reader that Jesus knew about this person ἐξ ἀρχῆς. For the moment the identity of the betrayer is left open. In 6.70 Jesus asks, 'Have I not chosen you twelve and one of you is a devil?' Judas is named in the very next verse as the one who is to betray Jesus. At the anointing in Bethany, Judas opposes the action of Mary. This protest prompts the narrator to confide that Judas had no interest in the poor but was concerned about money because he was a thief and regularly pilfered from the common purse. In 13.2 Satan puts the matter of betrayal into Judas's heart. Verse 11 notes that Judas remained unclean even after the footwashing. John 13.18-30 describes the unveiling of the betrayer, v. 27 asserting that Satan entered into Judas at this point. The pericope ends with Judas going out into the darkness. In 17.12 Jesus refers to him as ὁ υἱὸς τῆς ἀπωλείας. Later, he reappears in the darkness with the Roman and Jewish authorities, completing his act of treachery. The last mention of Judas comes in 21.20 where the betrayer is mentioned as a way of identifying the Beloved Disciple, who had inquired of Jesus concerning the betrayer's identity.

The one-dimensional character of this description of Judas should not be allowed to obscure his importance in the development of the Johannine plot. The emerging image of Judas is one of an individual who succumbs to Satanic influences. His character is flawed (12.6), he receives into his heart the Devil's designs to betray Jesus (13.2),[2]

---

1. As Brown notes, δείπνου γινομένου is grammatically followed by v. 3, with the remainder of v. 2 being regarded as a parenthetical statement (*The Gospel according to John*, II, p. 551).

2. K. Hein appears to support the idea of Judas's gradual corruption when he notes, 'John xiii.2 certainly says no more than that Judas is of a mind to betray Jesus' ('Judas Iscariot: Key to the Last Supper Narratives?', *NTS* 17 [1970–71], pp. 227-32). Cf. especially p. 228 n. 2.

Satan enters into him (13.27), and finally Judas betrays Jesus. This development of plot suggests that Judas's response relates to true belief as an antithetical paradigm which grows gradually in the Fourth Gospel. In contrast to the Beloved Disciple (21.20), who is always faithful and believes Jesus, Judas is the representative defector[1] who demonstrates how one is 'cut off', just as the unproductive branches are pruned from the vine (15.6).[2] The appearance of Judas ominously foreshadows the betrayal of Jesus. Verses 2 and 27 appear to describe the process by which Satan overwhelms Judas absolutely.[3] Verse 2 describes the poisoning of Judas's heart, whereas v. 27 documents his complete domination by Satan. The Devil, who has been a murderer from the beginning (8.44), enters with his corruptive influences into the very seat of Judas's will.[4] The purpose of such an all-out assault is the betrayal of Jesus. As D.A. Carson notes, 'the devil and Judas are now in a conspiracy of evil to bring Jesus to the cross'.[5] In referring to the betrayal John accomplishes two things. First, he heightens the drama of the scene by inserting into the narrative a form of παραδίδωμι, a term which is solely used in the Fourth Gospel for the betrayal of Jesus.[6] Second,

> The betrayal is mentioned in 2 precisely so that the reader will connect the footwashing and the death of Jesus. Jesus undertook this action symbolic of his death only after the forces had been set in motion that would lead to crucifixion.[7]

Clearly, John desires the following action to be viewed within the shadow of the cross.

Verse 3. Verses 2-3 serve to introduce the footwashing pericope in a

1. Culpepper, pp. 124-25.
2. For examinations of Judas in the Fourth Gospel cf. B. Gärtner, *Iscariot* (Philadelphia: Fortress Press, 1971), pp. 8-11, 16-17, 22-23, 25-29; and W. Volger, *Judas Iskarioth* (Berlin: Evangelische Verlagsanstalt, 1983), pp. 93-118.
3. Grossouw, p. 127. Owanga-Welo (p. 229), together with a number of other scholars, takes βαλεῖν as reflexive so that Satan puts it into his own heart in v. 2 while actually entering Judas in v. 27. In this way, too, the progress is preserved.
4. Cf. E. Stauffer, 'εἰς', *TDNT*, II, p. 425; J. Behm ('καρδία', *TDNT*, III, p. 425), notes that καρδία signifies the 'seat of the will, the source of resolves'.
5. Carson, p. 462.
6. Grossouw, p. 127.
7. Brown, *The Gospel according to John*, II, p. 563.

direct fashion. It is the foreknowledge of Jesus, as mentioned in v. 1, that precipitates the footwashing which follows.[1] Such knowledge is part and parcel of the Fourth Gospel's view of Jesus. Specifically, in this context, Jesus' knowledge includes two aspects: (1) that the Father has placed all things into his hands, and (2) that he has come from God and he is about to return to the Father. The idea of the Father placing all things into Jesus' hands is one with which the reader is familiar owing to its previous occurrences (cf. 3.35; 6.39; 10.28-29). Here the author uses the phrase to emphasize Jesus' knowledge of his origin and destiny. In particular, v. 3 focuses attention upon Jesus as the Sovereign of the universe who prepares to perform an act of servitude.[2] Coming as it does at this point in the narrative, the verse hints at Jesus' charge to fulfill the salvific act of sacrificial death on the cross.[3] John continues to develop the theme of Jesus' coming from the Father and returning to him. Not only does the introduction of this motif demonstrate the superiority of the one who comes from the Father over God's adversary,[4] but it also supplies an additional reason for the footwashing, since Jesus will soon be leaving the disciples. John again relates the footwashing to the passion, this time by mentioning Jesus' return to God, i.e. his crucifixion and resurrection.[5] Therefore, both aspects of Jesus' foreknowledge (the arrival of his 'hour' and the fact that the Father has placed all things in his hands) prompt the footwashing and tie into the passion.

Verse 4. At this point the footwashing scene begins in earnest. Jesus' actions are represented as highly deliberate. He interrupts the meal by rising and laying aside his garments.[6] This action leaves Jesus attired

---

1. Brown asserts, 'The footwashing as an action symbolic of Jesus' death is performed because he knows that he has the power to save others and the power to lay down his own life for this purpose' (*The Gospel according to John*, II, p. 564).

2. Carson (p. 462) observes, 'With such power and status at his disposal, we might have expected him to defeat the devil in an immediate and flashy confrontation, and to devastate Judas with an unstoppable blast of divine wrath. Instead, he washes his disciples' feet, including the feet of the betrayer.'

3. G. Delling, 'ὑπάγω', *TDNT*, VIII, p. 506 n. 13.

4. Schnackenburg, III, p. 17.

5. Brown, *The Gospel according to John*, II, p. 564.

6. Schnackenburg (III, p. 16) notes that the appearance of ἐγείρεται ἐκ τοῦ δείπνου continues the idea that the meal was in progress.

as a servant.[1] Morris suggests that Jesus has stripped to a loin cloth.[2] If this suggestion is correct, John describes a scene wherein the agent of creation wears nothing but a loin cloth and a towel with which he will dry the feet of the disciples.[3] There is a foreshadowing in the footwashing of the humiliation and cleansing connected with Jesus laying down his life.[4] The stark reality of nakedness also presents a clear reference to the crucifixion. As Ahr concludes:

> The reference to the crucifixion is ever more clearly present in the statement about Jesus' nakedness: anyone familiar with the story of Jesus' death can grasp the reference to the removal of clothes, and, indeed, it is the very unexpectedness of this statement which points the reader to this reference.[5]

'All of this serves to relate the footwashing to the death of the Lord.'[6]

c. *Verse 5*. The action initiated in the previous verse is continued in v. 5, the use of εἶτα making this clear. John methodically underscores the significance of Jesus' actions by specifically mentioning the towel, the water and the washbasin. This emphasis foreshadows the servant motif which is made explicit later in v. 16. In particular, the pouring of water into the νιπτῆρα and the washing of feet extends the motif of

1. F. Selter, 'Ready', *DNTT*, III, p. 121. Lagrange (p. 354) compares Jesus' voluntary servitude with the actions of Roman senators forced to serve Caligula as servants, both with reference to dress (short linen tunics) and posture (at his feet). Cf. Suetonius, *Caligula* 26.

2. Morris, p. 615 n. 15.

3. A number of scholars have gone so far as to find in John's use of τίθημι a direct reference to Jesus' death, since the term has this meaning in over half its Johannine occurrences (10.11, 15,17, 18; 13.17, 38; 15.13; 1 Jn 3.6). Cf. Barrett, *The Gospel according to St John*, p. 439; Brown, *The Gospel according to John*, II, p. 551; Dunn, p. 248; Sanders and Mastin, p. 306; and P.G. Ahr, 'He Loved Them to Completion?: The Theology of John 13–14', in *Standing Before God: Studies on Prayer in Scripture and in Tradition* (ed. A. Finkel and L. Frizzell; New York: Ktav, 1981), p. 77.

4. Barrett, *The Gospel according to St John*, p. 439. Zweifel (p. 95) observes that even the choice of the term λέντιον is not by chance but serves to underscore Jesus' role as servant.

5. Ahr, p. 77. M. Hengel, *Crucifixion* (trans. J. Bowden; Philadelphia: Fortress Press, 1977), p. 29 nn. 21 and 87 notes that often crucifixion victims died naked.

6. Brown, *The Gospel according to John*, II, p. 551.

servanthood which begins with the laying aside of the clothes in v. 4. There can be no doubt that footwashing was the domain of slaves. The historical survey in Chapter 3 demonstrates that servants were involved in the entire process: drawing the water, washing the feet, and disposing of the water. It appears that a slave could not refuse to render this service, no matter how old the servant might be. There is so much an identification of servants and footwashing that the footbasin comes to function figuratively as a sign of servitude; consequently, footwashing could be and was understood as synonymous with slavery. Clearly, to wash another's feet acknowledged a subjugation to that person. But to see only servitude here would be to miss a further dimension of John's emphasis. On extremely rare occasions an individual, without obligation, might take this chore upon him or herself as an act of deep love and sincere honor. In John 13 such service issuing from love is evident, both from the emphasis on servitude and also from the prominence given in v. 1 to Jesus' love for his own, which is mentioned twice, once with εἰς τέλος. Yet, Jesus' action remains unparalleled in ancient literature, for no other master (superior) condescends to perform this act for a subordinate.[1]

Water (ὕδωρ) is a word used frequently in Johannine literature, appearing 20 times in the Gospel, twice in 1 John, and 17 times in the Apocalypse, which also appears to come from the Johannine circle. The total of its occurrences in these three works is greater than that of the rest of the New Testament combined.[2] In the Fourth Gospel water comes into play in connection with baptism (1.26, 31, 33; 3.23) and in the story of its transformation into wine (2.1-11). Water also appears with Spirit in the discussion about 'birth from above' (3.5), and the Spirit comes to be identified as the 'Living Water' which quenches thirst forever (4.7-15). Water is associated with miraculous healings (5.1-9; 9.1-34), and it is miraculously walked upon by Jesus (6.16-21). Later at his death (19.34), water will issue forth from Jesus' side. Given its rather extraordinary associations, the appearance of ὕδωρ here creates an attitude of expectancy on the readers' behalf, for they are aware that its presence may well indicate that something

---

1. Ordinarily, those prompted by love to wash another's feet are subordinates or peers, never those in a superior position.
2. O. Bocher, 'Water', *DNTT*, III, p. 989.

significant is about to transpire.[1] The water is poured into νιπτῆρα. Brown takes νιπτῆρα, a New Testament *hapax*, to mean a pitcher, a normal meal utensil. From 2 Kgs 3.11 he concludes, 'In the ancient Near East washing was not normally done in a basin of standing water but by pouring water over the part of the body'.[2] Brown's suggestion seems logical, but the text considered in 2 Kings describes one who poured water on the hands of Elijah. Nothing is said about the feet, although it is possible that they might be washed in the same fashion as the hands. Second, most artistic depictions of footwashing portray the feet of the guest in a large water pot, with water poured upon them. Finally, many of the footbaths unearthed by archaeology are round basins with a support in the center on which the foot could rest. In the light of this evidence, it appears the νιπτῆρα might better be understood as a footbasin or washbasin.

John highlights the washing by using a form of ἄρχω, which 'usually draws attention to a particular element in the story'.[3] Here the use of ἄρχω suggests the beginning of an action which will be interrupted. Not only does Jesus wash the feet of the disciples but he carefully wipes them with his makeshift clothing, the towel. One additional note serves to emphasize the servanthood motif in this verse. At the Passover, the disciples would be reclining on couches which encircled the table. Since they would be facing the table, their feet would be behind them. In this way servants could go about their business with minimal disturbance of the meal. In such a situation, Jesus would have made his way round the outside of the circle, further highlighting his servant-like actions. At this point, the narrative setting gives way to the dialogue in vv. 6-11.

2. *The Dialogue (vv. 6-11)*

a. *Verses 6-8. Verse 6.* 'Next to Jesus, *Peter* is the most complex character'[4] in the Fourth Gospel. He is introduced in v. 6 as Jesus' dialogue partner. The reader has a positive impression of Peter to this point in the narrative due to his two previous appearances. Although

---

1. Cf. the discussion in Joseph Shultz, *The Soul of the Symbols* (Grand Rapids: Eerdmans, 1966), pp. 67-68. Cf. also Culpepper, pp. 192-95.

2. Brown, *The Gospel according to St John*, II, p. 551.

3. G. Delling, 'ἄρχω', *TDNT*, I, p. 478.

4. Culpepper, p. 120.

he is not the first disciple to follow Jesus or confess his messianic status (in the Fourth Gospel), Peter's importance is anticipated by the reader due to the new name Jesus gives him (1.42). He is specifically identified in only one other passage (6.68) in the Book of Signs. On this occasion Simon Peter affirms his (and the disciples') faith in Jesus' words of eternal life. This confession is all the more significant since it stands in the context of mass defections from the ranks of discipleship. Consequently, the implied reader is favorably disposed toward Simon Peter at this point in the narrative (13.6) and is, no doubt, quite unprepared for what transpires. It should be observed that this pericope is very significant for Peter's own story within the Fourth Gospel. In many ways it is pivotal.[1]

Although there is too little evidence to be certain, it appears that Peter is not the first disciple to whom Jesus comes; v. 5 implies that Jesus has already commenced the action. In fact, it is possible that Peter is to be seen as the last one to receive the washing, for immediately after his encounter with Jesus over the matter, the disciples are pronounced to be clean. As Jesus approaches Peter, he is unable to fulfill his purpose. Jesus' attempt to wash Peter's feet prompts a negative reaction in the disciple. In the light of the social understanding of footwashing, Peter is embarrassed by the fact that Jesus desires to perform this menial service for him. Peter mistakes Jesus' action as mere

---

1.   It may be appropriate to regard 13.6 as the beginning of Peter's decline in the Fourth Gospel. For after the footwashing, Jesus predicts Peter's denials (13.36-38), Peter demonstrates that he misunderstands Jesus by defending him with a sword (18.10), and eventually Peter denies his Lord (18.15-18, 25-27). However, from this point Peter slowly recovers. In 20.1-10, he goes to the empty tomb (although preceded by the Beloved Disciple). 21.1-14 finds Peter swimming from his fishing boat to Jesus (after the Beloved Disciple reveals Jesus' identity), and 21.15-19 describes Peter's reinstatement and commissioning by Jesus. The final mention of Peter contrasts him with the Beloved Disciple (21.20-23). It is possible to see in the character of Peter an example of one who believes in Jesus, betrays his Lord, and overcomes his failures, finally being reconciled with Jesus. This figure stands in sharp contrast to that of Judas, who never recovers from his own act of betrayal. It is also possible to discern a contrast between the Beloved Disciple and Peter in the Fourth Gospel. Perhaps 21.20 combines the Beloved Disciple, Peter, and the Betrayer for the purpose of contrasting their respective responses to Jesus. For works which deal with Peter in the Fourth Gospel, cf. *Peter in the New Testament* (ed. R.E. Brown, K.P. Donfried, and J. Reumann; Minneapolis: Augsburg, 1973), pp. 129-47, and Maynard, 'The Role of Peter in the Fourth Gospel', pp. 531-48.

hospitality. The placement of the terms κύριε, σύ, and μου 'at the beginning of the sentence strongly accents the incongruity of the situation as Peter saw it'.[1] Peter does not understand, and consequently opposes Jesus.

Verse 7. The tension reflected in Peter's question in v. 6 continues to mount as a personal confrontation between Jesus and Peter is easily detected, due to the emphatic nature of the pronouns, ἐγώ and σύ.[2] In his reply, Jesus gives the first clue that the footwashing which he performs is more than a simple washing. The disciples cannot understand what is taking place until μετὰ ταῦτα. This reply poses two most difficult questions: When will the disciples understand and exactly what will they know? The occurrence of μετὰ ταῦτα is neither uncharacteristic of the Fourth Gospel nor does its appearance demand that the passage be divided into two separate interpretations to make sense (section E. below, present chapter). There is clearly a future dimension to μετὰ ταῦτα. As with many crucial Johannine episodes the footwashing can only be understood fully after the crucifixion and resurrection. Yet, those scholars who altogether rule out some sort of immediate understanding[3] on the part of the disciples fail to reckon with the explanation which is available (vv. 12-17) and the perspective of the community reading the document. On a much sounder course are those interpreters who reckon with the explanation made available in vv. 12-17.

As is evident in v. 8, the footwashing is extremely important to the disciples. They gain a partial understanding through the experience and the discourse which follows. In addition, there is a definite pattern in the Johannine narrative in which salvific words are spoken in advance, and not held back until the death and resurrection have been related. As Michaels observes, 'In John's Gospel, "post-resurrectional truths"... have a way of making their appearance already within Je-

---

1. Michaels, p. 231. Cf. also Morris, p. 617; Brown, *The Gospel according to John*, II, p. 552; and Lindars, p. 450, who notes, 'the words *you* and *my* are juxtaposed in the Greek, emphasizing the paradoxical reversal of roles'.

2. Schnackenburg, III, p. 18.

3. Cf. Bultmann, p. 467; Richter, 'Die Fusswaschung Joh 13, 1-20', p. 21; Brown, *The Gospel according to John*, II, p. 552; Lindars, p. 450; and Schnackenburg, III, p. 19.

sus' ministry, especially as the passion draws near'.[1] All in all it is best to take μετὰ ταῦτα as having a double reference. The disciples are given an explanation immediately (v. 12) but understand fully after the Passion.[2]

Verse 8. Jesus' statement elicits an extremely strong response from Peter. Whether he will understand in the future or not, Peter is apparently more opposed to the idea than ever. In no uncertain terms, he answers that Jesus will never wash his (Peter's) feet. Not only is 'οὐ μή with the... future indicative... the most definite form of negation regarding the future',[3] but the addition of εἰς τὸν αἰῶνα serves to make even more emphatic this denial. Quite ironically, the other passages in John which contain the formula οὐ μή + aorist subjunctive/future indicative + εἰς τὸν αἰῶνα (4.14; 8.51; 10.28; 11.26) are all words from Jesus concerning eternal life.[4] In a twist as ironic as Caiaphas's prophecy, Peter uses the very formula Jesus has used to offer life *to refuse* Jesus' offer (of continued life and belief). It is also possible to see some emphasis in the position of μου, which would take on 'more significance if Jesus had already washed the feet of the others'.[5] Peter's message is clear; no matter what Jesus means, Peter will have no part of the footwashing. If Peter's hesitation (v. 6) is due to embarrassment, his refusal (v. 8) appears to be more calculated.

Previously (v. 7), Jesus has hinted that there is more to his action than meets the eye. Through Jesus' very stern rebuke, Peter discovers both that footwashing is not optional,[6] and that it has far-reaching significance: 'if I do not wash you, you have no μέρος with me'. Obviously, the importance attached to footwashing is tied to the

1.   Michaels, p. 226. Haenchen (II, p. 108) asserts:

> [T]he Evangelist, who elsewhere is given to conflating the times of Jesus' earthly activity and that of the community, cannot wait here, as an author, until he has related Jesus' death and resurrection. He has to say now what Jesus' enigmatic act means, and cannot have the resurrected Jesus return to the footwashing in chapter 20.

2.   Lohse, I, p. 122.
3.   Blass, Debrunner, Funk, p. 365 (2).
4.   The only exception is found in 8.52 where Jesus' opponents repeat his words in the form of an accusation.
5.   Tasker, p. 157.
6.   Michaels, p. 224. Cf. also Hultgren, p. 541.

understanding of μέρος in this verse.

One of the first things the implied reader must see in μέρος with Jesus is a share in eternal life. Not only has the prologue promised such to those who believe (1.12), but it has also been stated that Jesus bestows eternal life upon those who are placed in his hands (cf. 3.35-36; 6.40; 10.28-29). The immediate referent is found in v. 3, where the reader is reminded of Jesus' knowledge that all things have been placed in his hands by the Father. This interpretation is supported by the many New Testament texts where μέρος appears in contexts which deal with the issues of eternal life and eternal punishment (cf. Mt. 24.51; Rev. 20.6; 21.8; 22.19).[1] Therefore it seems safe to assume that one idea conveyed by μέρος with Jesus in Jn 13.8 is eternal life. Yet, this understanding does not exhaust the significance of μέρος. The closest structural parallels to this verse, found in Mt. 24.51, Ignatius's *Epistle to Polycarp*, and the *Martyrdom of Polycarp* 14.2, suggest that to share a person's μέρος was to share his or her identity or destiny. Matthew (24.51) describes the unfaithful servant as being assigned

> a place with the hypocrites (καὶ τὸ μέρος αὐτοῦ μετὰ τῶν ὑποκριτῶν), where there will be weeping and gnashing of teeth (par. Lk. 12.46).

In affirming the legitimacy of ecclesiastical offices, Ignatius claims:

> Give heed to the bishop, that God may also give heed to you. I am devoted to those who are subject to the bishop, presbyters, and deacons; and may it be mine to have my lot with them in God (καὶ μετ' αὐτῶν μοι τὸ μέρος γένοιτο σχεῖν ἐν θεῷ). Labour with one another, struggle together, run together, suffer together, rest together, rise up together as God's stewards and assessors and servants.[2]

As part of his last prayer, Polycarp gives thanks:

> I bless thee, that Thou has granted me this day and hour, that I may share, among the number of the martyrs (τοῦ λαβεῖν με μέρος ἐν ἀριθμῷ τῶν μαρτύρων) in the cup of thy Christ, for the Resurrection to everlasting life, both of soul and body in the immortality of the Holy Spirit.[3]

---

1.   For the later eschatological connotations of μέρος, cf. P. Dreyfus, 'Le thème de l'héritage dans l'Ancien Testament', *RSPT* 42 (1958), pp. 3-49; Boismard, p. 9; Brown, *The Gospel according to John*, II, p. 565.
2.   Cited according to the translation of K. Lake, *The Apostolic Fathers* (Cambridge, MA: Harvard University Press, 1912), I, pp. 273-75.
3.   Cited according to the translation of K. Lake, *The Apostolic Fathers*

If anyone has cast their lot with Jesus in the Fourth Gospel, it is the disciples. To have a share in his destiny includes not only eternal life, but also being sent as Jesus himself was sent (4.31-38; 20.21-23), resurrection at the last day (6.40), and being hated by the world (15.18–16.4). In Peter's case, this sharing of Jesus' destiny may even involve martyrdom (cf. 13.37-38, 21.18-19). Since suffering and exaltation are at the heart of Jesus' destiny according to the Fourth Gospel, it is not surprising that they should be presented as part and parcel of the disciples' share in that destiny. Simply put, it appears that μέρος here denotes continued fellowship with Jesus,[1] and a place in his community[2] which ultimately results in uninterrupted residence in the Father's house (14.1-14).[3] Such a view of μέρος dovetails neatly with 15.1-17, where remaining in Jesus is the key to life. Without such remaining, one's fate is like that of unproductive branches which are cut off and cast out to be burned. Consequently, the footwashing is a sign which points beyond itself to some deeper meaning.[4] Two things point to the crucifixion–exaltation as essential to that deeper meaning.[5] First, the qualities represented by μέρος (eternal life, identity with Jesus, sharing his destiny, mission, resurrection and martyrdom) are ultimately secured through Jesus' death. Second, Jesus' act of humiliation in washing the disciples' feet foreshadows his ultimate act of humiliation on the cross. These hints in the narrative make it easier to understand the importance of footwashing. By refusing the footwash-

(London: William Heinemann, 1913), II, p. 331.

   1.   Cf. Segovia: 'John 13.1-20, The Footwashing in the Johannine Tradition', p. 43: 'an acceptance of that which the washing symbolizes grants the disciples continued union with Jesus'. The context of belief, the Book of Glory, demonstrates that the footwashing does not initiate fellowship, but continues it. Cf. the discussion in v. 10.

   2.   Michaels, p. 231, and Lindars, p. 450.

   3.   Hultgren, p. 542.

   4.   For the idea that footwashing is a sign, cf. Richter, 'The Washing of Feet in the Gospel of John', p. 200; Dunn, p. 247; Segovia, 'John 13.1-20, The Footwashing in the Johannine Tradition', p. 43.

   5.   For an identification of footwashing with the passion, cf. Richter, 'The Washing of Feet in the Gospel of John', p. 200; Barrett, *The Gospel According to St John*, p. 441; Dunn, pp. 248-50; Schnackenburg, III, p. 19; Brown, *The Gospel according to John*, II, pp. 565-66; Segovia, 'John 13.1-20, The Footwashing in the Johannine Tradition', p. 43 n. 32.

ing, Peter is ultimately refusing the effects of the cross.[1] The emphatic language of v. 8 removes all doubt concerning footwashing's importance. Without it Peter will have no μέρος with Jesus.

b. *Verse 9*. Jesus' stern rebuke prompts an immediate response by Peter, 'Lord, not my feet only but also (my) hands and head.' Many interpreters are quick to identify Peter's request as motivated by a desire for complete washing.[2] Unfortunately, there has been little to no exploration of the specific choice of the hands and head for washing.[3] In other words, there has been no attempt to demonstrate how the hands and head come to signify complete washing. Unless these bodily parts were chosen at random, their mention by Peter is significant. Consequently, some attention must be devoted to them here.

Peter's mention of the hands and head might simply be due to the fact that, along with the feet, they are the only parts of the body normally left exposed, not covered by clothing. But to leave the inquiry at that point is to ignore the fact that it is because of their 'vulnerable' state that each of these bodily parts come to be regarded as especially worthy of washing or anointing in Judaism.

One of the most obvious points concerning the Synoptic Gospels' Pharisees is that they are scrupulous about washing their hands before eating. Mk 7.3 confirms this.

> The Pharisees and all the Jews do not eat unless they give their hands a
> ceremonial washing, holding to the tradition of the elders. . .

Not only do the disciples come under the scrutiny of the Pharisees on this issue (cf. Mk 7.1-23; Mt. 15.1-20), but Jesus himself is challenged on this point (cf. Lk. 11.37-44). As Jacob Neusner observes, 'There can be no doubt whatsoever that Pharisees washed hands before eating'.[4] According to Josephus (*War* 2.133), the Essenes also practiced some sort of washing before meals (ζωσάμενοί τε σκεπάσμασιν λινοῖς οὕτως ἀπολούονται τὸ σῶμα ψυχροῖς ὕδασιν).

---

1.   Barrett, *The Gospel according to St John*, p. 441.
2.   Cf. Brown, *The Gospel according to John*, II, p. 566, and Lindars, p. 451.
3.   However, cf. Carson, p. 464.
4.   J. Neusner, *A History of the Mishnaic Law of Purities: Part Twenty-two. The Mishnaic System of Uncleanness* (Leiden: E.J. Brill, 1977), p. 89.

The reason for washing the hands is made explicit in the Mishnah, *Yad.* 3.1-2. This tractate, which Neusner assigns to the Yavnean period,[1] records discussions concerning the degree to which the hands become unclean in a variety of situations. Owing to their suceptibility to uncleanness, resulting from contact with a number of items, the hands are eventually regarded as always being unclean 'in the second remove',[2] unless they have just been washed. The ultimate implication of all this is that the hands can render the entire person unclean (cf. *Ḥag.* 2.5; *'Ed.* 3.2).

When Peter requests that his hands be washed, he is suggesting that if any part of the body is in constant need of washing, it is the hands.

Peter's suggestion that the head be washed is also significant. In ancient Greek κεφαλή came to represent the whole person, life itself. For this reason curses are called down upon the head.[3] The same basic idea develops in the LXX where 'The head can be used as the equivalent of the person and his (/her) whole existence'.[4] In other words, κεφαλή is used to express the whole person, and so becomes the body part (standing for the whole) upon which blessings (Gen. 48.14, 18; 49.26), curses (2 Sam. 1.10; 3.29; Ezek. 33.4; Joel 3.4, 7: Obad. 15), dust and ashes (Josh. 7.6; Neh. 9.1; Lam. 2.10), and anointings (Exod. 29.8; Lev. 8.12; 1 Sam. 10.1) are placed. In the New Testament two uses are significant: anointing (Mt. 6.17; 26.17; Mk 14.3; Lk. 7.46) and judgment (Acts 18.6). Peter's request that his head be washed expresses the view that the head represents the person.[5] Since this is the case, it makes sense to Peter that an efficacious washing should be devoted to the head. According to Peter's viewpoint, both the hands

---

1.   J. Neusner, *Judaism: The Evidence of Mishnah* (Chicago: University of Chicago Press, 1981), pp. 105-106.

2.   For a discussion of the transmission of uncleanness, cf. Neusner, *The Mishnaic System of Uncleanness*, p. 160.

3.   H. Schlier, 'κεφαλή', *TDNT*, III, p. 675.

4.   K. Munzer, 'Head', *DNTT*, II, p. 158. Relevant passages include: 2 Kgs 25.27; Ps. 3.3; Ezek. 9.10; 33.4; 1 Sam. 25.39.

5.   Munzer concludes, 'In wanting to have his head washed (Jn 13.9), Peter wanted his whole life to be cleansed' ('Head', *DNTT*, II, p. 159).

and the head are appropriate for such significant washings.[1]

Clearly, Peter has misconstrued the entire episode. At first, he misunderstands Jesus as performing an act of hospitality. Then, when he is convinced of the necessity of the washing, he seeks to suggest the particular kinds of washings most appropriate. In typical Johannine fashion, his misunderstanding awaits the discourse by Jesus for clarification.

c. *Verse 10.* In this most strategic verse, Jesus reveals the true significance of the footwashing. 'The one who has bathed (λελουμένος) has no need to wash (νίψασθαι), except the feet, but is wholly clean; and you are clean, but not all of you.' Of central importance for discerning the meaning of this verse is the relationship between the verbs λούω and νίπτω. Those who opt for the omission of εἰ μὴ τοὺς πόδας are forced to conclude that λελουμένος refers to the footwashing. Therefore, λούω and νίπτω are held to be synonyms.[2] *P. Oxy.* 840, a fourth-century document, is sometimes appealed to as evidence that λούω and νίπτω could be used as synonyms (cf. Lagrange, p. 355; Bultmann, p. 470; and Schnackenburg, III, p. 404 n. 54). Since this is the only text cited as such evidence, it deserves special attention. *P. Oxy.* 840 states:

(7) And he took them (8) with him into the place of purity itself and (9) walked in the Temple enclosure. And there came near

(10) a Pharisee, a chief priest, Levi (11) by name, and met them and said (12) unto the Saviour: 'Who hath given thee leave (13) to tread this place of purity and to (14) look upon these holy vessels without thy first bathing thyself (λουσα[μ]έν[ῳ]) and

(15) even without thy disciples having washed ([βα]πτισθέντων) their (16) feet? But clean as thou art (17) hast thou walked in the Temple enclosure, which is a clean (18) place, wherein no one walketh but one that hath (19) bathed himself (λουσάμενος) and (or) changed his clothes

---

1.   Zweifel (pp. 110-11) argues that ritual purity is the context in which to understand this verse. Weiss (p. 317) is in basic agreement: 'Peter's excessive denial is pure Johannine irony, and his offer of his hands and head (xiii 9) is a clear polemic against the Jewish phylacteries worn as marks of faithfulness to Jahweh indicating that the wearer had been marked by Jahweh for a part in the inheritance'.

2.   For an explicit statement to that effect cf. Barrett, *The Gospel according to St John*, p. 442.

(20) nor presumeth to look upon these (21) holy vessels?' And straight-
way the Saviour stopped (22) with his disciples and answered: (23) 'How
is it then with thee? For thou art in the Temple. Art thou then (24) clean?'
He said unto him: 'I am clean, for I have bathed (ἐλουσάμην)

(25) myself in the pool of David, and went down (26) into it by the one
stair and came up by the other, (27) and have put on white and clean (28)
raiment and (only) then came I hither (29) and looked upon these holy

(30) vessels'. Then said the Saviour (31) unto him: 'Woe unto you ye
blind that (32) see not! Thou hast washed thyself (ἐλούσω) in water (33)
that is poured forth, in which dogs and swine (34) lie night and day, and
didst

(35) wash (νιψάσμε[ν]ος) and scour thine outer skin, which (36) harlots
also and flute girls (37) anoint, bathe, scour, and (38) beautify to arouse
(39) desire in men, but inwardly

(40) they are filled with (41) [all matter of ev]il. But I and (42) [my disci-
ples], of whom thou sayest, that we had not (43) [bathed, have bath]ed
ourselves (βεβα[μμένους, βεβά]μμεθα) in the liv[ing, (44) clean?]
water, which cometh down from [the] (45) [Father in heaven, B]ut woe
unto them. . . ' [1]

Obviously, the use of λούω and νίπτω in this text is important for the
claims that these terms are used as synonyms.

Generally, λούω is used for a complete washing or bath (cf. lines
14, 19, and 24-25). But in line 32, it is possible that ἐλούσω is used
for a partial washing, for this washing has been accomplished with
water that has been 'poured forth' (τούτοις τοῖς χεομένοις
ὕ[δ]ασι(ν)). If λούω does here refer to a partial washing then it is
theoretically possible that in Jn 13.10 λελουμένος could refer to the
footwashing. However, two points stand against such an interpretation.
(1) The context of the word makes clear that this washing, which the
Pharisee claims, occurs in the pool of David, which was designed and
used for bathing (cf. especially lines 24-29). (2) It appears that the
designation 'poured forth water' is a means of emphasizing its
ordinary quality. As Jeremias observes, the poured forth water has
reference 'to external, earthly... water in general, which as such
has no real cleansing power'.[2] Therefore, it is likely that even

---

1. Cited according to the translation of Jeremias, *Unknown Sayings of Jesus*,
pp. 37-39.
2. *Ibid.*, p. 44.

here λούω means a complete washing.

On the other hand, the only occurrence of νίπτω (lines 34-35) appears to suggest that this verb is here used to describe a complete washing. If Jesus is speaking about the same act of washing in both places (lines 32 and 34-35), then in this one text λούω and νίπτω function as synonyms for washing. However, it should not go unnoticed that Jesus' dual mention of washing may be a response to the two-fold accusation made by Levi, in lines 14-16; (1) that Jesus had not bathed, and (2) that his disciples had not washed their feet. If Jesus is responding to this two-fold charge, the meanings of λούω and νίπτω become clear and conform to their usage in other texts.

Therefore, given the late date of the papyrus (fourth century), the ambiguity of its meaning, and the absence of other supporting evidence, it is unlikely that *P. Oxy.* 840 can bear the weight it must for those who argue that λούω and νίπτω were clearly used as synonyms in the latter part of the first century CE.

In point of fact, John appears to intend a distinction between these two verbs.[1] This observation is based on several considerations. First, in classical Greek, the LXX and the New Testament, νίπτω designates a partial washing (e.g. hands, face, feet).[2] Second, in passages where both verbs occur together (e.g. *T. Levi* 9.11 and Tob. 7.9b), νίπτω 'is widely attested to be necessary even after one has bathed'.[3] Third, in the available evidence examined in Chapter 3 (above), λούω is never used to describe footwashing. Fourth, the practice in sacred and domestic contexts reveals that often a bath (λούω) (Exod. 29.4; Lev. 8.6) was followed by partial washings (νίπτω) (Exod. 30.17-21; 40.30-32; 1 Kgs 7.38; 2 Chron. 4.6). All these points indicate that— far from being synonymous—these verbs are distinct, signifying two different types of washing.

Jesus' explanation, which uses these two verbs, draws upon the ancient custom of the day. A traveller or guest would bathe at home before leaving on a trip. During the course of the journey, dirt and dust

---

1. Cf. C.H. Dodd, *Interpretation of the Fourth Gospel* (Cambridge: Cambridge University Press, 1953), p. 401 n. 3; Schnackenburg, III, pp. 21-22; Segovia, 'John 13.1-20, The Footwashing in the Johannine Tradition', p. 44 n. 34.

2. F. Hauck, 'νίπτω', *TDNT*, IV, p. 946. Cf. also H.G. Liddell and R. Scott, *A Greek–English Lexicon* (Oxford: Clarendon Press, 1966), pp. 1061-62.

3. Owanga-Welo (pp. 15-16) cites the uncertain *P. Oxy.* 840 at this point.

would become attached to the feet. Upon arrival the host would offer water to remove the soil of the journey. There would be no reason to bathe again, but only to wash those parts of the body which had become soiled.[1] Owanga-Welo (p. 241) illustrates the proverbial or parabolic character of John 13.10a by pointing to a parallel found in Seneca (*Epistulae Morales* 86.12):

> It is stated by those who reported to us the old-time ways of Rome that the Romans washed only their arms and legs daily—because those were the members which gathered dirt in their daily toil—and bathed all over once a week.[2]

Together with the evidence surveyed in Chapter 3, this text demonstrates the common character of the practice. The analogy is used by Jesus to convey the deeper meaning attached to the action. Since Jesus has already made clear that the footwashing is of far-reaching significance (v. 8), it is imperative that the intended nuances of the analogy be enunciated in order to interpret the pericope properly.

The initial question is, to what is Jesus alluding when he speaks of a complete bath that makes someone clean? For the disciples in the narrative there is one option that seems most likely: *baptism*. Not only do the first disciples come from the Baptist's circle (which would imply an acquaintance with and appreciation of baptism), but Jesus himself (3.22) and his disciples (4.2) are said to have baptized others and to have been more successful than John. Regardless of the way in which the apparent tension between 3.22 and 4.2 is handled, the implication is the same. Baptisms are either performed by Jesus or under his auspices. Whether John's baptism (which is of divine origin: cf. 1.33) is being exalted by the subsequent actions of Jesus and the disciples, or whether his baptism is being superseded by the later practice, the implication for 13.10 remains the same. It is extremely likely that the disciples, who baptize others, would have experienced baptism themselves, either at the hand of Jesus or John.

The readers, presumably familiar with baptism and its role, might nonetheless be able to discern another meaning for λελουμένος. On the basis of the post-resurrection perspective of several statements in the narrative, the reader may suspect that the bath which cleanses has

---

1. Michaels, p. 224.
2. Cited according to the translation of Gummerie, *Seneca: Epistulae Morales*, II, p. 317.

reference to the death of Jesus. Other passages in Johannine literature testify to the connection between Jesus' death and cleansing. Owing to the special qualities of Jesus' blood in Johannine thought (Jn 6.53-56; 1 Jn 1.7-9; Rev. 1.5; 5.9; 19.13) and to the remarkable usages of water in the Fourth Gospel (cf. the discussion of 13.5 above), it is difficult to avoid interpreting the water and blood which come from Jesus' side in 19.34 as having reference to the life giving and cleansing qualities of his death.[1] 1 Jn 1.7-9 gives clear evidence of the connection between cleansing from sin and the blood of Jesus:

> But if we walk in the light as he is in the light, we have fellowship with one another and the blood of Jesus his Son cleanses (καθαρίζει) us from all sin. If we say that we have no sin, we deceive ourselves and the truth is not in us. If we confess our sins, he is faithful and righteous to forgive us (our) sins and cleanse (καθαρίση) us from all unrighteousness.

There can be little doubt that such statements are based upon reflection about the crucifixion of Jesus. In Rev. 7.14, one of the elders responds to John concerning the identity of certain ones who are dressed in white clothes:

> These are the ones who are coming out of the great tribulation, and have washed their clothes and made them white in the blood of the Lamb.

Again the cleansing efficacy of the blood should be noted. The readers, then, might already see the significance of λελουμένος in terms of Jesus' death, especially in the light of μετὰ ταῦτα. But it is unlikely that the cleansing through baptism and through the blood would have been seen as mutually exclusive.

One or both of the suggested meanings for λελουμένος stand as the only viable options for the disciples in the narrative or for the implied readers. However, the author knows of another possibility which the reader will encounter in 15.3. In this verse Jesus tells the disciples, 'Already you are clean (καθαροί) because of the word which I have spoken to you'. If it were legitimate to take λελουμένος in 13.10 as the referent of τὸν λόγον in 15.3, then perhaps the difficulty would be solved. On one occasion in the LXX (Judg. 3.19), λόγος does refer to a 'prophetic' action, when Ehud tells King Eglon that he has a λόγος for him in private and then kills the king. However, such a

---

1. For an overview of the scholarly debate concerning this dimension of 19.34, cf. Brown, *The Gospel according to John*, II, pp. 945-52.

parallel (if it be a parallel) is far too removed to explain 15.3. In addition, it appears that the λόγος of 15.3 has reference to Jesus' collective teaching, not one specific event. Approaching 13.10 in the light of 15.3, Bultmann argues that cleansing comes on the basis of the Revealer's word and on that basis alone. Therefore, λελουμένος is used to describe the bath in the word which makes cleansing with water secondary at best.[1] However, one of the difficulties in explaining 13.10 on the basis of 15.3 is the difference in context. While 13.10 speaks of cleansing from some uncleanness or defilement, 15.3 uses cleansing in the sense of pruning the branches in order to produce good fruit.[2] Although there does not seem to be sufficient evidence to demand that 13.10 must be interpreted by means of 15.3, there may be a deeper connection between cleansing by means of pruning and cleansing through washing. Rather than playing 13.10 and 15.3 off against one another, the two statements about cleansing should be allowed to speak independently, perhaps at different levels of meaning. Perhaps C.H. Dodd offers the best analysis through comparison with a similar dilemma found elsewhere in the Fourth Gospel:

> The disciples are καθαροί through washing with water: they are καθαροί, also, διὰ τὸν λόγον. Similarly, eternal life comes by eating the flesh and blood of the Son of Man (vi 54) and also, τὰ ῥήματα ἃ λελάληκα ὑμῖν are ζωή. The treatment of the two sacraments are analogous.[3]

So for the evangelist, cleansing takes place through water and the word, and both are dependent on the cleansing effects of Jesus' death.

---

1. Bultmann, p. 472 and p. 534.
2. Cf. Schnackenburg, III, p. 48.
3. Dodd, p. 402 n. 1. Cf. also Brown's comments:

> A dichotomy between the salvific action of Jesus and his salvific word is not true to John. Nor was there any necessary dichotomy in the mind of the Johannine writer between Baptism and the working of the word of Jesus through the Paraclete. The Christians to whom this *mashal* was addressed would have become branches in Jesus through Baptism. This would make them fruit bearing because it would give them life begotten from above and would make them clean according to the symbolism of xiii 10 (*The Gospel according to John*, II, p. 677).

Despite certain dissenting views,[1] it appears that λελουμένος most likely has reference to baptism (and Jesus' death). Several additional pieces of evidence tend to corroborate this decision. One of the reasons for this identification is to be gleaned from the effects of the bathing. Jesus says, 'The one who has bathed (λελουμένος)...is wholly clean'. In early Christian literature no rite signifies complete cleansing from sin as obviously as does baptism. Certainly, the crucifixion is that event which accomplishes the cleansing, but it is baptism which signifies the cleansing. The occurrence of λελουμένος fits well with such a theme. Second, Jesus declares that there is no reason to repeat the complete bath one has received. Likewise, baptism is a rite which is once-and-for-all.[2] Additional support for this nuance is the tense of λελουμένος. In the light of the significance of the perfect tense, which designates a past action with abiding results,[3] it is difficult to assign the choice of tense to coincidence. Finally, there is some philological support for taking λούω as a reference to baptism. In several New Testament passages λούω and its cognates are probable references to baptism (Heb. 10.22; Eph. 5.26) or are closely related to it (Acts 22.16; 1 Cor. 6.11; Tit. 3.5).[4] Therefore, it seems likely that the readers would make the connection between λελουμένος and baptism.[5]

1. Cf. G. Beasley-Murray, 'Baptism', *DNTT*, I, p. 152 and especially Richter, 'The Washing of Feet in the Gospel of John', p. 201. Cf. also Bultmann, pp. 469-70.

2. Cf. Cullmann, pp. 108-10; F. Hauck, 'καθαρός', *TDNT*, III, p. 426; and A. Oepke, 'λούω', *TDNT*, IV, p. 306.

3. Blass, Debrunner, Funk, p. 342.

4. As P. Grelot concludes, 'When one gives thought to this background, it is difficult not to see a baptismal allusion in the declaration by Jesus...' ('L'interprétation penitentielle du lavement des pieds', in *L'homme devant Dieu. I. Mélanges offerts au père Henri Lubac* [Paris: Aubier, 1963] p. 86). Obviously, there are other passages which do not equate λούω with baptism. For example, cf. Acts 9.37 and 16.33.

5. Most scholars consider λελουμένος to convey some sort of baptismal overtones. So R. Brown, *New Testament Essays* (New York: Paulist Press, 1965), p. 63; Cullmann, pp. 108-10; Dodd, p. 401 n. 3; F. Hauck, 'καθαρός', *TDNT*, III, p. 426; A.J.B. Higgins, *The Lord's Supper in the New Testament* (London: SCM Press, 1960), p. 84; Hultgren, p. 544; Lightfoot, p. 261; G.H.C. MacGregor, 'The Eucharist in the Fourth Gospel', *NTS* 9, (1963), pp. 111-19; Maynard, 'The Role of Peter in the Fourth Gospel', pp. 534-35; Maynard, *The

By following the ancient banquet practice to its completion the deeper meaning of the footwashing comes into view. The one who travels any distance at all on the dusty paths in the ancient orient accumulates dust which must be removed. If, in the analogy Jesus uses, λούω represents baptism, then it makes best sense to take the function of the footwashing as an additional act of cleansing. Dodd concludes:

> In xiii 10 λούεσθαι, to take a bath, is contrasted with νίπτειν, to wash a part of the body. Baptism is a bath (λουτρόν, Eph. v. 26; Tit. iii, 5). The Christian reader is assured that having undergone the λουτρόν he is καθαρός, yet may need some kind of recurrent washing.[1]

More than one interpreter has seen in the footwashing an allusion to forgiveness of post-baptismal sin.[2] This association is due in part to the occurrence of καθαρός in this verse. A cognate of this term appears elsewhere in Johannine literature (1 Jn 1.7, 9) with explicit reference to forgiveness of sin through the blood of Jesus. In addition, a multitude of ancient texts use καθαρός (and its cognates) in contexts which describe the forgiveness of sins. The LXX [Lev. 16.30; Pss. 18.14 (19.13); 50.4 (51.2)], and certain para-biblical literature (Sir. 23.10; 38.10; Josephus, *Ant.* 12.286; *T. Reub.* 4.8) use καθαρός in such a fashion.[3] Although καθαρός may designate other kinds of cleansing,[4] its frequent associations with forgiveness of sin make it

---

Function of Apparent Synonyms and Ambiguous Words in the Fourth Gospel, pp. 329-30; A. Oepke, 'λούω', *TDNT*, IV, p. 306; Schnackenburg, III, p. 21; H. Seeseman, 'ὅλος', *TDNT*, I, p. 175.

1. Dodd, p. 401 n. 3.
2. Westcott, p. 191; B.W. Bacon, 'The Sacrament of Footwashing', *ExpT 43* (1931–32), p. 221; Cullmann, pp. 108-10; Dodd, p. 401 n. 3; Hauck, 'καθαρός', *TDNT*, III, p. 426; Higgins, p. 84; W.L. Knox, 'John 13.1-30', *HTR* 43 (1950), p. 163; MacGregor, p. 76; Maynard, 'The Role of Peter in the Fourth Gospel', pp. 534-35; *idem*, *The Function of Apparent Synonyms and Ambiguous Words in the Fourth Gospel*, pp. 329-30; A. Oepke, 'λούω', *TDNT*, IV, p. 306.
3. For additional evidence see W. Bauer, *A Greek–English Lexicon of the New Testament and Other Early Christian Literature* (ed. W.F. Arndt and F.W. Gingrich; Cambridge: Cambridge University Press, 1952), pp. 388-89; R. Meyer and F. Hauck, 'καθαρός', *TDNT*, III, pp. 413-81; and H.-G. Link and J. Schattenmann, 'καθαρός', *DNTT*, III, pp. 102-108.
4. Jewish purity concerns are also designated by καθαρός (cf. Jn 2.6). However, John rejects such cleansing as invalid.

likely that the readers of the Fourth Gospel would have understood καθαρός to have reference to forgiveness of sin. Thus, while sin is not explicitly mentioned in v. 10, its presence is implied. Such an interpretation fits well with Jesus' emphatic language in v. 8. On this view, Peter is told that he would have no μέρος with Jesus because of (post-baptismal) sin which had not been removed by cleansing.[1] This meaning would become clear to Peter μετὰ ταῦτα. Another point concerns the Book of Glory, this understanding of footwashing fits well within the overall context of belief in which ch. 13 takes part. The disciples are not being initiated into belief in this passage, but are continuing in their belief. Their earlier baptism, which the community probably understood as being at the hands of John (1.19-39) or possibly Jesus (3.22, however cf. 4.1-2), would designate initial belief and fellowship with Jesus, whereas footwashing would signify the continuance of that belief and fellowship.[2] As a sign of preparation for Jesus' departure, footwashing signifies the disciples' spiritual cleansing in preparation both for a continuing relationship with Jesus and for taking on his mission in the world.

Yet another point concerns evidence from Chapter 3 above, which demonstrates that footwashing could be used in a sacred or cultic way (Exod. 30.17-21; 40.30-32; 1 Kgs 7.38; 2 Chron. 4.6). For Jesus to treat footwashing as a religious rite would not be wholly without precedent. Finally, the efficacious nature of the washing is emphasized by the way the footwashing 'foreshadows the self-giving involved in Jesus' death on the cross'.[3] In the light of the preceding considerations, an identification of footwashing with the cleansing from the sin contracted through daily life in this world is an appropriate one. Just as a banquet guest would bathe at home and only wash the feet at the

1. Maynard concludes, 'Whatever the symbolism, it is clear that "the footwashing is something that makes it possible for the disciples to have eternal life with Jesus"' ('The Role of Peter in the Fourth Gospel', p. 535).

2. Carson (pp. 465-66) remarks, 'In his first epistle, addressed to Christians, to people who have already believed (1 John 5.13) and received eternal life (2.25), John insists that continuing confession of sin is necessary (1.9), as is continued dependence upon Jesus Christ, who is the atoning sacrifice for our sins (2.1, 2). The thought of Jn 13.10 is not dissimilar.'

3. Michaels, p. 227. Cf. also Beasley-Murray, *John*, p. 235 and *DNTT*, I, p. 154; Brown, *The Gospel according to John*, II, p. 586; Bruce, p. 283; Grossouw, pp. 129-30.

house of the host or hostess to remove the dust accumulated on the road, so Peter (the believer) who experiences baptism (which signifies a complete cleansing from sin) does not need to be rebaptized, but undergoes footwashing, which signifies the removal of sin that might accumulate as a result of life in this sinful world. In a sense, footwashing is an extension of baptism, for it signifies the washing away of post-baptismal sins in Peter's (the believer's) life.

In view of these considerations, ἀλλ' ἔστιν καθαρὸς ὅλος may be taken to mean that as a result of the just completed washing the disciples are wholly clean. However, such an interpretation not only faces the philological difficulty of interpreting λελουμένος as having reference to the just completed footwashing, but it also violates the context of the phrase. For over against the view that ὅλος rules out the need for additional (foot)washing, the main point of the banquet analogy is that the one who has bathed at home is wholly clean; only one's feet need to be washed. Instead of forcing ὅλος into a rigid exclusivity, the term must be interpreted in the light of the philological and contextual evidence. In all likelihood, the term ὅλος is related to Peter's suggestion (v. 9) that in addition to the feet his hands and head be washed. The one who has bathed (λελουμένος) has no need for such partial washing, for the whole body is clean, except the feet. Instead of the cleansing power of the footwashing, this phrase refers to baptism. On the other hand, the next phrase (καὶ ὑμεῖς καθαροί ἐστε)[1] does appear to refer to the just completed washing. Such an understanding preserves the integrity of Jesus' response to Peter as well as emphasizes the effects of the footwashing, which are essential (v. 8). Despite the baptism and footwashing not all the disciples were clean. The strong negative οὐχί serves to emphasize this point. Obviously, the reference is to Judas. In addition to identifying Judas, this clause demonstrates that neither baptism nor footwashing works in a mechanical fashion in bringing cleansing.[2] In point of fact, Jn 13.10 illustrates the point that it is possible to experience both efficacious washings, baptism and footwashing, and still not be clean.[3]

---

1. Owanga-Welo (pp. 158-59) declares that the phrase καὶ ὑμεῖς καθαροί ἐστε 'is structurally a pronouncement which confers a spiritual or moral quality upon the disciples'.

2. Barrett, *The Gospel according to St John*, p. 442.

3. Carson (p. 466) observes, 'If this proves anything beyond the unfathomable

d. *Verse 11*. At first glance v. 11 looks rather superfluous, coming as it does on the heels of such a strategic section. However, this short verse contains much for the reader to ponder. First, v. 11 contrasts being clean with betraying, thereby demonstrating that being clean involves remaining loyal to and in fellowship with Jesus. Second, the author reiterates that one may be a disciple and even be washed by Jesus, and yet still not be clean,[1] just as in the synoptics, where Judas partakes of the bread and wine without sharing in the reality they signify. Third, mention of Jesus' knowledge reminds the reader of what is now in Judas's heart. Finally, there is also here present 'the gradual and increasingly distinct characterization of the traitor'.[2] By this time the reader has learned to pay careful attention to Judas, owing to the contexts in which he appears in the Fourth Gospel up to this point: near the 'eucharistic words' in 6.71, in the story of the anointing (footwashing) at Bethany in 12.4, and three times in 13.1-20. At this point the dialogue gives way to the explanatory discourse.

3. *The Discourse (vv. 12-20)*
a. *Verses 12, 13. Verse 12*. After Jesus completes the washing of the disciples' feet, he dresses and returns to his position at the meal. As he has done throughout the Fourth Gospel, Jesus counterbalances the disciples' misunderstanding with additional teaching. Picking up on the ideas expressed in v. 7, Jesus asks the disciples if they understand the significance of the event. Such a question suggests that the disciples have not learned what was intended from the experience. Of course the readers also must be a bit bewildered by this point. The eternal Logos, the Agent of creation and Savior of the world, stooping to wash the feet of the disciples, speaking of the μέρος at stake and about a bath which brings cleansing—who could comprehend it all? But such deep theological reflection via dialogue and action is part and parcel of the Fourth Gospel. The question in v. 12 not only is required in the narrative, but is needed by the reader. The literary unity

love and forbearance of the Master, it is that no rite, even if performed by Jesus himself, ensures spiritual cleansing. Washed Judas may have been; cleansed he was not (cf. 6.63f.).'
1. Bultmann, p. 473.
2. Schnackenburg, III, pp. 22-23.

of the passage implies that vv. 12-20 are provided as commentary,[1] explanation, and command for the community.[2]

Verse 13. Jesus' words in this verse contrast the disciples' correct estimate of his person and status with the action he has just performed. His words are directed to the entire group, as the second person plural personal pronoun, ὑμεῖς, exhibits. Throughout the Gospel, Jesus has been referred to as Teacher and Lord. In almost every instance where διδάσκαλος appears, there is an emphasis upon his position. It is interesting that Jesus is never referred to as διδάσκαλος except by those who already believe in him (11.28; 20.16) or who will come to believe (1.38; 3.2). The impression left by Jesus' use of the term here, along with the confessional nature of the term in the Fourth Gospel, is one of honor, authority, and even exaltation. κύριος is a term used for Jesus throughout the Fourth Gospel. Initially, it seems to mean no more than 'sir' (although, cf. the textually uncertain use in 4.1). However, as the book progresses the term takes on a distinctively Christological orientation, as the generic sense all but disappears (cf. 6.68; 11.27; 20.18, 28). In particular, Jesus responds to Peter's use of the title in vv. 6 and 9. The disciples' use of the title reflects insight into his person, for they are correct in their usage. Jesus does not repudiate the titles.[3] On the contrary, he takes them up himself in this initial section of the Book of Glory, and this is part of the self-revelation which characterizes chapters 13–17. John seems further to emphasize this point by placing the titles in the nominative case (a very rare construction).[4]

b. *Verses 14-17. Verse 14*. Contrasting his own person and status with that of the disciples, and underscoring this contrast by the repetition of διδάσκαλος and κύριος, Jesus now gives explicit instructions about the practice of footwashing among the disciples. It may be that the order of κύριος and διδάσκαλος has been reversed for empha-

---

1. Owanga-Welo (p. 250) observes, 'Due to the fact that John 13.12-20 interprets or comments on John 13.1-11, its function is metalinguistic. That means that it is a commentary on another portion of the text.'
2. Schnackenburg, III, p. 23.
3. Lindars, p. 452.
4. Blass, Debrunner, Funk, p. 143.

sis.[1] Οὖν serves to make clear the connection between Jesus' own actions and the following commands. In the light of his actions, καὶ ὑμεῖς ὀφείλετε ἀλλήλων νίπτειν τοὺς πόδας. The emphasis of his instruction is borne out by the appearance of καί, also, and the emphatic use of the personal pronoun, ὑμεῖς. The verb ὀφείλω further highlights the mandatory nature of the act. ὀφείλω carries with it the idea of necessity or obligation. Its force can be seen from elsewhere in the Johannine literature. According to Jn 19.7, in an attempt to convince Pilate that Jesus should be crucified, the Jews say, 'We have (the) Law, and according to the Law he must (ὀφείλει) die...' In the epistles ὀφείλει is used to describe the mandatory nature of moral conduct (1 Jn 2.6) and Christian service to other brothers and sisters (1 Jn 3.16; 4.11; 3 Jn 8). The only other time Jesus uses the term in the gospels is also in a context of mandatory service, that of a slave to a master (Lk. 17.10). Normally, in the other New Testament uses of ὀφείλω the nuance is that of:

> an obligation towards men which is deduced and which follows from the experienced or preceding act of God the Saviour. In many instances the sentence construction indicates the connection between human obligation and the experienced act of salvation.[2]

Here, the directive to service is based upon the salvific action of the Lord and Master,[3] for 'now that Jesus, their *Lord and Teacher*, has washed his disciples' feet—an unthinkable act!—there is is every reason why they *also should wash one another's feet*, and no conceivable reason for refusing to do so'.[4] The disciples have received cleansing at the hands of Jesus. Now, they are instructed to preserve this practice (as a sign of cleansing from sin). The stress of this verse lies upon washing one another's feet. Because of the connection of these verses with vv. 6-10 there is the implicit and contextual directive that the disciples receive this service and sign (from one another) as well as rendering it. There is nothing in this to suggest that footwashing be extended beyond the limits of the disciples (i.e. the believers).[5]

---

1. Brown, *The Gospel according to John,* II, p. 553.
2. F. Hauck, 'ὀφείλω', *TDNT*, V, p. 563. Zweifel (p. 131) asserts, '[ὀφείλετε]...is an order, not (simply) good advice'.
3. Cf. Schnackenburg, III, p. 24.
4. Carson, pp. 467-68.
5. Sanders and Mastin, p. 309.

By definition, it is to be a distinctively Christian act.

Verse 15. The force of Jesus' command that the disciples practice footwashing among themselves is strengthened by reference to the footwashing as a ὑπόδειγμα. But what does ὑπόδειγμα mean in this context? Is it a call to imitate the humble service of Jesus in general, or does it serve as a definite mandate for the disciples to wash one another's feet? In other words, how would the readers understand ὑπόδειγμα? Although a general call to humble service cannot be ruled out altogether, thère are three reasons to think that the readers would see in ὑπόδειγμα a reinforcement of the direct command to wash one another's feet. The first consideration is the context of this verse. In v. 14, it has been clearly stated that the disciples are to wash one another's feet. Following so closely upon this explicit command, it is likely that ὑπόδειγμα would be taken in a specific fashion. Second, this is the first (and only) ὑπόδειγμα given by Jesus which the readers will encounter in the Fourth Gospel.[1] Third, the combination of καθώς... καί emphasizes the intimate connection between Jesus' action (washing the disciples' feet) and the action of his disciples (washing one another's feet).[2] They are to act precisely as he acted. The instructions to wash one another's feet are rooted and grounded in the actions of Jesus in vv. 4-10. Therefore, the footwashing is far more than an example. 'It is a definite prototype.'[3] In all probability, the readers, as well as the disciples in the narrative, would take ὑπόδειγμα with reference to footwashing in particular, not to humble service generally.

Verse 16. Again there is an appeal to the person and status of Jesus as the basis of the command to wash one another's feet. This time it comes in the form of a saying that also appears in a Synoptic context (Mt. 10.24). The authority of the statement is underlined by the double ἀμήν which precedes the rest of the saying. The ἀμὴν ἀμήν

---

1.   Schultz, p. 62.
2.   Morris, p. 621 n. 36.
3.   H. Schlier, 'ὑπόδειγμα', *TDNT*, II, p. 33. Apollonius of Citium uses ὑπόδειγμα on a number of occasions with the sense of 'illustration, (or) picture showing how something is to be done' (Liddell–Scott, p. 1878). Cf. especially Apollonius Citiensis, *In Hippocratio De Articulis Commentarius* (ed. F. Kudlien; Berlin: Akademie Verlag, 1965), pp. 38, 60-64, 112.

formula denotes a particularly solemn saying which issues forth from Jesus' own authority. As Schlier concludes:

> The point of the Amen before Jesus' own sayings is... to show that as such they are reliable and true, and that they are so as and because Jesus Himself in His Amen acknowledges them to be His own sayings and thus makes them valid.[1]

Having already identified himself as Teacher and Lord (vv. 12-13), Jesus here expands upon the implication of his Lordship. Since as Lord he has washed the feet of his disciples, they have no choice but to take similar action, on account of their own position as slaves in relation to Jesus. Their own status and consequent actions cannot hope to be on a higher level than that of their superior. Another maxim-like saying underscores the point. 'No one who is sent is greater than the one who sends him.' Again, the clear emphasis is upon the authority of Jesus' actions in relation to the similar activity of the disciples. It is difficult to determine whether John's use of ἀπόστολος is intended to inspire thoughts of 'the Twelve' in a technical sense,[2] for this possibility must be balanced by John's avoidance of the term ἀπόστολος as a designation of the Twelve. What may be safely assumed is that the phrase οὐδὲ ἀπόστολος μείζων τοῦ πέμψαντος αὐτόν prepares the readers for v. 20, which clearly has reference to the disciples' mission.[3] This interpretation of the master–slave language, which agrees perfectly with the context, is much to be preferred over reading back service into v. 15 and thereby making it simply an ethical example. In any event, the full authority of Jesus is given to the injunction to wash one another's feet.

Verse 17. A final exhortation is given in order that the disciples might not fail to carry out the footwashing among themselves. This time the command takes the form of a blessing. It is not enough for the disciples to know what to do; they must actually do it in order to be considered blessed.[4] The grammar of this verse bears out the idea that the

1. H. Schlier, 'ἀμήν', *TDNT*, I, p. 338. Lindars (p. 48) asserts, 'the sayings introduced by the formula [amen, amen] preserve very primitive, and for the most part certainly authentic, tradition of the words of Jesus'.

2. Cf. Brown, *The Gospel according to John*, II, p. 553 and Lindars, p. 453.

3. Michaels, p. 228.

4. Cf. Barrett, *The Gospel according to St John*, p. 444; Bruce, p. 286;

disciples possess some understanding of the footwashing, now that Jesus has given this explanation, but that they must now follow through with action. This contrast is accomplished by the use of a first-class conditional clause, which indicates a future possibility.[1]

μακάριος normally implies 'an approving proclamation of fact, involving an evaluative judgment'.[2] The use of μακάριος in this context clearly underscores the importance of acting out Jesus' commands to wash one another's feet. Such emphasis is similar to that of v. 8, where Peter is warned that μέρος with Jesus is dependent upon reception of the footwashing. Therefore, not only have the disciples received footwashing from Jesus as a sign of continued fellowship with him, but they are now also instructed to continue this practice. In the light of its earlier meaning, it is likely that the footwashing to be practiced by the disciples would convey a similar significance: continued fellowship with Jesus.[3] Obedience to Jesus' commands to wash one another's feet makes one the recipient of Jesus' declaration of μακάριος.

In sum, the narrative contains not one, but three directives to the disciples to practice footwashing. It seems improbable that either the disciples (in the narrative) or the implied readers would understand such emphatic language as not having as its primary reference the actual practice of footwashing.

c. *Verses 18-20. Verse 18.* In some ways this verse serves the same function for vv. 12-17 as vv. 10b-11 do for vv. 6-10a. As in vv. 10a-11, Jesus distinguishes between the betrayer and the other disciples. In the earlier verses the readers are told that Judas is not clean, even though the other disciples are clean. Here, Judas is singled out as the one disciple who will not enjoy the blessing which results from obedience to Jesus' instructions concerning footwashing. In language reminiscent of 6.70, emphasis is placed upon Jesus' choice of Judas and his knowledge beforehand of Judas's future action. In this verse,

Michaels, p. 228; Sanders and Mastin, p. 310; and Schnackenburg, III, p. 25.

1.   Blass, Debrunner, Funk, p. 372 (3); Michaels, p. 232; W.D. Chamberlain, *An Exegetical Grammar of the Greek New Testament* (Grand Rapids: Baker, 1941), p. 198.

2.   Brown, *The Gospel according to John*, II, p. 562.

3.   Segovia, p. 46.

the selection of Judas as a disciple is justified theologically as fulfillment of Scripture.[1] The formula ἵνα ἡ γραφὴ πληρωθῇ is one of several formulae which John uses to denote the fulfillment of Scripture. As Brown notes, 'The Johannine fulfillment texts are all in the context of "the hour", i.e. of the passion—this is true even of xii 38, the sole fulfillment in the Book of Signs'.[2] Collectively, these texts serve to highlight the divinely ordained sequence of events which make up the passion.

The quotation of Ps. 41.9 contains several pieces of information pertinent to the story. ὁ τρώγων μου τὸν ἄρτον is the first explicit mention of bread at this meal. Together with v. 26, this phrase suggests that the meal is still in progress, at least until the action depicted in 13.30. The appearance of τρώγω in the quotation instead of ἐσθίω, which occurs in the LXX and Mk 14.18, picks up on its earlier use in ch. 6. This employment serves to identify further the meal as the traditional 'Last Supper'. However, the primary function of the quotation is to communicate to the readers the heartfelt anguish which Judas' treachery brings to Jesus. To raise one's heel to an enemy was quite an insult in antiquity. The injury was much more severe when directed to a friend, for it seems to have been a most contemptuous gesture.[3] Here, the very heel that had been washed by Jesus was raised against him in contempt. Through this quotation Jesus begins to reveal to the disciples that he well suffer betrayal. Therefore, v. 18 provides a brief transition to vv. 21-30, where the betrayal motif is expanded considerably.

It scarcely needs to be observed that the example of Judas demonstrates that one must be prepared to accept what the washing stands for and not simply the footwashing itself. No doubt Judas had been bathed and received the footwashing. However, not only does he fail to maintain μέρος with Jesus, but he performs the heinous deed of betrayal.

1.   For a discussion of John's use of Ps. 41.9, cf. G. Reim, *Studien zum alttestamentlichen Hintergrund des Johannesevangeliums* (Cambridge: Cambridge University Press, 1974), pp. 39-41.
2.   Brown, *The Gospel according to John*, II, p. 554.
3.   For the contemptuous nature of this action cf. E.F. Bishop, '"He that eateth bread with me hath lifted up his heel against me."—Jn xiii. 18 (Ps. xli. 9)', *ExpT* 70 (1958–59), pp. 331-33.

Verse 19. The rationale for Jesus' revelation of his betrayal to the disciples is given in this verse. By disclosing the fact beforehand, not only does Jesus hope to minimize the betrayal's adverse effects upon the disciples, but he transforms this apparent threat to his claims about himself into a means by which such claims may be vindicated. As Schnackenburg notes:

> Despite the incomprehensible fact of the betrayal, Jesus continues to be the one sent by God and, after the event of the cross has taken place, it will be clear that the disciple's betrayal and the plan devised by Satan even served Jesus' exaltation.[1]

It would appear that the footwashing has helped to prepare the disciples for the disclosure of Jesus' betrayal and their future mission. Verse 19 is the first of several admonitions (also cf. 14.29 and 16.4) that the disciples should remain steadfast when these dreadful events occur, for they can be secure in the knowledge that Jesus knew of them beforehand and, therefore, they must be divinely ordained. The ἵνα clause makes clear the purpose of Jesus' disclosure; it should result in belief. In the light of the disciples' earlier faith, πιστεύσητε, the better attested of the two readings, perhaps indicates a new impulse in their faith.[2]

Rather than undermining the disciples' faith in Jesus, knowledge of these events will confirm that ἐγώ εἰμι. There can be little doubt that the absolute of ἐγώ εἰμι implies divinity. Deutero-Isaiah appears to provide the appropriate context for interpreting these passages (Isa. 43.25; 45.18; 51.12; 52.6; 53.10). Brown concludes, 'Against this background the absolute Johannine use of ἐγώ εἰμι becomes quite intelligible. Jesus is presented as speaking in the same manner in which Yahweh speaks in Deutero-Isaiah'.[3] Jesus' claims will prove to be vindicated in the strongest possible fashion.

Verse 20. At first glance, it is possible to take v. 20 as an interruption to the progression of the story.[4] For if v. 20 is omitted, v. 19 and v. 21 allow for a smooth transition. However, the link between v. 16

---

1. Schnackenburg, III, p. 26.
2. Schnackenburg, III, p. 403 n. 78.
3. Brown, *The Gospel according to John*, I, p. 537. Cf. also the fuller discussion on pp. 533-38.
4. *Ibid.*, II, p. 571.

and v. 20 is difficult to overlook. Lindars gives a typical assessment:

> The connection is so close that one cannot escape the conclusion that these two sayings had already been linked together in the underlying tradition, before John welded them into his Last Supper narrative.[1]

The double ἀμήν is one major similarity between the verses. Such a literary device not only captures the attention of the disciples, but serves to underscore the importance of the following words for the readers. Another common theme is that of mission and 'being sent'. Yet, whereas v. 16 only suggests this motif as it concerns the disciples, v. 20 makes obvious the disciples' future mission. As a whole the verse re-emphasizes the unity of Father and Son, as well as the unity between Jesus and his disciples. The words anticipate much of the material which follows (Jn 14–17, but cf. also 4.31-38), but they especially foreshadow 20.21, where the commission of the disciples occurs. Standing in this context, the verse suggests that the footwashing not only prepares the disciples for Jesus' departure, but also prepares them for their mission after his departure.

D. *Conclusions*

Several observations may here be offered as a way of emphasizing some of the major issues raised in the literary-exegetical analysis.

1. The account of the footwashing is located in an intricately constructed section of the Fourth Gospel. Footwashing is a sign of preparation generally in antiquity, and as the subject of the initial pericope in the farewell materials, it becomes the first part of the disciples' preparation for Jesus' departure. Standing first in the Book of Glory, the footwashing is inextricably bound to the passion of Jesus and its implications for the disciples.

2. In an act unrivalled in antiquity, Jesus, the Lord and Teacher, strips himself and begins to perform the most menial task for his disciples. The enormous extent of his love leads to Jesus taking upon himself the role of the slave, in defiance of normal social custom.

3. Jesus makes clear that the footwashing is not optional, but

1. Lindars, p. 455.

necessary for the disciples to maintain a share in his identity. Footwashing appears to convey a cleansing which supplements the bath that earlier produced a more fundamental cleansing. Therefore, the footwashing by Jesus' hand serves as a sign of continued fellowship with Jesus and additional cleansing in the disciples' lives.

4. In the wake of his own action, Jesus, in three distinct commands, directs the disciples not only to follow his example of humble service, but specifically to wash one another's feet. How else such a point could be made is difficult to envision.

5. If the disciples in the Fourth Gospel are instructed to observe footwashing in an ongoing fashion, perhaps the act is best understood as a sign of preparation for mission which denotes fellowship with Jesus, made possible by continual cleansing.

E. *Implications for the Literary Unity of John 13.1-20*

Before turning to the historical pursuits of Chapter 5, it is necessary to explore the implications of this reading for the literary unity of Jn 13.1-20. Such a course of action is needed because, as noted briefly earlier, the literary unity of this passage has been widely disputed. In the view of many scholars the first section, vv. 1-11, is incompatible with the second section, vv. 12-20. The interpretations of the action of Jesus given in these two portions of the narrative are said to be different, and many assert that the meaning of the pericope cannot be understood without dividing the passage. These suspicions are often substantiated by reference to other supposed tensions.

One of the first scholars to identify two different interpretations of the footwashing in Jn 13.1-20 was M.-E. Boismard. He proposes:

> 1. The account of washing the feet demands a sacramental interpretation in reference to baptism (vv. 6-10); 2. it equally demands a moralistic interpretation (vv. 12-17); 3. these two interpretations are not homogeneous with each other, but the primitive account (moralistic interpretation) has been reinterpreted, at a later stage of the development of the Johannine traditions, so that it became a narrative with sacramental significance.[1]

Boismard concludes that there are two interpretations, side by side,

---

1. Boismard, p. 6.

such that 'there exists a double introduction and a double conclusion to the narrative'.[1] In developing the notion of a double introduction, Boismard comments, 'The double εἰδώς is particularly characteristic and reveals the doublet...v. 1 corresponds very well with the moralistic interpretation...(while) v. 3 announces and prepares for the sacramental interpretation...'[2] The two interpretations, found in vv. 6-10 and 12–17 are sacramental and moralistic, respectively. Both end with betrayal predictions, vv. 10b-11 (sacramental) and vv. 18-19 (moralistic). Boismard concludes that though neither interpretation represents secondary editing, the moralistic interpretation is probably 'the more archaic', while the sacramental interpretation is 'the more developed form'.[3]

A variation of this proposal is offered by Richter. He suggests several reasons why the footwashing passage cannot be a literary unit.

1. According to vv. 6ff. it (footwashing) is a symbol, that, as every other symbol in the Gospel of John, has a Christological and salvation-historical meaning, but according to vv. 12ff. it is an example for humble service.

2. According to the first interpretation, the symbolic character of the footwashing can only be seen later (μετὰ ταῦτα v. 7), and all pertinent commentaries (correctly) understand the μετὰ ταῦτα as meaning 'after Easter', in the same manner as the other signs of Jesus could only be understood in their Christological and soteriological meaning after his glorification and after the sending of the Paraclete. And yet the second interpretation follows immediately after the action.

3. The question by Jesus in v. 12 ('Do you understand what I have done to you?') does not consider the word of Jesus in v. 7 ('What I do, you do not understand now, but you will understand it later') and vice versa, so that one has to assume or at least can assume, that both interpretations are indepen-

---

1. Boismard, p. 22.
2. *Ibid.*
3. *Ibid.* It appears that Boismard understands the two interpretations as coming to the Evangelist at the same time.

dent from one another and that neither knows about the other.

4. In the first interpretation the assurance of salvation ('You are clean', v. 10) occurs, based on the act of salvation by Jesus, which is symbolized by the footwashing; however, in the second interpretation ('Blessed are you if you do it', v. 17) it is based on the act of the disciples which consists of the imitation of the example given by Jesus.[1]

Richter goes on to point out that either interpretation could be omitted, and the story would still cohere.[2] Boismard's suggestion that vv. 1-3 serve as dual introductions is followed by Richter. However, he disagrees with Boismard's conclusion that the second interpretation is the more ancient. There are two primary reasons for his view. (1) The first interpretation bears external and internal similarities to the compositional tendencies of the Fourth Evangelist. The standard narrative structure in the Fourth Gospel includes: 'dialogue, misunderstanding of Jesus' words, symbolic character of Jesus' actions, later understanding'.[3] Richter suggests, 'only the first interpretation corresponds with the purpose of the Gospel'.[4] (2) He observes that John nowhere else uses one and the same action of Jesus both as symbolic of a spiritual truth and as an act to be imitated by the disciples.[5] Richter also disagrees with Boismard about how the two interpretations were joined together. Richter believes the second interpretation was added to a document which already contained the first interpretation. The editor who added the second interpretation was probably the member of the Johannine school who also added the second farewell discourse (Jn 15).[6] Consequently, Richter holds that there are two independent footwashing interpretations, one later than the other, placed in the Fourth Gospel by two different hands.

Brown also thinks the footwashing pericope contains two independent interpretations of the footwashing. Describing Boismard's re-

---

1. G. Richter, 'Die Fusswaschung Joh 13, 1-20', *MTZ* 16 (1965), p. 21. The arguments have been numbered here for the sake of clarity.
2. *Ibid.*
3. *Ibid.*, p. 22.
4. *Ibid.*, p. 23.
5. *Ibid.*
6. *Ibid.*

construction as 'too rigorously systematic', Brown rejects the idea of two introductions in vv. 1-3. He prefers to take verse one as an introduction to the entire 'Book of Glory'.[1] While noting that the question of age is not necessarily tied to the question of which tradition appeared in the original edition of the Gospel, Brown agrees with Richter that the interpretation in vv. 6-11 is original.

> Format alone would suggest that the first interpretation (6-11) is more original. We have seen that, when in the course of editing or redacting another unit of Johannine material has been added to the Gospel, there is a tendency to tack this onto the end of a section rather than to break up the already existing unit (cf. iii 31-36, vi 51-58, xii 44-50; also xv–xvi below). In the instance under discussion 6-11 is much more closely tied to the action of the footwashing than is 12-20 which could easily have been appended. The dialogue in 6-10 has no other possible reference than to the footwashing, while some of the sayings in 12-20 are general and appropriate to other moments in Jesus' career.[2]

Brown identifies the first interpretation as 'a prophetic action symbolizing Jesus' death in humiliation for the salvation of others'.[3] The second interpretation was current in Johannine circles and viewed the footwashing 'as a moral example of humility to be imitated by others... This section was appended to 2-10a probably at the same time that xv–xvi were appended to xiv in the formation of the Last Discourse'.[4]

These scholars are prominent among many who maintain that two different interpretations are present in Jn 13.1-20.[5]

1. Brown, *The Gospel according to John*, II, p. 560.
2. *Ibid.*, p. 561.
3. *Ibid.*, p. 562.
4. *Ibid.*
5. In addition to Boismard, Richter and Brown, a number of others argue in favor of two interpretations. Cf. Weiss, pp. 298-325; Hultgren, pp. 539-46; Segovia, 'John 13.1-20, The Footwashing in the Johannine Tradition', pp. 31-32, 37; and Zweifel, pp. 64-66. Bultmann (p. 462) also sees two differing interpretations in Jn 13.1-20. He identifies vv. 12-20 as (apophthegm material) present in John's source, while vv. 6-10 bear the marks of being the work of the evangelist. On the relationship of the two interpretations Bultmann concludes, 'The fact that the evangelist uses this apophthegm and gives it a new interpretation, does not mean that he wants to exclude the old one, but to establish it afresh. It is the task of exegesis to demonstrate the inner unity of the two interpretations'. Schnackenburg (III, pp. 14-24) argues that vv. 5-10 belong to 'the evangelist's fundamental

However, several scholars have remained unconvinced by such arguments and have sought to demonstrate that Jn 13.1-20 ought to be regarded as a literary unit.

David Daube has pointed out the similarity between Jn 13.1-20 and a tripartite story pattern found in a variety of ancient literature which includes rabbinic literature. The triad is composed of 'a mystifying gesture, a question, and an interpretation'. Daube notes:

> John is an accomplished writer—the tripartite framework and the setting we have ascribed to it are quite plain. A master is surrounded by his circle. The former deliberately acts in a way for the moment unintelligible to the latter, in a way that must seem paradoxical, though its significance will ultimately be made clear. . . and once the significance is revealed, the master's practice turns out to have been right and worth imitating.[1]

Viewed in this light, Jn 13.1-20 is not a combination of two differing interpretations, but a coherent unit which is in tune with the literary conventions of the time.

Other scholars argue that the original tradition incorporates elements from what some have seen as two traditions. Lindars notes that the pericope as a whole fits the basic pattern of other Johannine passages and bears distinctive Johannine characteristics. He offers a different assessment regarding the material which may be assigned to the original tradition. Instead of holding vv. 2-11 as a unit and regarding vv. 12-15 as 'a second interpretation of the washing', Lindars suggests that only the information in vv. 4, 5, and 12-15 was a part of the tradition available to the evangelist. Lindars charges that Brown disregards 'John's methods of building on traditional material, expanding it with dialogue, and often singling out a particular person'.[2] Since, according to Lindars, John is doing here what he does in other places, there is no need to see any diametric opposition in the pericope as a whole. If the evangelist himself is responsible for the passage, as Lindars argues, then it stands to reason that the passage is intelligible without dividing it up.

---

stratum', while 12b-16 have been inserted. However, while 'these texts look suspiciously like editorial additions. . . they fit well into the evangelist's language. . . and they are theologically in accordance with his intentions'.

1. D. Daube, *The New Testament and Rabbinic Judaism* (New York: Arno, 1973), pp. 182-83.

2. Lindars, p. 447.

Michal Wojciechowski also challenges the idea that two distinct interpretations have been combined in Jn 13.1-20.[1] By means of a thorough literary examination, he postulates the existence of a source which includes vv. 1, 4-6a, 8-9, 12, and 17. Verses 10a, 13, and 16 are classified as authentic logia that have been inserted here, whereas vv. 14-15 are regarded as Johannine creations which present Jesus' actions as an example for the disciples. Wojciechowski views these verses as additions which make application of the actions of Jesus to the situation of the disciples, and thus finds no real tension present in the narrative.

Although appreciative of Wojciechowski's proposal, Robert T. Fortna goes so far as to suggest that attempts to isolate a source behind John 13 are made in vain:

> I earlier suggested the verses in chapter 13 most likely to contain vestiges of this pre-Johannine account (*TGOS*, 155-57). But the material has evidently been so rewritten, perhaps more than once. . . that reconstruction of the source now seems too tenuous to be practicable. Thus an interpretation of the pre-Johannine form of the story is no longer possible. And while on the other hand a number of Johannine themes can be perceived in chapter 13, they now are so intimately interwoven with the earlier traditions that our understanding of the chapter's meaning cannot be informed by redaction-critical studies.[2]

Such a position certainly questions the legitimacy of dividing the passage into two interpretations in order to explain it.

In addition to these challenges on basic issues, some of the individual points offered by Richter as evidence for dividing the passage have not gone undisputed. The statement that the disciples will understand the significance of Jesus' action 'after these things' is said to necessitate the separation of the pericope. Richter and others argue that since μετὰ ταῦτα means the disciples must wait until the resurrection for an understanding of Jesus' actions, the explanation given in vv. 12-20 is artificial and incompatible. However, Lohse asserts that to ask whether μετὰ ταῦτα is related to the meaning in vv. 12-17 or to the passion and resurrection is superfluous. He contends that μετὰ ταῦτα

---

1. M. Wojciechowski, 'La source de Jean 13.1-20', *NTS* 34 (1988), pp. 135-41.

2. R.T. Fortna, *The Fourth Gospel and its Predecessor* (Edinburgh: T. & T. Clark, 1989), pp. 148-49, 323.

has reference to both present and future understanding. While full understanding of Jesus' actions comes after the passion, the explanation offered in vv. 12-17 anticipates the understanding which will come later. Rather than obstructing the literary unity of 13.1-20, μετὰ ταῦτα ties the footwashing together with the rest of the passion narrative.[1]

The related question concerning the ability of the disciples to understand before (v. 7) and then after (v. 12) the footwashing presents far less of a problem than Richter suggests. Certainly there is a future understanding involved in v. 7. However, such a comprehension does not preclude a present (if only a partial) understanding. Schneiders concludes:

> In v. 7 Jesus says that what *he is doing*, i.e., the relation of his action at the supper to his death, cannot be understood until after the crucifixion. Nevertheless, the disciples can understand immediately what *Jesus explains to them* in vss. 13-15, viz., that his relation to them in the footwashing is the pattern of their relation to each other. Only after glorification will they understand that the relationship between Jesus and themselves was literally service unto death.[2]

A partial understanding is available in v. 12 but fuller revelation must wait until the crucifixion and resurrection. However, since the members of John's audience stand in a post-resurrection setting, they do not have to wait until chs. 19 and 20 to figure out what this event means.

Still another argument, that there are two incompatible interpretations in John 13, fails to convince when examined closely. Richter has asserted:

> in the entire Gospel no example can be found where the Evangelist uses the same incident out of the life of Jesus first as a symbol and then immediately as an example which should be followed.[3]

He therefore concludes that one of the interpretations is the work of a later editor. However, Weiser argues that Richter's assertion is too sweeping. In opposition to Richter's position, Weiser suggests that there is at least one other place where such an example appears, Jn

---

1. Lohse, I, p. 122.
2. Schneiders, p. 82 n. 26.
3. Richter, *Die Fusswaschung im Johannesevangelium*, p. 310.

12.24-25. When the passage is compared with Jn 13.1-20, Weiser notes several identical elements:

1. A Christological-soteriological statement in the first part;
2. A statement which calls for imitation in the second part;
3. The statement which calls for imitation originates from tradition;
4. However, the two parts are in tension with one another. How can the once and for all act of salvation, which is in the death of Jesus, be imitated by the disciples of whom is asked the same?
5. Nevertheless, both statements are connected with one another and in 12.24 it is very clear that not only has the Evangelist taken over the formulations, but he has even recorded them (maybe even the joining of the two verses originates with him). But the most important thing is: He has not removed the tension between the Christological statement and the statement calling for duplication in the life of the disciple. The same relationship exists with Jn 13.6-10 and 12-17.[1]

Weiser notes that the two actions joined in 13.1-20 are not entirely out of keeping with John's practice elsewhere. It is therefore unwarranted to demand that the passage be divided in order to interpret it properly.

Others have claimed not only that Jn 12.24-25 offers a parallel to the two dimensions of the footwashing pericope, but also that a similar pattern has been found in several other New Testament passages. For example, Robinson has suggested that Mk 10.32-45 is a synoptic equivalent to Jn 13.1-20.[2] There is an emphasis in both passages upon Jesus' humble, loving service exemplified in his own death, but also an emphasis upon the identification of the Lord and disciples through similar actions. Similar patterns are also found in 1 Jn 3.16, Phil. 2.5-11, and 1 Pet. 2.21-25. Although the sacrificial death of Jesus cannot be repeated, various kinds of acts based upon it can and should be. In the light of these parallels, Dunn concludes:

1. Weiser, 'Joh 13, 12-22: Zufügung eines späteren Herausgebers?', *BZ* 12 (1968), p. 254.
2. Robinson, p. 146 n. 2.

> In short, Boismard and Richter are mistaken in thinking that the soterio-
> logical-Christological significance of the first part cannot be harmonized
> with the moral-ethical interpretations of the second part. On the contrary,
> the union of the two interpretations in the complete presentation is neither
> artificial nor unexpected, but is entirely of a piece with one particular
> strand of *imitatio Christi* which appears both elsewhere in John's writings
> and in other New Testament books.[1]

Of course, many of these scholars recognize that it is possible to assign the two sections of 13.1-20 to different hands. However, in the
light of evidence to the contrary, they regard such a course of action
as highly questionable. Weiser warns:

> Does there not exist the danger that we approach the Gospel too much
> with our own understanding and determine ourselves why it should have
> been and why it should not have been written? As long as the text allows a
> meaningful explanation, and statements of other passages contribute to a
> non-contradictory understanding, one has no right to interpret the text in a
> mutually exclusive sense and to draw out of it a conclusion for the literary
> critical judgment.[2]

C.K. Barrett comes to a similar conclusion:

> Certainly no one can deny the possibility that these may have been two ac-
> counts of the one event. It is equally certain that this cannot be proven,
> and it is in fact improbable, since what is beyond question, since it lies on
> paper before us, is that John wishes the one event, and that which it sym-
> bolizes, to be understood in both ways:. . .effective and exemplary.[3]

This survey has shown the way in which scholarship has been preoccupied with the literary unity of Jn 13.1-20. While some scholars insist that the passage must be divided for it to make sense, others are

---

1.   Dunn, p. 249. Cf. also the critique of Richter by R.P. Martin (*New
Testament Foundations* [Exeter: Paternoster Press, 1975], I, p. 308):

> But his arguments are not conclusive, since it is always problematical to call in a
> redactor to smooth out alleged stylistic differences. Nor is there any compulsion
> to see verses 12-20 as saying something different from the earlier section.
> Rather, Jesus' words to the disciples as a group reinforce what has just taken
> place. There is little force in Richter's argument that the christological-
> soteriological significance of verses 5-11 cannot be harmonized with the ethical
> connotation of verses 12-20.

2.   Weiser, p. 356.
3.   C.K. Barrett, *Essays on John* (Philadelphia: Westminster Press, 1982),
p. 96. For a similar assessment, cf. Carson, pp. 458-60.

convinced that not only is such an approach unwarranted methodologically, but that the text as it stands makes sense.

The reading of Jn 13.1-20 offered in this work has shown the limitations of such preoccupation with the redactional history of the pericope. The tensions in the text of the Fourth Gospel have justifiably caused many Johannine scholars to look for sources as a means of explaining the aporias. However, in the light of this reading, it appears that some scholars have been too eager to find differing sources in John 13. The reading of Jn 13.1-20 offered here makes it improbable that two contradictory traditions have been combined, and it even further undermines the necessity of searching for two sources in the first place. By over-emphasizing the seeming incongruities and supposed tensions, the traditio-historical approach has obscured the fact that Jn 13.1-20 is coherent and allows for a sensible explanation. At the same time, such artificial division of the passage has impeded exploration of the text's meaning for its readers. For ordinarily, when vv. 12-20 are looked upon as a later addition, these verses are discarded as being a mere lesson in humility. Unfortunately, their meaning for the community is left unexplored by most commentators.

On the other hand, when the passage is read as a unit, the commands in vv. 14, 15 and 17 must be explained in the light of the first half of the pericope. In large part, the meaning of the commands to wash feet is determined by the degree to which vv. 12-20 are informed by vv. 6-11. This reading suggests that whatever tradition history or redactional activity lies behind the narrative, the pericope as it now stands has a coherent meaning. Therefore, interpreters can no longer be satisfied with speculation about the redactional history of the passage alone. Instead of playing vv. 6-11 off against vv. 12-20, they must seek to explain vv. 12-20 in the light of vv. 6-11, or at least attempt to demonstrate why the implied readers could not understand the text as a coherent unit. In any case, the reading of 13.1-20 offered here has significant implications for the literary unity of the passage.

Chapter 5

HISTORICAL RECONSTRUCTION

A. *Footwashing and the Johannine Community*

This chapter seeks to move from literary analysis to historical analysis, from the text of John 13 to the practice of the Johannine community. The fundamental question to be raised is this: did religious footwashing have a place in the practice of the Johannine community? L. William Countryman offers an opportune challenge with the observation:

> One cannot say whether the original Johannine audience would have understood Jesus to be instituting footwashing as a rite or whether they would have taken the passage solely as a metaphor or acted prophecy.[1]

Is Countryman correct in his assessment? Or might it be possible to draw back the curtains that conceal the practice of the Johannine community in order to determine their understanding of Jn 13.1-20? This chapter takes up the latent challenge of Countryman's observation by attempting to discover the significance of footwashing for the Johannine community.

Unfortunately, in the majority of works on the Fourth Gospel or the Johannine community, one looks in vain for the slightest degree of interest in the practice of footwashing. For despite the explicit and emphatic commands recorded in Jn 13.14-17, the function of footwashing in the Johannine community has received surprisingly little attention. In the major commentaries there is absolutely no reflection about the practice in the Johannine community. Most commentators simply take the commands to wash feet as symbolic of the attitude of humble service the disciples should exhibit. Yet in the majority of

---

1. L.W. Countryman, *The Mystical Way in the Fourth Gospel* (Philadelphia: Fortress Press, 1987), p. 89.

cases where such humble service is delineated, footwashing is not included in the discussion. Brown is representative of this treatment of vv. 14-17. In a general comment he suggests that 'vss. 12-20 contain another interpretation of the footwashing current in Johannine circles whereby it was looked on as a moral example of humility to be imitated by others'.[1] In a detailed note Brown observes:

> [T]he disciples must be willing to do similar acts of service for one another. That the practice was taken seriously is attested in 1 Timothy 5.10 where one of the qualifications for a woman to be enrolled as a widow is that she have shown hospitality and have 'washed the feet of the saints'.[2]

Although Brown offers considerable notations on the other dimensions of these verses, nothing else is said about the practice of footwashing in the community. Even though meagre, Brown's comments are more exhaustive than those to be found in the other major commentaries. In the light of the explicit commands to continue the practice (13.14-17), such a lack of reflection is both surprising and disappointing.

Given such a state of affairs, this investigation must of necessity raise new questions and reconsider previously examined evidence which may have a bearing on the question. Therefore, in the following sections a historical reconstruction of the Johannine belief and practice about footwashing is proposed. Although the nature of the inquiry necessitates some historical reconstruction, the attempt is made to fashion the reconstruction on the basis of what might reasonably be deduced from the relevant materials, circumstantial as some of the evidence may be.

1. *John 13.14-17 and the Actual Readers*

The most appropriate place to commence this inquiry is the text of Jn 13.14-17. The primary question at this point is: would the actual readers in the community have understood these verses to mean that Jesus instituted footwashing as a rite—or would they 'have taken the passage solely as a metaphor or an acted prophecy'?[3]

It has been suggested in the literary and exegetical analysis of Chapter 4 that the implied readers would understand vv. 14-17 in a

1. Brown, *The Gospel according to John*, II, p. 562.
2. *Ibid.*, p. 569.
3. Countryman, p. 89.

literal fashion. This assessment is due in large part to the straightforward character of the language. After all, the text does indeed contain explicit commands for the disciples to wash one another's feet. These commands are not inferences in these verses but the clear wording of the text. Such explicit language prompts Weiss to observe. 'The community would not have preserved the command, "you also ought to wash one another's feet" (xiii 14b), if it had not been obeying the command'.[1] The fact that these commands follow Jesus' own action of washing the disciples' feet also suggests a literal understanding of 13.14-17.

In addition, when the commands of 13.14-17 are read against the cultural context of western antiquity, it seems even more probable that the first readers (members of the Johannine community) would have taken vv. 14-17 as calling for literal compliance on their part. The survey of footwashing in antiquity (cf. Chapter 3 above) indicates that footwashing was both widely practiced and diverse in its significance. In the light of these points, it is reasonable to assume that the readers of the Fourth Gospel would be familiar with footwashing of one kind or another through actual participation. The first readers are in a very different position than modern western readers, who—due to their unfamiliarity with the practice of footwashing—seem unable to take seriously that a literal fulfillment of the command is in view. The first readers' familiarity with the practice in general increases the likelihood that, after reading Jn 13.14-17, they would be inclined to carry out its literal fulfillment.

A final consideration relevant to this inquiry concerns the setting of vv. 14-17. It seems highly likely that the first readers would know the meal during which the footwashing took place as the traditional 'Last Supper'.[2] This context would raise the readers' expectations in regard to words of institution. In other words, the 'eucharistic' setting would prepare the readers for the institution of a sacred rite. Read against this backdrop, vv. 14-17 sound very much like words of institution.

Of course, the obvious place to look for evidence of the community's attitude toward Jn 13.14-17 is the Johannine epistles. Unfortunately, these documents show remarkably little interest in the

---

1. Weiss, p. 300.
2. Cf. the discussion in Chapter 4, Section C.1.b, above.

community's rites as such, choosing instead to focus attention upon its beliefs and ethical conduct.

Despite this fact, there is a good deal of material available which documents the way in which other actual readers understood Jn 13.14-17. Most of this evidence comes from writers and churches familiar with the Fourth Gospel, but a few texts will be examined whose relationship to the Fourth Gospel is less certain.

2. *John 13 and Some Actual Readers in the Early Church*

A number of early Christian texts give evidence of the regularity with which a reading of Jn 13.14-17 resulted in the practice of footwashing. In these cases, the relationship of the practice to John 13 is explicit.

Tertullian not only stands as one of the first writers to exhibit a knowledge of the footwashing pericope (cf. *On Baptism* 12), but he also indicates (*De Corona* 8; written c. 211) that footwashing was practiced as part of Christian worship:

> I must recognize Christ, both as He reclines on a couch, and when He presents a basin for the feet of His disciples, and when He pours water into it from a ewer, and when He is girt about with a linen towel—a garment specially sacred to Osiris. It is thus in general I reply upon the point, admitting indeed that we use along with others these articles, but challenging that this be judged in the light of the distinction between things agreeable and things opposed to reason because the promiscuous employment of them is deceptive, concealing the corruption of the creature, by which it has been made subject to vanity.[1]

Several aspects of this passage indicate the continued practice of footwashing. (1) The context of Tertullian's remarks concerns the event described in John 13. (2) He acknowledges that the use of a linen towel is also of significance in the mystery religion associated with Osiris. (3) Tertullian admits that Christians continue to make use of the basin, water, and the towel, presumably in the observance of footwashing. This final point underscores the probability that footwashing was important for the community, since Tertullian is willing to risk similarity with the Osiris cult in order to defend the practice.

The evidence from Tertullian suggests that the commands of Jn

---

1. Cited according to the translation of A. Roberts and J. Donaldson, *Ante-Nicene Fathers* (Grand Rapids: Eerdmans, 1951), III, p. 98.

13.14-17 resulted in the literal observance of footwashing. In other words, Tertullian and his readers understood Jn 13.14-17 to call for a literal fulfillment, confirming the conclusions reached earlier about implied readers and actual readers.

According to the Canons of Athanasius (written c. 366–73), several times a year the bishop is to demonstrate his service to those in his charge, among other things, by washing their feet:

> This bishop shall eat often with the priests in the Church, that he may see their behavior, whether they do eat in quiet and in the fear of God. And he shall stand there and serve them; and if they be weak (if he can), he shall wash their feet with his own hands. And if he is not able to do this, he shall cause the archpriest or him that is after him to wash their feet. Suffer not the commandment of the Savior to depart from you, for all this shall ye be answerable, that they likewise may see the lowliness of the Savior in you.[1]

It is clear from the reference to 'the commandment of the Savior' that the practice of footwashing in this community is the direct result of Jn 13.14-17. Thus, another group of 'readers' understands the text to call for literal compliance.

In comments upon the actions of Jesus on the eve of his death, John Chrysostom (*Homilies on John* 71; written c. 391) urges Christians to imitate the actions of Jesus, even to the point of washing the feet of slaves:

> 'Let us wash one another's feet' He said. 'Those of slaves, too?' And what great thing is it, even if we do wash the feet of slaves? For He Himself was Lord by nature, while we were slaves, yet He did not beg off from doing even this. . . Yet what shall we then say, we who have received the example of such great forbearance, but do not imitate it even slightly, and who, on the contrary, adopt the opposite attitude: both magnifying ourselves unduly and not rendering to others what we ought? For God made us debtors to one another—after He Himself had begun this process—and debtors in regard to a smaller amount. He Himself, to be sure, was Lord, whereas if we perform an act of humility we do it to our fellow slaves. Accordingly, He made an indirect reference to this very thing, also, by saying: 'If therefore, I the Lord and Master', and again: 'So you also'. Indeed, it would have followed logically for us to say:

---

1.   Chapter 66, cited according to the translation of W. Riedeland and W.E. Crum, *The Canons of Athanasius of Alexandria* (London: Williams and Norgate, 1904), pp. 43 and 131.

'How much rather we slaves', and He left this conclusion to the conscience of His hearers.[1]

Jn 13.14-17 seems to have such an unambiguous meaning for Chrysostom that he cannot help but call for the literal practice of footwashing, despite is apparent absence among his hearers.

Ambrose is another reader who understands John 13 as calling for literal fulfillment. In his *Of the Holy Spirit* (1.15) Ambrose affirms:

> I, then wish also myself to wash the feet of my brethren, I wish to fulfill the commandment of my Lord, I will not be ashamed in myself, nor disdain what He Himself did first.[2]

Clearly, the actions and commands of Jesus, as depicted in Jn 13.1-20, are responsible for Ambrose's interpretation.

Augustine may also be added to the list of those who read Jn 13.14-17 as advocating a literal observance. In a discussion of Jn 13.10-15 Augustine (*John: Tractate* 58.4) advocates the continued practice of footwashing:

> And wherever such is not the practice among the saints, what they do not with the hand they do in heart. . . But it is far better, and beyond all dispute more accordant with the truth, that it should also be done with the hands; nor should the Christian think it beneath him to do what was done by Christ. For when the body is bent at a brother's feet, the feeling of such humility is either awakened in the heart itself, or is strengthened if already present.[3]

That Augustine equates humble service with footwashing is apparent. However, without denying that humility can be exhibited in other ways ('in heart'), he emphatically asserts that footwashing is worthy to be continued.

In the *Apostolic Constitutions* (3.19), which date to the latter half of the fourth century, one of the characteristic roles of a deacon is footwashing:

---

1. Cited according to the translation of T.A. Goggin, *Saint John Chrysostom: Commentary on Saint John the Apostle and Evangelist, Homilies 44–88* (New York: Fathers of the Church, 1960), p. 261.
2. Cited according to the translation of P. Schaff and H. Wace, *Nicene and Post-Nicene Fathers*, X, p. 95.
3. Cited according to the translation of Schaff, *Nicene and Post-Nicene Fathers*, VII, p. 306.

> We ought therefore also to serve the brethren, in imitation of Christ. For says He: 'He that will be great among you, let him be your minister; and he that will be first among you, let him be your servant'. For so did He really, and not in word only, fulfill the prediction of, 'serving many faithfully'. For 'when He had taken a towel, He girded Himself. Afterward He puts water into a basin; and as we were sitting at meat, He came and washed the feet of us all, and wiped them with the towel'. By doing this He demonstrated to us His kindness and brotherly affection, that so we also might do the same to one another. If, therefore, our Lord and Master so humbled Himself, how can you, the labourers of the truth, and administrators of piety, be ashamed to do the same to such of the brethren as are weak and infirm?[1]

Here the example of Jesus is the paradigm for the practice of footwashing on the part of the deacons. Clearly, this understanding is based on a reading of Jn 13.1-20.

John Cassian (360–435) (*Institute of the Coenobia* 4.19) reveals that in the community of which he was a part, John 13 was interpreted as calling for the practice of footwashing:

> But each one who undertakes these weeks is on duty and has to serve until supper on Sunday, and when this is done, his duty for the whole week is finished, so that, when all the brethren come together to chant the Psalms (which according to custom they sing before going to bed) those whose turn is over wash the feet of all in turn, seeking faithfully from them the reward of this blessing for their work during the whole week, that the prayers offered up by all the brethren together may accompany them as they fulfill the command of Christ. . . [2]

It is evident from the mention of 'the command of Christ' that the footwashing was inspired by the text of John 13.

In the monastic sphere of Pachomias (*Rules* 51–52; written in 404), visiting clerics and monks are to be received with footwashing:

> When people come to the door of the monastary, they are to be received with greater honor if they are clerics or monks. Their feet shall be washed, according to the Gospel precept, and they shall be brought to the guest house and offered everything suitable to monks.[3]

---

1.   Cited according to the translation of Roberts and Donaldson, *Ante-Nicene Fathers*, VII, p. 432.

2.   Cited according to the translation of *Nicene and Post-Nicene Fathers*, Second Series, XI, pp. 224-25.

3.   Cited according to the translation of A. Veilleux, *Pachomian Koinonia*, II

From this text, it is clear that the practice of the community was the direct result of the 'Gospel precept', no doubt a reference to John 13.

Caesarius of Arles (c. 470–542), an ardent defender of footwashing, makes plain that his belief is based upon the reading of John 13. In *Sermon* 202 he exhorts:

> Today, dearest brethren, we are going to hear the Evangelist say that 'when the Lord had risen from the meal, he took off his cloak, tied a towel around himself, and began to wash his disciples' feet'. What shall we say about this occasion, most beloved? Or what excuse will we be able to offer, we who scorn to give strangers the service which He deigned to offer to His servants? Possibly there are some powerful and noble men or delicate women who scorn to bend down to the footstep of the saints who are sojourning in this world. Not only do they themselves refuse to wash the feet of strangers, but neither do they command any of their servants to do it for them. Perhaps Christian men or women blush to touch the feet of the saints in this world with their delicate hands, because the prerogative of birth does not allow it. Wicked nobility, which makes itself ignoble before God through pride! The noble and mighty blush to wash the feet of saints and strangers in this world, but if they do not amend their lives, they will have to be separated from companionship with them in the future life. Then they will be tormented without any remedy of repentance, when they shall see those whom they despised receive the kingdom because of their humility, while they on account of their pride have merited punishment. Let us fear, brethren, what the blessed Apostle Peter feared, when he heard the Lord say: 'If I do not wash you, you will have no share in my heritage'. For if, perchance, we disdain to wash the feet of the saints, we will not merit to have a share with them. Let us rather bend down the feet of the saints or of strangers; because when we fulfill this service with holy humility, indeed we are not merely touching their feet with our hands, but we are cleansing the meanness and filth of our souls through faith and humility, and we are cleansing not only the smallest, but even the most serious of our sins.[1]

In another sermon (86.5) Caesarius gives a strong admonition to practice footwashing:

(Kalamazoo: Cistercian Publications, 1981), p. 153.

1.   Cited according to the translation of M.M. Mueller, *Saint Caesarius of Arles: Sermons* (Washington, DC: Catholic University of America Press, 1973), III, pp. 65-66.

Welcome strangers and do not be ashamed to wash their feet; do not blush
to do as a Christian what Christ deigned to perform.[1]

These texts demonstrate that Caesarius felt as though footwashing
should be especially encouraged, but at the same time, they demonstrate that the reason for such conduct is the action of Jesus as
recorded in Jn 13.1-20.

3. *The Practice of Footwashing in the Early Church*

In addition to the testimony which comes from the actual readers of
John 13, evidence for the practice of footwashing in the early church
is also relevant to this investigation. For although the precise relationship between these practices and that text is unknown, such activities
suggest that the practice is not unrelated to it.

Tucked away almost incidentally in the Pastorals is a reference to
footwashing (1 Tim. 5.9-10). Placed within the broader context of
discussions about widows in the church (1 Tim. 5.3-16), these verses
lay out certain prerequisites which a widow must meet in order to
qualify for support from the church.[2] In addition to the stipulations
about age and marital fidelity, the widow's life must testify of good
works, 'whether (εἰ) she has brought up children, (εἰ) shown hospitality, (εἰ) washed the saints' feet, (εἰ) helped those experiencing
trouble, (εἰ) devoted herself to every good work'. In an attempt to
ascertain the significance of footwashing in this text several things
must be noted.

To begin, each of these good works share in common the fact that
they are services rendered by widows to particular groups of people.
This observation suggests that, instead of being randomly chosen acts
which serve as examples of good works in general, each example may
have been chosen because it represents a particular kind of service
which, together with the others, offers various proofs of the widow's
faithfulness in a wide range of duties and relationships. Approached in
this light, the works take on new significance. The rearing of children
would represent the fulfillment of the widow's domestic duties. The

---

1. Cited according to the translation of M.M. Mueller, *Saint Caesarius of Arles:
Sermons* (New York: Fathers of the Church, 1956), II, p. 29.

2. For an overview of the questions about the unity of 1 Tim. 5.3-16, cf. D.C.
Verner, *The Household of God: The Social World of the Pastoral Epistles* (Chico,
CA: Scholars Press, 1983), pp. 161-66.

rendering of hospitality, earlier mentioned as a characteristic of the bishops (1 Tim. 3.2), would accord well with the general admonition to hospitality put forward by Paul (Rom. 12.13), Heb. (13.2), and the *Didache* (12.1-5). But it will also have had a special place in the community's life, because successful evangelization efforts by itinerant prophets and ministers were dependent upon such support (Mt. 10.11-15; Rom. 16.1, 2; Acts 16.15; 3 Jn 5–8; *Did.* 11.1-6). The comforting of those in need of help is mentioned in the teaching of Jesus (Mt. 25.34-46) and in the Pauline tradition (cf. 2 Cor. 1.3-4), as well as in the writings of other early Christian communities (cf. *Did.* 4.5-8). It is possible that such activity included visiting those in prison (Mt. 25.31-46; Heb. 13.3) as well as comfort generally. Perhaps such activity is to be seen as related to the spiritual gifts of encouragement (Rom. 12.8) or helps (1 Cor. 12.28). If rendering hospitality and helping those in need extended beyond the bounds of the church, then part of the reason for their inclusion here might stem from the desire for a good name in the community, a consideration which seems to have been important for the bishops as well (1 Tim. 3.7).

But what does εἰ ἁγίων πόδας ἔνιψεν mean in this context? It is possible that this phrase is to be taken as a specific example of hospitality which the widow was to have performed. While such an understanding of εἰ ἁγίων πόδας ἔνιψεν may be correct, three considerations suggest that this assessment does not go far enough. (1) Each of the other examples of good works appear to describe specific kinds of action which differ from one another. This implies that εἰ ἁγίων πόδας ἔνιψεν signifies a particular kind of good work, apart from hospitality. (2) The mention of footwashing in a list of duties is a rarity. For although footwashing was generally the domain of servants, the historical survey offered in Chapter 3 turned up no lists which mentioned footwashing.[1] In other words, this unique placement of footwashing in a list of qualifications for a specific position or office implies that there is something particular about the rite. (3) The footwashing is distinguished from the other good works in that this service is restricted to the household of faith, for it is the feet of the saints that are to be washed. If this footwashing is simply an illustra-

---

1. As E. Schüssler Fiorenza notes, 'Unusual is the requirement that "she must have washed the feet of the saints", a duty usually performed by slaves or servants' (*In Memory of Her* [New York: Crossroad, 1983], p. 311).

tive reference to hospitality, why is it restricted to the saints?[1]

In the Pauline circle there is no mistaking that ἁγίων refers to believers.[2] Such language implies that the footwashing performed by the widow was a distinctively Christian rite.[3] If this practice was a religious act of the community, it is likely that it was based upon knowledge of the tradition upon which John 13 is based. One of the most compelling reasons for this deduction is that, according to the historical survey of footwashing in antiquity offered in Chapter 3, there is little evidence that women who were not slaves washed the feet of guests. The exceptions (Abigail and Aseneth) are those who explicitly offer to function as servants. Since few would want to argue that the widows were the slaves of the community, what accounts for their action unless it has been prompted by Jesus' own example?[4] For there is no reason for the widows to perform this function for the community unless it has been redefined in the light of Jesus' action. Many scholars acknowledge the activity described in 1 Tim. 5.10 as dependent in some way upon Jn 13.1-20 or the tradition which lies behind it.[5] In

---

1. Cf. H.A. Kent, Jr, *The Pastoral Epistles* (Chicago: Moody Press, 1982), p. 167.

2. Cf. Rom. 1.2, 7; 8.27; 12.13; 15.25, 26, 31; 16.2, 15; 1 Cor. 1.2; 6.1, 2; 14.33; 16.1, 15; 2 Cor. 1.1; 8.4; 9.1, 12; 13.3; Eph. 1.1, 15, 18; 2.19; 3.8, 18; 4.12; 5.3; 6.18; Phil. 1.1; 4.21, 22; Col. 1.1, 4, 26; 3.12; 2 Thess. 1.10; Phlm. 5, 7).

3. Cf. especially the comments of G. Holtz, *Die Pastoralbriefe* (Berlin: Evangelische Verlagsanstalt, 1972), p. 118, who asks, 'But should a cultic act perhaps be thought of? After John 13.15 the footwashing is conceivably, with the Lord's Supper, an early custom. A connection is often made between the rite and baptism. . .' Holtz even goes so far as to suggest that women's participation at the footwashing was on the same level as their service at baptism and eucharist. He provides no documentation for this claim, however.

4. Cf. especially Kent, p. 167.

5. Cf. the following works: N.J.D. White, *The First and Second Epistles to Timothy and the Epistle to Titus* (Grand Rapids: Eerdmans, 1910), p. 131; C.P. Spicq, *Les Epîtres Pastorales* (Paris: Gabalda, 1947), p. 170; Lagrange, p. 153; Kötting, p. 761; D. Guthrie, *The Pastoral Epistles* (Grand Rapids: Eerdmans, 1957), pp. 102-103; J.N.D. Kelly, *A Commentary on the Pastoral Epistles* (New York: Harper & Row, 1963), p. 117; H. Ridderbos, *De Pastorale Brieven* (Kampen: J.H. Kok, 1967), p. 132; N. Brox, *Die Pastoralbriefe* (Regensburg: Friedrich Pustet, 1969), p. 193: Holtz, p. 118; P. Donier, *Les Epîtres Pastorales* (Paris: Gabalda, 1969), pp. 90-91; H. Bürki, *Der erste Brief des Paulus an Timotheus* (Wuppertal: R. Brockhaus, 1974), p. 172; U. Borse, *1. und 2.*

commenting upon the command to practice footwashing in Jn 13.12-20, Brown observes:

> That the practice was taken seriously is attested in 1 Tim. v. 10 where one of the qualifications for a woman to be enrolled as a widow is that she have shown hospitality and have 'washed the feet of the saints'.[1]

Barrett's comments on 1 Tim. 5.10 are even more explicit:

> The allusion here (to footwashing) makes it very probable that the author either had read John 13.14, or had heard some oral tradition to the same effect.[2]

If the practice mentioned in 1 Tim. 5.10 is ultimately based upon the story found in John 13,[3] then some of the earliest actual 'readers' of the footwashing pericope, outside the Johannine community, understood the 'text' to call for a literal fulfillment. Such an understanding confirms the implications of Jn 13.14-17 for the actual readers suggested above.[4]

Timotheusbrief. Titusbrief (Stuttgart: Katholisches Bibelwerk, 1986), p. 59; J. Roloff, *Der erste Brief an Timotheus* (Zürich: Benziger Verlag, 1988), p. 295. Richter, *Die Fusswaschung im Johannesevangelium*, p. 319 and Schnackenburg, III, p. 24 are less certain but suggest this relationship as possible. Cf. also the following two footnotes.

1. Brown, *The Gospel according to John*, II, p. 569. Cf. also B.B. Thurston, *The Widows: A Women's Ministry in the Early Church* (Philadelphia: Fortress Press, 1989), p. 49, who concludes, 'Behind the "good deeds" required of widows stand the words of Jesus: "If I then, your Lord and Teacher, have washed your feet, you also ought to wash one another's feet" (John 13.14). The "real widows" will be expected to follow the example of humble service set by Christ. They will be to the church what the woman with the ointment was to Jesus in Luke 7.36-50.' Cf. also O. Bangerter, 'Les veuves des épîtres pastorales, modèle d'un ministère féminin dans l'église ancienne', *Foi et Vie* 83 (1984), pp. 27-45, especially pp. 36-39.

2. C.K. Barrett, *The Pastoral Epistles* (Oxford: Clarendon Press, 1963), p. 76. Curiously, in the second edition of his commentary on John (p. 443), when Barrett refers to 1 Tim. 5.10, he treats the phrase εἰ ἀγίων πόδας ἔνιψεν as a metaphor. Schüssler Fiorenza (p. 324) notes, 'Whereas in the Pastorals the enrolled widows are required "to have washed the feet of the saints", in the Fourth Gospel this is Jesus' action of love to be followed by *all* his disciples'.

3. The role of the footwashing tradition, lying behind Jn 13.1-20 is discussed in section 5 below.

4. Cf. section 5.A.1 above. The close geographical promixity of these documents in terms of place of composition (traditionally identified as Asia Minor) confirms the idea that the community would know of the footwashing tradition. In

Another reference to footwashing may be contained in the *Martyr-dom of Polycarp* (written in 156). In ch. 13, just before Polycarp is tied to a stake to be burned, the following actions are noted:

> When the fire was ready, and he had divested himself of all his clothes and unfastened his belt, he tried to take off his shoes, though he was not heretofore in the habit of doing this because the faithful always vied with one another as to which of them would be first to touch (ἄψηται) his body (his skin = τοῦ χρωτὸς αὐτοῦ). For he had always been honored, even before his martyrdom, for his holy life (13.2).[1]

Several factors suggest that this passage may allude to the practice of footwashing. First, only the description of the removal of the shoes prompts the comment about the competition of the faithful to touch Polycarp's skin, not the description of the removal of his clothes nor the unfastening of the belt. Second, the author specifically states that Polycarp went to great lengths to avoid taking off his shoes because so many wanted to touch his skin. Third, there is philological evidence to suggest that in certain contexts, ἅπτω means 'to wash'. Homer (*Odyssey* 19.344, 348) twice describes footwashing as 'to touch my foot'. Odysseus responds to Penelope's offer of hospitality by saying:

> Aya, and baths for the feet give my heart no pleasure, nor shall any woman touch (ἅψεται) my foot of all those who are serving-women in thy hall, unless there is some old, true-hearted dame who has suffered in

addition, many scholars are convinced that 1 Timothy and the Fourth Gospel share a close temporal proximity as well, as most scholars date the Pastorals to the latter part of the first century CE. Cf. P.N. Harrison, *The Problem of the Pastoral Epistles* (London: Oxford University Press, 1921); G. Herdan, 'The Authorship of the Pastorals in the Light of Statistical Linguistics', *NTS* 6 (1959–60), pp. 1-15; M. Dibelius and H. Conzelmann, *The Pastoral Epistles* (Philadelphia: Fortress Press, 1972). However, several scholars argue for a date near the end of Paul's life. Cf. B.M. Metzger, 'A Reconsideration of Certain Arguments against the Pauline Authorship of the Pastoral Epistles', *ExpT* 70 (1958), pp. 91-101; D. Guthrie, *New Testament Introduction* (Downers Grove, IL: InterVarsity, 1970), pp. 584-622; E.E. Ellis, *Paul and his Recent Interpreters* (Grand Rapids: Eerdmans, 1961), pp. 49-57; J.N.D. Kelly, *A Commentary on the Pastoral Epistles* (Grand Rapids: Baker, 1981), pp. 30-36; G.D. Fee, *1 and 2 Timothy, Titus* (San Francisco: Harper & Row, 1984), pp. 80-81.

1. Cited according to the translation of C.C. Richardson, *Early Christian Fathers* (New York: Macmillan, 1970), p. 154.

her heart as many woes as I; such a one I would not grudge to touch (ἄψασθαι) my feet.[1]

Obviously, 'touching the feet' and 'washing the feet' are used interchangeably by Homer.

An example from the New Testament demonstrates that this verb carries the same connotation even without specific mention of the feet as the object. Lk. 7.36-50 describes Jesus' visit to the home of a Pharisee named Simon. While there, a sinful woman from the village approaches Jesus and begins to wash his feet with her tears, and to dry them with her hair. Simon thinks to himself, 'If this man were a prophet, he would know who is touching (ἄψασθαι) him and what kind of woman she is—that she is a sinner'. It is clear that the woman is washing Jesus' feet, yet Simon observes that she is touching Jesus. Apparently, 'touching' is an idiom for 'washing' in certain contexts.

In the light of such philological evidence it appears that the *Martyrdom of Polycarp* would indirectly reflect the continued practice of footwashing. If there is any connection between Polycarp and 'John' (as early church tradition indicates: cf. Irenaeus, *Against Heresies* 2.33.3; Eusebius, *Ecclesiastical History* 5.20.4) then perhaps this practice was carried out as a result of John 13.[2]

It may be that footwashing was a common part of the Agape meal for Tertullian's community. In connection with a discussion on the Agape meal (*The Apology* 39; written in 197), Tertullian mentions a 'manual ablution':

> Our feast explains itself by its name. The Greeks call it agape, i.e. affection. Whatever it costs, our outlay in the name of piety is gain, since with the good things of the feast we benefit the needy; not as it is with you, do parasites aspire to the glory of satisfying their licentious propensities, selling themselves for a belly-feast to all disgraceful treatment,—but as it is with God himself, a peculiar respect is shown to the lowly. If the object of our feast be good, in the light of that consider our further regulations. As it is an act of religious service, it permits no vileness or immodesty. The participants before reclining, taste first of prayer to God. As much is eaten as satisfies the craving of hunger; as much is drunk as befits the chaste. They say it is enough, as those who remember that even during

1.   Cited according to the translation of Murray, *Homer: The Odyssey*, I, p. 253.
2.   I am indebted to Jackie Johns for calling my attention to this passage in the *Martyrdom of Polycarp*.

the night they have to worship God; they talk as those who know that the Lord is one of their auditors. After manual ablution, and the bringing in of lights, each is asked to stand forth and sing, as he can, a hymn to God, either one from the holy Scriptures or one of his own composing—a proof of the measure of our drinking.[1]

It is just possible that 'manual ablution' refers to footwashing,[2] for manual may mean 'by hand', rather than 'of the hand', in this context. If so, then such an expression would coincide with similar language in Augustine and John Cassian, who both make explicit the obvious fact that footwashing was to be carried out by hand.

Additional evidence for the practice of footwashing occurs in a discussion of marriage, where Tertullian (*To His Wife* 2.4, written c. 200–206) notes the hardship placed upon a believing woman married to an unbelieving husband:

For who would suffer his wife, for the sake of visiting the brethren, to go round from street to street to other men's, and indeed all the poorer, cottages? Who will willingly bear her being taken from his side by nocturnal convocations, if need so be? Who, finally, will without anxiety endure her absence all the night long at the paschal solemnities? Who will, without some suspicion of his own, dismiss her to attend the Lord's Supper which they defame? Who will suffer her to creep into prison to kiss a martyr's bonds? Nay, truly, to meet any one of the brethren to exchange the kiss? to offer water for the saints' feet? to snatch (somewhat for them) from her food, from her cup? to yearn (after them)? to have (them) in her mind? If a pilgrim brother arrive, what hospitality for him in an alien home?[3]

In the light of the previous reference to footwashing, it is likely that either women (among others) performed the footwashing for the believers at the Agape meal, or that women performed a Christian act of hospitality for other believers. If the latter is true, then the list of those who would perform this function has been expanded from the widows in the Pastorals reference to include women generally—that

1. Cited according to the translation of Roberts and Donaldson, *Ante-Nicene Fathers*, III, p. 47.
2. For a similar conclusion cf. W. Farag, 'Religious Footwashing in Doctrine and Practice with Special Reference to Christianity' (Dissertation, the Dropsie University, 1970), p. 73.
3. Cited according to the translation of Roberts and Donaldson, *Ante-Nicene Fathers*, IV, p. 46.

is, unless at the time of the Pastorals everyone, or at least every woman, was already expected to wash the feet of the saints.

These texts from Tertullian confirm that footwashing was practiced in his circles. In all likelihood this practice was not unrelated to his reading of John 13.

Origen also advocates the practice of footwashing in Christian circles as a sign of hospitality (*Genesis Homily* 4.2). In a discussion of the reception which Abraham gives to the three men (angels), Origen notes:

> Abraham, the Father and teacher of nations, is, indeed, teaching you by these things how you ought to receive guests and that you should wash the feet of guests. Nevertheless, even this is said mysteriously. For he knew that the mysteries of the Lord were not to be completed except in the washing of feet. But he was not unaware of the importance of that precept, indeed in which the Saviour says: 'If any shall not receive you, shake off even the dust which clings to your feet for a testimony to them. Truly I say to you that it shall be more tolerable for the land of Sodom in the day of judgement than for that city'. He wished, therefore, to anticipate that and to wash their feet lest perhaps any dust should remain, which, shaken off, could be reserved 'In the day of judgment' for a testimony of unbelief. For that reason, therefore, wise Abraham says: 'Let water be received and your feet be washed'.[1]

Though the primary focus of the text is upon Abraham's example, it is clear that Origen expected similar action on the part of his hearers.[2]

Similarly, in remarks to bishops, elders, and deacons Cyprian the Bishop of Carthage calls for good works and humility in spirit:

> Let them imitate the Lord, who at the very time of His passion was not more proud, but more humble. For then He washed His disciples' feet, saying, 'If I, your Lord and Master, have washed your feet, ye ought also to wash one another's feet. For I have been given you an example, that ye should do as I have done to you'.[3]

Although it is highly probable that Cyprian is merely advocating

---

    1. Cited according to the translation of R.E. Heine, *Origen: Homilies on Genesis and Exodus* (Washington, DC: Catholic University Press, 1982), pp. 105-106.

    2. *Epistle* 5.3 (written c. 200–208). Cf. also the discussion of Origen's *In Librum Judicum homilia*, 8 in section B.1.b (4) below, present chapter.

    3. Cited according to the translation of Roberts and Donaldson, *Ante-Nicene Fathers*, V, p. 283.

humble service, the passage leaves the impression that Christian leaders should follow their Lord's example (and his commands in Jn 13.14-17) by washing the feet of their fellow believers.

The 48th Canon of the Synod of Elvira (c. 305) offers some evidence that certain clerics in Spain were washing the feet of the newly baptized:

> It has pleased (the Synod) to amend (the rule), that those who are being baptized should not put coins in the vessel, as used to be done, so that the priest should not seem to demand as a price that in fact he received as a present. Nor should their feet be washed by priests or clerics.[1]

Although the Synod disavows such a practice, the denunciation itself is additional evidence that early in the fourth century footwashing was being practiced.

Ambrose indicates that footwashing took place immediately after baptism in Milan. He makes this clear by noting (*Sacraments* 3.4):

> You came up from the fount. What followed? You heard the reading. The girded priest—for although the presbyters also do this the highest priest, girded, I say, washed your feet.[2]

It appears that in the Milanese church those who were baptized immediately received the footwashing.

Augustine (*Letter* 55.33; written c. 400) provides evidence that a number of the churches, with which he was familiar, practiced footwashing:

> As to the feetwashing. . . the question has arisen at what time it is best, by literal performance of this work, to give public instruction in the important duty which it illustrates, and this time [of Lent] was suggested in order that the lesson taught by it might make a deeper and more serious impression. Many, however, have not accepted this as a custom, lest it should be thought to belong to the ordinance of baptism; and some have not hesitated to deny it any place among our ceremonies. Some, however, in order to connect its observance with the more sacred association of this solemn season, and at the same time to prevent its being confounded with baptism in any way, have selected for this ceremony either the eighth day

---

1.   Cited according to the translation of A.S.S. Dale, *The Synod of Elvira and Christian Life in the Fourth Century* (London: Macmillan Co., 1882), p. 330.

2.   Cited according to the translation of R.J. Defferrai, *Saint Ambrose: Theological and Dogmatic Works*, p. 291.

itself, or that on which the third eighth day occurs, because of the great significance of the number three in many holy mysteries.[1]

Such negative testimony gives evidence that footwashing was commonplace during Augustine's lifetime. It should also be noted that Augustine assumes footwashing should continue to have a place in the church's worship.

Martin of Tours, a French monk of the late fourth century, personally washed the feet of his biographer, Sulpicius Severus (c. 360–c. 420), who was visiting him:

> And at this time it is scarcely credible with what humility and with what kindness he received me; while he cordially wished me joy, and rejoiced in the Lord that he had been held in such high estimation by me that I had undertaken a journey owing of my desire to see him. Unworthy me! (in fact, I hardly dare acknowledge it), that he should have deigned to admit me to fellowship with him! He went so far as in person to present me with water to wash my hands, and at eventide he himself washed my feet; nor had I sufficient courage to resist or oppose him doing so. In fact, I felt so overcome by the authority he unconsciously exerted, that I deemed it unlawful to do anything but acquiesce in his arrangements.[2]

Although John 13 is not mentioned in the text, it seems likely that Martin's washing the feet of a confessed 'inferior' was based upon the example of Jesus. Otherwise, it is difficult to understand the motivation for such an action.

Sozomen (*Ecclesiastical History* 1.11.10, written c. 439–50) records that footwashing was observed in the home of Bishop Spyridon of Trimythus. His custom of receiving strangers and caring for them is documented on one occasion as follows:

> The reception Spyridon gave to strangers will appear from the following incident. In the quadragesima, it happened that a traveler [was] upon a journey to visit him. . . Perceiving that the stranger was much fatigued, Spyridon said to his daughter, 'Come, wash his feet and set meat before him'.[3]

---

1. Cited according to the translation of Schaff, *Nicene and Post-Nicene Fathers*, I, p. 314.

2. Cited according to the translation of P. Schaff and H. Wace, *Nicene and Post-Nicene Fathers* (Grand Rapids: Eerdmans, 1957), XI, p. 16.

3. Cited according to the translation of P. Schaff and H. Wace, *Nicene and Post-Nicene Fathers* (Grand Rapids: Eerdmans, 1957), II, p. 247.

This text is important in that it describes the reception of guests by footwashing as common in the home of Spyridon. Unfortunately, it is difficult to determine whether the practice was inspired by John 13 or was simply an act of hospitality. But as Kötting has noted, 'it is not possible to separate footwashing as a welcome for guests from that of the emulation of the brotherly mindedness of Christ'.[1] This account is the first to identify a daughter as the one who renders this service.

In an exposition of Abraham's generous gesture of hospitality in Genesis 18, which included footwashing, John Chrysostom (*Genesis Homily* 46), urges his audience to similar actions:

> Let us learn, and let us seek the virtue of the righteous one (Abraham). For if we act in this manner, it is reasonable for us also to obtain such booty; we always attain even much more, if we desire. For on account of this, the benevolent Master says, in order that we might not hesitate toward such hospitality nor that we overdo those things which ought to be neglected. Whoever receives one of these least ones in my name, receives me. . .Listen husbands, listen wives: Therefore husbands, in order that in this manner those who live with you might be completely educated, whenever some spiritual gain might be present, do not complete this through the house-slaves, but accomplish this all yourselves. And wives, in order that you might eagerly desire to share with (your) husbands (in) such successful accomplishments, and not be ashamed of the hospitality and the service unto them, but imitate Sarah the elderly lady, the one who accepts in such a time of life to toil, and to accomplish the works of the servant girls. . .Let us all imitate this (man), and let us make every effort concerning hospitality, not in order that we might receive only the exchange of the perishable and corruptible things, but in order that we might even lay aside the enjoyment of the immortal goods themselves.[2]

Chrysostom does not mention footwashing explicitly here, but the implication is that Christians ought to practice hospitality, which includes performance of lowly deeds that slaves ordinarily are required to offer. In view of the text upon which these comments are based, footwashing may well be implied.

No one in the early church made as many references in sermons to washing the feet of foreigners and travellers as Caesarius of Arles (c. 470–542). Ordinarily, the admonition to wash feet is part of a stock

---

1.   Kötting, p. 768.
2.   Migne, *Patrologia Graeca*, LIII, pp. 379, 381, 384.

list of suggested actions. One such example (*Sermon* 60.4) should suffice for the present study:

> Moreover, according to our strength we ought to engage frequently in fasting, vigils, and prayers with perfect charity, visit the sick and seek those washing their feet but also generally supplying their necessities as far as we can.[1]

On another occasion, in admonitions to godparents, Caesarius (*Sermon* 104.3) notes that footwashing accompanied baptism:

> As often as the Paschal feast comes, if any men or women spiritually receive sons from the sacred fount, they should realize that they are bondsmen for them in the sight of God, and therefore should bestow on them the solicitude of true love. . . [As to the duties of the baptized] Let them receive strangers and, in accord with what was done for themselves in baptism, wash the feet of their guests.[2]

According to Caesarius, reflection upon one's baptism should prompt a willingness to continue to practice footwashing. When this passage is taken together with the previous texts from Caesarius, it becomes evident not only that footwashing was practiced by his hearers, but that such action was based upon the text of John 13.

In the monastic rule produced by Benedict of Nursia (*Regula Monachorum* 35; written c. 540), footwashing appears to have been a regularly assigned activity in the community:

> XXXV—Of the Weekly Servers in the Kitchen: Let the brethren so serve each other in turn that no one be excused from the work of the kitchen unless on the score of health. . .Let him who is ending his week's service clean up everything on Saturday. He must wash the towels with which the brethren wipe their hands and feet: and both he who is finishing his service, and he who is entering on it, are to wash the feet of all. . .On Sunday, as soon as Lauds are ended, both the incoming and outgoing servers for the week shall cast themselves on their knees in the presence of all and ask their prayers.[3]

1.   Cited according to the translation of M.M. Mueller, *Saint Caesarius of Arles: Sermons* (New York: Fathers of the Church, 1956), I, p. 299. For nearly identical comments, cf. Sermons 1.12; 10.3; 14.2; 16.2; 19.2; 25.2; 67.3; 146.2.

2.   Cited according to the translation of Mueller, *Saint Caesarius of Arles: Sermons*, III, pp. 73-74.

3.   Cited according to the edition of P. Delatte, *The Rule of St Benedict* (trans. J. McCann; London: Burns, Oates, and Washbourne, 1921), pp. 254-57.

Not only was footwashing a part of the community's internal life, but visitors were also to be received in this fashion (*Regula Monachorum* 53):

> LIII—Of the Reception of Guests: Let all guests that come be received like Christ Himself. . . Let the Abbot pour water on the hands of the guests; let both the Abbot and the whole community wash the feet of all guests. When they have been washed let them say this verse: '*Suscepimus, Deus, misericordiam tuam, in medio templi tui*'.[1]

It is likely that the example of Jesus was the basis for the practice, which involved this entire community.

4. *Conclusions*

Although most scholars have not explored the possibility that the Johannine community practiced footwashing in accordance with the commands of Jn 13.14-17, there is nonetheless a significant amount of evidence to make this suggestion plausible. The only viable way to gauge the plausibility of whether the Johannine community engaged in the practice of footwashing as a religious act has been to examine the text of the Fourth Gospel and to survey a number of its actual readers. It does little good to catalogue those ancient authors (and texts) who make no mention of footwashing as a rite[2]—as though the possibility of discovering the practice of the Johannine community were contingent upon confirmation from such texts. Such a procedure assumes too much. For on the one hand, the absence of a particular practice or belief in early Christian texts is no absolute proof that such a practice or belief played no part in that particular community's life. After all, despite the fact that most scholars are convinced that the observance of the eucharist was widespread in early Christianity, there is only one certain mention of it outside the gospels in the New Testament (1 Cor. 11.17-34). Its omission from the other New Testament epistles and Acts (2.42?) demonstrates that the occasional nature of the documents, rather than the practice of the community, determines the content of the composition. On the other hand, it is possible that the Johannine community was distinctive in some of its practices, as well as its life and thought. Therefore, the Fourth Gospel, its readers, and those who

---

1.   Delatte, pp. 330-37.
2.   Farag (pp. 53-65) gives a helpful survey of this material, but he then goes on to trace the practice in some circles.

seem to have some knowledge of the tradition upon which John 13 is based must be the starting point. Such a procedure should not be taken to imply that there is no place for a comparison of the Johannine community's practice with that of other early Christian communities: what it does imply is that the Johannine community's practice must be explored first and allowed to speak on its own terms.

When the Fourth Gospel is taken as the starting point, there is every reason to believe that footwashing was practiced as a religious rite in the Johannine community. Not only does the literary and exegetical analysis reveal that the implied readers would have understood Jn 13.14-17 as calling for a literal compliance, but the cultural environment of western antiquity demonstrates that readers of the Fourth Gospel would have been predisposed to practice footwashing as a result of reading Jn 13.1-20. The evidence from early Christianity demonstrates that a number of people read the text in just such a fashion. Not only is the geographical distribution of the evidence impressive—in that it comes from North Africa (Tertullian), Egypt–Palestine (Origen), Asia Minor (1 Timothy, *Martyrdom of Polycarp*, John Chrysostom), Italy (Ambrose, Augustine), and Gaul (Caesarius)—but the diverse contexts in which the commands were obeyed are also noteworthy, in that they range from the church, to the monastery, to the home. Enough examples have been given to show both that the implications drawn from the reading of Jn 13.1-20 were somewhat consistent, and that the practice of footwashing was widespread.

The evidence for a footwashing practice based on John 13 is of sufficient strength to conclude that—in all likelihood—the Johannine community engaged in religious footwashing as the direct result of reading Jn 13.1-20, or conceivably, as a result of contact with the tradition that lies behind it. Indeed, it could be argued that instead of scholars needing to demonstrate the probability of the practice in the Johannine community, the burden of proof is on those who would deny such a probability.

5. *Footwashing in the Johannine Community*

This study is concerned with what can be known about the Johannine community's practice of footwashing at the time of the final edition of the Fourth Gospel. Such an approach is merited by the fact that the final form of the Gospel stands as the single extant form. Despite the various theories which seek to explain the Fourth Gospel's composition, it is clear that the final form of the text circulated in the early church with little significant variation. Consequently, the logical place to begin is at the point where knowledge of the text is most certain.

As noted earlier, the relevant data show that in all probability the Johannine community did engage in the practice of footwashing as a religious rite. Yet, before moving to an investigation of footwashing's meaning and significance, perhaps a few comments should be devoted to the question of the community's practice prior to the gospel's final form, although such an inquiry lies outside the specific focus of this study.

When entrance is sought into the history of the Johannine community prior to the final version of the gospel, one steps into very shadowy and uncertain terrain—as the differing attempts at reconstruction testify. Therefore, extreme caution must be used in order to avoid becoming lost in the maze of hypothetical speculation. Nevertheless, perhaps a few plausible observations may be given.

If the community observed footwashing owing to the impact of Jesus' action and commands (Jn 13.1-20), then it is likely that the community began the observance at the time when the tradition became part of the community's Jesus-traditions. But is such a moment identifiable? A precise answer cannot be given, but perhaps the history of tradition enterprise can be of assistance here. For example, no matter what *else* is said about earlier sources, in those scholarly reconstructions which identify successive stages in the history of the Fourth Gospel's composition, a footwashing narrative is always included in the first edition. If such assessments are correct, then some part of the footwashing tradition is at least a little earlier than the first edition of the gospel. Since—as this study has shown—the footwashing pericope is not a combination of two differing traditions but a coherent unit as it stands, the likelihood increases that the bulk of the tradition behind the pericope should be considered this early. If this tradition is as early as most, then in all probability it came to the community at about the same time as other Jesus traditions.

This assessment leads to a related question; When did the Johannine community begin? An accurate response is most difficult to make here, because so much uncertainty surrounds the formation of the community. Since most scholars date the beginning period of the Johannine community between 55 to 70 CE, and since most scholars feel that many of the Johannine Jesus-traditions came to the community

early, if not at the beginning, then it is not unjustified to point to such
a period as the time when the practice of religious footwashing began
in the community.

Simply put, it appears that both the tradition behind John 13 and the
practice of footwashing may well be as old or older than the community itself.[1]

B. *The Meaning of Footwashing for the Johannine Community*

If there is good reason to believe that the Johannine community practiced footwashing as a religious rite, then what was its meaning and
significance? As with the first major question in this chapter, the
starting point is the delicate transition from the implied readers to the
actual readers. One way to make this move is to identify the assumptions of the first readers regarding the significance of footwashing.
The historical survey in Chapter 3 revealed that footwashing had several distinct functions or meanings in antiquity. In addition to preparation generally, footwashing could serve as a sign of hospitality, of
hygiene, of ritual purity and of subordination or servitude, as well as
being an expression of deep love. It is quite probable that the first
readers would have been acquainted with most of these dimensions of
footwashing.

However, the meaning of footwashing for the Johannine community
is tied up with the meaning of Jn 13.1-20. A particularly relevant
question is this: how much would the commands in vv. 14-17 have
been read in the light of the significance attached to footwashing by
Jesus in vv. 6-10? Two points suggest that vv. 14-17 would be read
very much in the light of 13.1-10. First, the literary and exegetical
analysis has shown that, against much of Johannine scholarship, Jn
13.1-20 can and should be read as a literary unit. Such a hermeneuti-
cal shift necessitates that vv. 14-17 be read in the context of the first
ten verses of the passage. When vv. 12-20 are no longer read in isolation, the relevance of vv. 1-10 becomes apparent. Second, it is in-
conceivable that a community, engaged in a rite instituted by Jesus,

---

1.   As for the ultimate origin of the footwashing tradition, it should not go
unnoticed that this act, whereby a superior washes the feet of an inferior, has no
known parallel in antiquity. Any theory about the tradition's origin must account
adequately for this extraordinary aspect.

would practice it without taking fully into account the explanation which Jesus offered regarding its significance. Therefore, the significance of footwashing for the Johannine community is tied to the meaning of 13.1-10 (especially vv. 6-10).

Several aspects from 13.1-10 are most important for determining the meaning of footwashing for the community. (1) The context of the footwashing is a description of Jesus' supreme love for his own (v. 1). (2) Jesus' actions are described in such a way as to emphasize his identification with servitude and humiliation (vv. 4, 5). (3) In v. 7 Jesus informs Peter that the significance of this event will only become clear μετὰ ταῦτα, i.e. after the death/exaltation. (4) Peter is told, in no uncertain terms, that his continued μέρος (fellowship and participation) with Jesus is dependent upon receiving the washing (v. 8). (5) The footwashing is said to supplement (or extend) the effects of a previous bath (v. 10). (6) Both the bath and the footwashing signify cleansing and/or purification (v. 10).

These statements would force the actual readers to reassess their assumptions about the significance of footwashing. Both by ruling out certain possible meanings (hospitality and hygiene) and by enlarging their sphere of possible meanings (as a sign of continual fellowship and through the transformation of the act in the anomaly of a superior washing the feet of a subordinate), the readers' understanding of footwashing would be brought into clearer focus.

The literary and exegetical analysis has shown that as a sign of preparation for Jesus' departure, the footwashing signifies the disciples' spiritual cleansing for a continued relationship with Jesus. As such, the footwashing functions as an extension of the disciples' baptism in that it signifies continual cleansing from the sin acquired (after baptism) through life in a sinful world. This act then is a sign of continued fellowship with Jesus, but it also functions as a sign of their continued readiness for participation in his mission.

A few scholars have reflected about the possible meaning of the practice of footwashing in the Johannine community. Their assessments are particularly relevant for this inquiry.

On the basis of 1 Tim. 5.10, B.W. Bacon suggests that footwashing must have been observed in Ephesus. He explains the practice as based on the custom of a bride washing her feet before her wedding. In giving a new sense to the annual Christian passover, the Fourth Evangelist emphasizes the purification of the church:

instead of the washing of hands belonging to the Jewish Kiddush he substitutes a rite of the Ephesian Church, a washing of the feet of the Bride. In 13.10 it is interpreted to symbolize removal of post-baptismal sin, that all the Church's members may be sanctified, cleansed by the washing of water with the word. Thus the Bridegroom, in due time, will 'present her to himself a glorious bride, holy and without blemish'.[1]

According to Bacon, John omits the account of the Last Supper because of his quartodeciman dating of the Passover. His substitution of the footwashing for the Last Supper is because of his desire to institute a ceremony that would re-establish the importance and sanctity of the eucharist, which had become a 'mere grace before meat'. The footwashing would then prepare the believer to eat the eucharistic meal.

Although Bacon is correct in seeing a connection between footwashing and the forgiveness of post-baptismal sin, his interpretation is not without its problems. The evidence he gives for the bridal footwashing is somewhat vague, Servian's comments on *Aeneid* 4.167 being cited along with certain 'rabbinic sources'. Bacon also gives little attention to the text of Jn 13.1-20 itself, choosing instead to emphasize the historical context in Ephesus. In addition, his inference that the footwashing was created from Lk. 22.24-27 begs a host of questions.

In the most comprehensive study devoted to this topic, Herold Weiss takes very seriously the function of footwashing in the Johannine community. Weiss observes, 'There can be no doubt, however, that the Johannine community must have performed this ceremony with some regularity and with a definite purpose in mind'.[2] According to Weiss, while other scholars have been side-tracked with a variety of interpretive issues, John A.T. Robinson has pointed in the right direction by interpreting Jesus' washing of the disciples' feet as a challenge to the disciples concerning their willingness to be baptized with his baptism (cf. Mk. 10.33-45). However, Robinson did not go far enough in his interpretation, for he sought to explain the footwashing's significance in the light of Jesus' Sitz im Leben, rather than that of the Johannine community.

Weiss seeks to explain the footwashing on the basis of a little known practice in the Hellenistic synagogue, which he proposes on the basis of five passages in Philo and one in the papyri, *P. Oxy.* 840. Weiss

---

1. Bacon, p. 221.
2. Weiss, p. 298.

acknowledges that footwashing is only 'tangentially referred to' in the Philonic passages, but after a discussion of *Quaestiones et Solutiones in Genesin* (4.60), he nonetheless concludes, 'It becomes quite obvious from this passage that in the Hellenistic synagogue there was speculation about footwashing as providing sanctification by the divine spirit and opening up the soul to the divine manifestation'.[1]

Following the lead of Wayne Meeks[2] and J.L. Martyn,[3] Weiss argues for a Johannine Sitz im Leben of persecution and martyrdom. He then reads John 13 in the light of this Sitz im Leben. Weiss concludes that Mary's anointing of Jesus not only prepares Jesus for his burial but also prepares him to meet God.

> Correspondingly the act of Jesus produces the sanctification of the disciples. He identifies himself with them, but he also prepares them to enter into the presence of God.[4]

Identifying 13.4, 5 and 12-15 as most probably the earliest footwashing material, Weiss draws attention to those verses which have synoptic parallels. The parallels, he notes, are found in persecution contexts, and in his eyes, this confirms his proposed Sitz im Leben for the community. Weiss goes on to interpret 13.10 by means of 15.3, arguing that being clean means to bear fruit—that is, to follow Jesus in death. Weiss concludes:

> Footwashing was certainly part of the praxis of the Johannine community. The practice may have had a place also within the mainstream of Christianity, but apparently its significance in the church at large was different from the one acquired within the Johannine group. It may very well have been the case that the significance given to the practice in other circles was the same which it had when it first came to the Johannine community. But just as the practice acquired new meaning within the Johannine community, it acquired new meaning also in other circles. . . within the Johannine community the footwashing ceremony . . . acquired a peculiar symbolic meaning in reference to the experience of martyrdom by members of

---

1. Weiss, p. 304.
2. W.A. Meeks, 'The Man from Heaven in Johannine Sectarianism', *JBL* 91 (1972), pp. 44-72.
3. J.L. Martyn, *History and Theology in the Fourth Gospel* (New York: Harper & Row, 1968).
4. Weiss, p. 314.

the community. Thus the cleansing produced by the act had eschatological
rather than ceremonial or sacramental meaning.[1]

Clearly, Weiss's article is to be commended as an example of the
many avenues of exploration which open up when the practice of
footwashing is taken seriously. Although much could be said about
many facets of Weiss's argument, the following comments identify
some of the major weaknesses of the proposal. (1) It is questionable
whether the Philonic materials can bear the weight they must for
Weiss's interpretation to be plausible. Chapter 3 of this study shows
that an interpretation of John 13 must take account of a broader range
of background materials than simply the Philonic passages. (2) Weiss
seems to overemphasize the theme of persecution and martyrdom.
While some evidence from the Fourth Gospel suggests that martyrdom and persecution figure in the Johannine Sitz im Leben in some
fashion, it is unwise to interpret the whole the of Fourth Gospel in the
light of those factors. (3) Instead of permitting Jn 13.10 to speak on
its own terms, Weiss makes the mistake of insisting that 13.10 be interpreted in the light of 15.3.[2] (4) Weiss may be too dependent on
source analysis. Rather than reading Jn 13.1-20 as a unit and then
moving to historical reconstruction, Weiss quickly dismisses part of
the passage (vv. 6-10) as irrelevant for determining the meaning of
footwashing for the community. As Chapter 4 has demonstrated, the
literary unity of the passage should not be summarily rejected—in
fact, recognizing this unity is key to a proper interpretation. (5) There
seems to be no evidence of this interpretation in the exegesis of the
early church. One would have expected some reflection of this interpretation to have survived, if it existed in the Johannine community.

The two most recent interpretations of the meaning of the practice
of footwashing come in the form of popular commentaries on the
Fourth Gospel. In a note on Jn 13.15, J. Ramsey Michaels proposes
that footwashing may have been part of the community's practice. In
commenting upon its possible meaning, he notes:

> Such a practice would be a way for the Christian community to dramatize
> the responsibility of its members to be servants to one another and so

1. Weiss, pp. 323-25.
2. For a discussion of the relationship between 13.10 and 15.3, cf. Chapter 2,
section C.2.c (on 13.10), above.

bring to full realization in the world the forgiveness and love of Jesus.[1]

Michaels goes on to suggest that perhaps footwashing was a preparation for the eucharist proper inasmuch as the imagery of cleansing is present in the footwashing pericope.[2]

It is indeed difficult to fault Michaels for failing to devote more attention to the meaning of the practice in view of the space limitations of the Harper Good News Commentary format—in spite of which he gives evidence of more reflection about this issue than any of the major commentaries. Suffice it to say that most of Michaels's comments indicate that he is on the right track, although he has not pressed far enough the relationship between footwashing and forgiveness of sin.

L. William Countryman also thinks that perhaps footwashing was a part of the practice of the Johannine community. As noted above, Countryman is not absolutely certain that the community engaged in the practice; nonetheless, he speculates earlier in his commentary about the practice's meaning. Countryman suggests:

> If footwashing was a regular rite in the Johannine communities, it could easily have been understood as a harking back to baptism and might even have played a role in the forgiveness of postbaptismal sin. Since the disciples have been baptized, they do not need another complete bath.[3]

Clearly, Countryman's interpretation is in line with the meaning of the practice offered in this study. As the earlier part of this chapter demonstrates however, Countryman's hesitancy about the practice of footwashing in the community is unwarranted.

It is significant that, of the few scholars who reflect upon the meaning of the practice of footwashing, each concludes that footwashing signifies purification of one kind or another. It is further significant that two of these interpreters explicitly identify footwashing as a sign of the forgiveness of post-baptismal sin.

But is there evidence either that the actual readers were concerned with post-conversion sin or that they would have interpreted Jn 13.1-20 in such a fashion? Although the evidence at this point is somewhat fragmentary, enough data exists to permit an attempted reconstruction.

---

1. Michaels, *John*, p. 232.
2. *Ibid.* Cf. also his discussion on p. 227.
3. Countryman, p. 88.

1. *Footwashing and Forgiveness of Sin*
a. *Post-conversion Sin and the Johannine Community*

One way to gauge whether the actual readers would have interpreted footwashing in this context is to determine the degree to which post-conversion sin was an issue for them.

In the Fourth Gospel there is little explicit information available on this topic, but perhaps Jn 20.23 may be of some help. After Jesus commands the disciples to receive the Holy Spirit he says, "If you forgive the sins of any they are forgiven them, if you retain the sins of any they are retained'. For the implied readers, this commission would be understood in the light of the earlier thoughts that just as Jesus brought judgment into the world (3.17-21) and revealed those blinded by sin (9.39-41), so the Paraclete, through the agency of the disciples, will convict the world of sin and unbelief (16.8). As Jesus' followers, the disciples now will continue his work. Therefore, on the narrative level, 20.23 is primarily concerned with the mission of the disciples.

However, when the move is made from implied readers to actual readers, a slight change in meaning may take place, for the actual readers are part of a community which would be familiar with both mission to the world and discipline within the community. Jn. 20.23 would then be read to include not only conversion, but forgiveness of those within the community.[1]

Fortunately, much more information about attitudes toward post-conversion sin is preserved in another community document, 1 John.[2] Three passages in particular have a bearing upon this discussion: 1 Jn 1.7-10; 2.1-2; 5.16-18. Each of these passages deals not only with the concept of sin, but specifically with sin committed by believers.[3]

---

1. For this association cf. the remarks of C.H. Dodd, *Historical Tradition in the Fourth Gospel* (Cambridge: Cambridge University Press, 1965), p. 348 n. 2; Brown, *The Gospel according to John*, II, p. 1044; Lindars, p. 613; Schnackenburg, III, p. 326; and Beasley-Murray, *John*, p. 384, Cf. also R.E. Brown, *The Epistles of John* (Garden City, NY: Doubleday, 1982), pp. 203-204.

2. Whether the Fourth Gospel and 1 John have a common author or not, it is very clear that they come from the same community. For not only are these documents more similar in style than any other two New Testament documents, including Luke and Acts (cf. Brown, *The Epistles of John*, p. 21), but their theological affinities are many.

3. Cf. the exceptional case made for this interpretation by Brown, *The Epistles*

Evidently, certain members of the community (whether opponents or those whom the opponents were hoping to influence) were claiming that on the basis of their relationship to Christ they were free from sin permanently. The author of 1 John asserts that those who make such claims deceive themselves, do not possess the truth, and make God a liar (1 Jn 1.8-10). Lest such a strong statement be misconstrued, the writer quickly makes known his intention that his readers avoid sin at all costs (1 Jn 2.1a). However, even though he desires moral perfection for his community, the author acknowledges the possibility of post-conversion sin and the necessity of remedying it through the same means by which their conversion was accomplished, appropriating the effects of the atoning death of Jesus Christ (1 Jn 2.1b). Brown, who envisages a communal context for this forgiveness of post-conversion sin, goes so far as to see an allusion here to John 13:

> Possibly the author found GJohn support for this in the washing of the feet by Jesus at the Last Supper, an action symbolic of the cleansing power of Jesus' death (13.8, 10; . . .) which has been interpreted on a secondary level as referring to the effects of baptism. There Jesus instructs his disciples that, if he has washed their feet, they must wash *one another's* feet (13.14). Thus communion with one another is a context for cleansing by Christ.[1]

1 Jn 5.16-18 makes even clearer that post-conversion sin was a concern among members of the Johannine community. For not only does the author anticipate sinful behavior on the part of believers, but he also instructs his readers to take an active role (through intercessory prayer) in the reconciliation of a sinning member.[2] These verses also indicate the possibility that a member of the community could forfeit his or her place by the 'sin unto death' (cf. the phrase ἁμαρτία μὴ πρὸς θάνατον). Although some scholars insist that the 'sin unto

---

of John, pp. 202-45, 610-22, 633-38. Cf. also R.E. Brown, *The Community of the Beloved Disciple* (New York: Paulist Press, 1979), pp. 124-27, and the similar, but independent, assessment of S.S. Smalley, *1, 2, 3 John* (Waco: Word, 1984), pp. 27-41, 297-304.

1.   Brown, *The Epistles of John*, p. 239. In a footnote (38), Brown points out that on the basis of the longer reading in Jn 13.10 a few scholars think that footwashing itself was practiced for post-baptismal sin.

2.   For the idea of intercession for sinners in the Old Testament cf. R. Schnackenburg, *Die Johannesbriefe* (Freiburg: Herder, 1975), pp. 275-76 and I.H. Marshall, *The Epistle of John* (Grand Rapids: Eerdmans, 1978), p. 246 n. 16.

death' is not a threat for the believers,[1] it is quite likely that the author makes this statement because such a possibility was all too real. As Rodney A. Whitacre has rightly observed:

> to demonstrate that the stress [in 1 John 5.16] is on ἁμαρτία μὴ πρὸς θάνατον is not to prove that the mention of ἁμαρτία πρὸς θάνατον is simply an aside with no function of its own other than as a contrast. Rather, it should be interpreted as an implied warning, which is made explicit a few verses later: 'Little children, keep yourselves from idols' (5.21). The author sees his readers as in danger of committing ἁμαρτία πρὸς θάνατον in that they are in danger of being deceived by lying spirits (4.1-6; 2.26), and there are some among them who do not love the brothers (3.17-18).[2]

The mention of the 'sin unto death' seems prompted by the writer's desire to motivate his readers to intercede in prayer on behalf of a sinning believer.[3]

Several concluding observations may be offered about the relationship between footwashing and post-conversion sin in the Johannine community. (1) 1 John exhibits a concern about post-conversion sin and is not hesitant about affirming its presence in the community. (2) There is the conviction that such sin is a serious matter which ultimately can affect one's standing in the community. The use of μέρος in Jn 13.8 expresses a very similar understanding of how sin can affect the believer's status. (3) The way in which the believer is to deal with post-conversion sin is to appropriate the provisions for forgiveness of sin based on the atoning death of Jesus. In like fashion, the significance of the footwashing receives its efficacy from Jesus' death. (4) Individual members of the community are encouraged to take an active role in the reconciliation of potentially estranged members. Just as those who wash the feet of others participate in conveying Christ's

---

1. Cf. especially D.M. Scholer, 'Sins Within and Sins Without: An Interpretation of 1 John 5.16-17', in *Current Issues in Biblical and Patristic Interpretation* (ed. G. Hawthorne; Grand Rapids: Eerdmans, 1975), pp. 230-46; Brown, *The Epistles of John*, pp. 613-19, 635-37; and J.R.W. Stott, *The Letters of John* (Grand Rapids: Eerdmans, 1988), pp. 188-93.

2. R.A. Whitacre, *Johannine Polemic: The Role of Tradition and Theology* (Chico, CA: Scholars Press, 1982), p. 140. Cf. also the comments of Smalley, *1, 2, 3 John* pp. 297-301, and Marshall, pp. 145-51.

3. For a good discussion of the relationship of post-conversion sin in 1 John and the footwashing of John 13, cf. Grelot, pp. 86-91.

forgiveness to fellow believers, so in 1 John the believer is also an active participant in reconciliation. Love is the motive in both contexts.

Although the practice of footwashing is not mentioned in 1 John, the identification of post-conversion sin and its consequences is clearly quite compatible with the conclusions reached in the literary and exegetical analysis of John 13.

b. *Footwashing and Forgiveness of Sin in Early Christianity*

Again, the writings of the early church may profitably be consulted in order to gain additional insight into the way the Johannine community would have understood the rite of footwashing. Unfortunately, the evidence is not as helpful as one would wish. On the one hand, not everyone who advocates the practice goes on to identify its significance, while on the other hand, not all who comment on the meaning of Jn 13.1-20 make clear whether or not they have engaged in footwashing as a religious rite. Therefore, in order to make best use of this evidence, these texts are presented in four categories, beginning with the data that is most directly relevant.

(1) *The Practice of Footwashing and the Forgiveness of Post-Conversion Sin*. There are a few writers in the early church who not only advocate the practice of footwashing, but go on to interpret its significance in terms of the forgiveness of post-conversion sin.

Ambrose (*Of the Holy Spirit* 1.15) explains that by washing another's feet, one receives cleansing from pollution:

> I, then, wish also myself to wash the feet of my brethren, I wish to fulfill the commandment of my Lord, I will not be ashamed in myself, nor disdain what He Himself did first. Good is the mystery of humility, because while washing pollution of others I wash away my own.[1]

This statement by Ambrose seems to imply that while the act of footwashing purifies the one who receives the footwashing, the one who performs the washing also receives forgiveness. This is a topic on which he has much more to say (cf. the discussion in the next section below). Since for Ambrose only a Christian would be performing this footwashing, such cleansing must be from post-baptismal sin.

Augustine (354–430) affirms that Jesus was referring to the washing

---

1. Cited according to the translation of Schaff and Wace, *Nicene and Post-Nicene Fathers*, X, p. 95.

away of sin when he said that the disciples had no need to wash except the feet. Augustine (*Homilies on John* 56.4) explains Jn 13.10 by appealing to the sin accumulated on the journey of this life:

> But what is this? What does it mean? And what is there in it we need to examine? The Lord says, The Truth declares that even he who has been washed has need still to wash his feet. What, my brethren, what think you of it? Save that in holy baptism a man has all of him washed, not all save his feet, but every whit: and yet, while thereafter living in this human state, he cannot fail to tread on the ground with his feet. And thus our human feelings themselves, which are inseparable from our mortal life on earth, are like feet wherewith we are brought into sensible contact with human affairs; and are so in such a way that if we say we have no sin, we deceive ourselves, and the truth is not in us.[1]

Augustine (*Homilies on John* 56.5; 58.5) goes on to speak of footwashing as a symbol of Christ's continual intercession on behalf of believers:

> And every day, therefore, is He who intercedeth for us washing our feet: and that we, too have daily need to be washing our feet, that is, ordering aright the path of our spiritual footsteps, we acknowledge even in the Lord's prayer, when we say, 'Forgive us our debts, as we also forgive our debtors'. For 'if', as it is written, 'we confess our sins', then verily is He, who washed His disciples' feet 'faithful and just to forgive us our sins, and to cleanse us from all unrighteousness', that is, even to our feet wherewith we walk on the earth. Accordingly the Church, which Christ cleanseth with the washing of water in the word, is without spot and wrinkle, not only in the case of those who are taken away immediately after the washing of regeneration from the contagious influence of this life, and tread not the earth so as to make necessary the washing of their feet, but in those also who have experienced such mercy from the Lord as to be enabled to quit this present life even with feet that have been washed. But although the Church be also clean in respect of those who tarry on earth, because they live righteously; yet have they need to be washing their feet, because they assuredly are not without sin. . . We remember that the way in which we commended to your attention the grandeur of this act of the Lord's, was that, in washing the feet of disciples who were already washed and clean, the Lord instituted a sign, to the end that, on account of the human feelings that occupy us on earth, however far we may have advanced in our apprehension of righteousness, we

---

1. Cited according to the translation of Schaff, *Nicene and Post-Nicene Fathers*, VII, p. 302.

might know that we are not exempt from sin; which He thereafter washes away by interceding for us, when we pray the Father, who is in heaven, to forgive us our debts, as we also forgive our debtors.[1]

Not only does Augustine affirm the connection between the footwashing and forgiveness of sin to symbolize Christ's forgiveness but he also considers the footwashing as a sign to that effect. He goes on to say that a brother may help in such a cleansing and, so to speak, be washing his brother's feet (*Homilies on John* 59.5):

> Can we say that even a brother may cleanse a brother from the contracted stain of wrongdoing? Yea, verily, we know that of this also we were admonished in the profound significance of this work of the Lord's that we should confess our faults to one another, and pray for one another, even as Christ also maketh intercession for us. . . For what else does the Lord apparently intimate in the profound significance of this sacramental sign, when He says, 'For I have given you an example, that ye should do as I have done to you'; but what the apostle declares in the plainest terms, 'Forgiving one another, if any man have a quarrel against any: even as Christ forgave you, so also do ye'? Let us therefore forgive one another his faults, and pray for one another's faults, and thus in a manner be washing one another's feet. It is our part, by His grace, to be supplying the service of love and humility: it is His to hear us, and to cleanse us from all the pollution of our sins through Christ, and in Christ; so that what we forgive even to others, that is, loose on earth, may be loosed in heaven.[2]

Whether Augustine encouraged actual footwashing to serve as a sign of forgiveness is difficult to ascertain. However, it is undeniable that Augustine sees a correlation between footwashing and forgiveness, at least on a symbolic level, and elsewhere he advocates the literal practice of footwashing (cf. *John: Tractate* 58.4, quoted in section A.2, above, present chapter).

John Cassian (c. 360–435) in describing the duties of the brother who serves as a kitchen attendant (*Institute of the Coenobia* 4.19) links footwashing to forgiveness of sin:

> But each one who undertakes these weeks is on duty and has to serve until supper on Sunday, and when this is done, his duty for the whole week is finished, so that, when all the brethren come together to chant the Psalms (which according to customer they sing before going to bed) those

1.   Schaff, *Nicene and Post-Nicene Fathers*, VII, pp. 302, 306-307.
2.   *Ibid.*, p. 307.

whose turn is over wash the feet of all in turn, seeking faithfully from
them the reward of this blessing for their work during the whole week,
that the prayers offered up by all the brethren together may accompany
them as they fulfill the command of Christ, the prayer, to wit, that intercedes for their ignorances and for their sins committed through human
frailty, and may commend to God the complete service of their devotion
like some rich offering.[1]

Apparently, the performance of footwashing (which 'fulfills the
command of Christ') combines with the prayers of all the brethren to
intercede for the ignorance and sins of those whose week of service
has ended. It would seem that the rendering of footwashing had some
connection with forgiveness of sin. It follows that this forgiveness was
for post-conversion sin, since these brethren are surely to be regarded
as believers.

Caesarius of Arles (c. 470-542) not only admonishes his readers to
wash the feet of others, but he can even say that the one who does not
perform the act will be found in torment without hope of repentance.
Such an extreme statement is possible because of the fact that one receives forgiveness of serious sins for oneself when washing the feet of
others (*Sermon* 202; for the full quotation, cf. section A.2 above):

Let us fear, brethren, what the blessed Apostle Peter feared, when he
heard the Lord say: 'If I do not wash you, you will have no share in my
heritage', For if, perchance, we disdain to wash the feet of the saints, we
will not merit to have a share with them. Let us rather bend down to the
feet of saints or of strangers; because when we fulfill this service with
holy humility, indeed we are not merely touching their feet with our
hands, but we are cleansing the meanness and filth of our souls through
faith and humility, and we are cleansing not only the smallest, but even
the most serious of our sins.[2]

Clearly, Caesarius sees the footwashing itself as active in the forgiveness of sin. Since he is addressing believers, the sin removed must be
regarded as post-baptismal sin.

These texts give additional support to the interpretation offered
above about the meaning of the practice of footwashing in the Johan-

---

1. Cited according to the translation of *Nicene and Post-Nicene Fathers*, Second
Series, XI, pp. 224-25.
2. Cited according to the translation of M.M. Mueller, *Saint Caesarius of Arles:
Sermons* (Washington, DC: Catholic University of America Press, 1973), III,
pp. 65-66.

nine community, for these texts not only come from authors who advocate, or give evidence of, the practice of footwashing in their communities, but they also interpret the practice's meaning as signifying the forgiveness of post-conversion sin.

(2) *The Practice of Footwashing and the Forgiveness of Sin.* The next group of texts demonstrates that in Milan, footwashing was practiced as a sign of the forgiveness of sin, but in this case it is hereditary sin which is forgiven. Ambrose notes that the one who submits to the washing receives cleansing by Christ himself (*Of the Holy Spirit* 1.13):

> Come, then, Lord Jesus. . . Pour water into the basin, wash not only our feet but also the head and not only the body, but also the footsteps of the soul. I wish put off all the filth of our frailty.[1]

Not only is cleansing achieved, but in some sense the effects of the Adamic curse are reversed so that spiritually one is already encountering eschatological conditions:

> Wash the steps of my mind that I may not sin again. Wash the heel of my soul, that I may be able to efface the curse, that I feel not the serpent's bite on the foot of my soul, but as Thou Thyself hast bidden those who follow Thee, may tread on serpents and scorpions with uninjured foot.[2]

The idea of washing away the poison of the serpent is developed further in another passage (*The Sacraments* 3.7). Here Ambrose explains Jn 13.10:

> Why this? Because in baptism all fault is washed away. So fault withdraws. But since Adam was overthrown by the Devil, and venom was poured out upon his feet, accordingly you wash the feet, that in this part, in which the serpent lay in wait, greater aid of sanctification may be added, so that afterwards he cannot overthrow you. Therefore, you wash the feet, that you may wash away the poisons of the serpent. It is also of benefit for humility, that we may not be ashamed in the mystery of what we disdain in obedience.[3]

---

1.   Cited according to the translation of Schaff and Wace, *Nicene and Post-Nicene Fathers*, X, p. 95.

2.   *Ibid.*

3.   Cited according to the translation of R.J. Deferrari, *Saint Ambrose: Theological and Dogmatic Works* (Washington, DC: Catholic University of America Press, 1963), p. 292.

The connection between baptism and footwashing is made with the assertion that baptism washes away personal sin, while footwashing washes away inherited sin. Such an implication is made explicit in Ambrose's discussion, *On the Mysteries* (6.32):

> Peter was clean, but he must wash his feet, for he had sin by succession from the first man, when the serpent overthrew him and persuaded him to sin. His feet were therefore washed, that hereditary sins might be done away, for our own sins are remitted through baptism.[1]

The logical conclusion is that footwashing is to be performed at least once in a convert's life. At Milan this ordinarily took place immediately after baptism (cf. *Sacraments* 3.4). However, it is possible, on account of the Ambrose text consulted earlier (*Of the Holy Spirit* 1.15), that footwashing continued to wash away sin, at least in the one washing the feet of others. At any rate, there is no question that Ambrose and the Milanese church attached sin-forgiving significance to the footwashing.

(3) *The Interpretation of Footwashing in John 13 as Forgiveness of Post-Conversion Sin.* Some additional writers in the early church interpret Jesus' washing the disciples' feet in John 13 as signifying the forgiveness of post-conversion sin. These writers do not indicate whether their communities practiced footwashing or not, but together with those who interpreted the practice of footwashing as signifying the forgiveness of post-conversion sin, they offer additional support for the proposal that the Johannine community would have interpreted John 13 this way and, consequently, would have viewed their own practice of footwashing in this way.

In a discussion of Isaiah 6, Jerome (*Epistle* 17A.12) compares Isaiah's need for cleansing his unclean lips with the disciples' need for cleansing their stained feet:

> For example, Our Lord in the Gospel is girt with a towel, He prepares a basin to wash the disciples' feet, He performs the service of a slave. Granted, it is to teach humility, that we may minister to each other in turn. I do not deny that. I do not reject it. What is it that He says to Peter upon his refusal? If I wash not thy feet, thou shalt have no part with me. And he replied: Lord, not only my feet, but also my hands and my head. Be-

---

1. Cited according to the translation of Schaff and Wace, *Nicene and Post-Nicene Fathers*, X, p. 321.

cause His apostles, as men walking the earth, still had feet stained by the
pollution of sin, the Lord being about to ascend to heaven, desires to free
them entirely from their transgressions, that the words of the prophet may
be applicable to them: How beautiful are the feet of those that preach
peace.[1]

Clearly, Jesus' footwashing removes the stain of sin's pollution accumulated by walking in a sinful world. The washing is also seen as
preparation for the disciples' mission. It seems that Jerome has in
mind the disciples' post-baptismal sin, for he describes the footwashing as freeing them *entirely* from their transgressions, implying an
earlier freeing from sin.

In explaining John 13.10-11, Theodore of Mopsuestia (*Commentary
on the Gospel of John the Apostle* 6.26-30) affirms that footwashing
removed the sins of the disciples which had been committed after their
baptism (at the hand of John the Baptist).

> This is not baptism in remission of sin (which they surely received once
> for all), neither again is there need for another baptism, for total cleansing
> is received the first time (it is performed). Now it is needful to wash only
> their feet in order to cover [sins], which things are committed again [i.e.
> after baptism] as you well know.[2]

Theodore's interpretation of Jn 13.10 agrees with the thesis of this
dissertation and gives additional weight to the likelihood that the Johannine community would have interpreted John 13 in this fashion.

Gregory the Great considers Jesus' footwashing to convey cleansing
from uncleanness. In commenting upon Job 29.6 (*Morals on the Book
of Job* 19.14) Gregory notes a correlation between this passage and Jesus' washing the feet of the disciples:

> Whom then do we take for 'the feet' of the Lord, but the holy Preachers.
> Of whom He saith, 'And I will walk in them: Thus 'the feet are washed
> with butter', because the holy Preachers are filled to the full with the fat-
> ness of good works. For as we have already said above, scarcely is the
> mere preaching itself carried on without something being done
> wrong. . .Whence the Apostles too had their feet washed, that from any

---

1.   Cited according to the translation of C.C. Mierow, *The Letters of St Jerome*
(New York: Newman, 1963), I, pp. 90-91.

2.   *Theodorei Mopsuesteni: Commentarius in Evangelium Iohannis Apostoli* (ed.
J.M. Voste; Louvain: Version, 1940), p. 183.

slight defilement contracted in the act of preaching itself they might be cleansed as from a sort of dust collected by a journey.[1]

Not only is such dust referred to as defilement, but Gregory does not hesitate to make clear that this dust is sin, more specifically the sin of pride (*Morals on the Book of Job* 1.23):

> Hence the Lord did well to wash the feet of the holy Apostles after their preaching, doubtless with this view, that He might shew plainly, both that very frequently in doing good the dust of sin is contracted, and that the steps of the speakers are often defiled by the same means whereby the hearts of the hearers are purified. For it often happens that some in giving words of exhortation, however poorly, are inwardly lifted up, because they are the channel, by which the grace of purification comes down; and while by the word they wash away the deeds of other men, they as it were contract the dust of an ill thought from a good course. What then was it to wash the disciples' feet after their preaching, but after the gloriousness of the preaching to wipe off the dust of our thoughts, and to cleanse the heart's goings from inward pride.[2]

As with so many others, Gregory believes that when Jesus washed the disciples' feet, he cleansed them from sin. Although he does not make it explicit, the implication is that, because it takes place in and after their preaching, such sin occurs after baptism.

(4) *The Interpretation of Footwashing in John 13 as Forgiveness of Sin*. A number of other early Christian texts testify to the frequency with which the footwashing in John 13 was interpreted as signifying the cleansing of the disciples from sin. While many of these texts do not specify the sin removed as post-conversion sin, they do show that an interpretation of footwashing as forgiveness or cleansing was not uncommon in early Christianity. Such evidence serves in a more general fashion to enhance the proposal that the Johannine community would have interpreted John 13 in a similar fashion.

The earliest extant interpretation of the footwashing account is one given by Irenaeus, Bishop of Lyons. In *Against Heresies* (4.22) he discerns a connection between footwashing and the forgiveness of sin:

---

1. Cited according to the anonymous translation, *Saint Gregory the Great: Morals on the Book of Job* (London: Oxford, 1845), II, pp. 412-13.
2. *Morals*, I, p. 49.

> Now in the last days, when the fulness of the time of liberty had arrived, the Word Himself did by Himself 'wash away the filth of the daughters of Zion', when He washed the disciples' feet with His own hands. For this is the end of the human race inheriting God; that as in the beginning, by means of our first (parents), we were all brought into bondage, by being made subject to death; so at last, by means of the New Man, all who having been cleansed and washed from things pertaining to death, should come to the life of God. For He who washed the feet of the disciples sanctified the entire body and rendered it clean.[1]

Clement of Alexandria (*The Instructor* 2.63) understands Jesus' action in washing the disciples' feet as cleansing them for their impending ministry:

> By washing the feet of His disciples with His own hands as He sent them forth to noble deeds, the Savior manifested in an excellent way their journeying to bestow graces upon the nations, and He purified that journeying in anticipation by His own power.[2]

Without an express mention of the forgiveness of sin, Clement implies that the disciples were in need of some sort of purification which the footwashing accomplished.

The idea that the footwashing prepares the disciples for their mission is continued by Origen (*Commentary on John* 32.7), who sees the fulfillment of Isa. 52.7 in the act:

> And what was it that Jesus did when washing the feet of the disciples? Did he make them beautiful through the washing of their feet and drying (them) with the towel which was worn (girded), as they were about to preach the good things? For when Jesus washed the feet of the disciples, then, I believe, the prophecy spoken long ago concerning his disciples was fulfilled: 'How beautiful are the feet of those who preach the good things'.[3]

As with Clement, it appears that Origen views the disciples as lacking something before they go to preach. This need is supplied in the footwashing. Origen (32.8) goes on to assert that the footwashing signifies

---

1. Cited according to the translation of Roberts and Donaldson, *Ante-Nicene Fathers*, I, p. 493.

2. Cited according to the translation of S.P. Wood, *Clement of Alexandria: Christ the Educator* (New York: Fathers of the Church, 1954), p. 148.

3. E. Preuschen (ed.), *Origenes Werke: Der Johanneskommentar* (Leipzig: Hinrichs, 1903), pp. 438-39.

a cleansing of the soul which the disciples will need as they travel in the world:

> The washing of your feet by me in which the feet (βάσεις) of your souls have been cleansed is a sign (σύμβολον), in order that you become beautiful, you are about to preach the good things and to walk with clean feet among the souls of men.[1]

The Isaiah passage is clearly in Origen's mind as he writes, but he explains this preparation as including a cleansing of the feet of the soul. The implication appears to be that sin is forgiven in this action. Such an idea becomes more apparent in another passage (32.6). Here Origen argues that Peter received the footwashing last because he did not need the cleansing as much as the other disciples:

> He did not begin with Peter. And one must speak to this because just as a physician serves by means of medicine to those who are fully sick, he makes the beginning of his healing from those who are depressed and who are suffering worse, in this manner the one who washes begins washing the feet of the disciples from those (needing) greater washing. And probably he came to Peter at last, as least of all needing the washing of feet.[2]

While Origen does not mention sin explicitly, it seems to be a logical conclusion that Jesus came to Peter last because he was less sinful than the other disciples.[3]

On occasion Origen discusses the footwashing in terms of cleansing. While describing the situations in which Joshua and Moses were instructed to remove their shoes because they were in the Lord's presence, Origen (*Homilia* 6.3) suggests that the Christian's ability to stand in God's presence is due to the footwashing:

> From what source do we suppose that we have strength and merit to approach the Lord and be made worthy? Because he said to us that by the feet we are made alive, because they are enslaved in mortal bonds. In that place are of course the feet which Jesus washed; which if he does not wash, you have no part with him. If, therefore, from our life and consciousness, all the chains of mortal cares are freed, we immediately rejoice because we are brought near to the presence of God.[4]

1. Preuschen, *Origines Werke*, p. 438.
2. *Ibid.*, p. 435.
3. Cf. Richter, *Die Fusswaschung*, p. 6.
4. W.A. Baehrens (ed.), *Origenes Werke* (Leipzig: Hinrichs, 1921), VII, p. 325.

In this passage there is a least the hint that sins are forgiven in Jesus' action.

Origen makes this understanding explicit in another passage (*In Librum Judicum, homilia* 8), where footwashing is said to signify the removal of sin.

> O Lord Jesu, Son of David, come I pray Thee, lay aside from Thee the nature wherewith Thou hast clothed Thyself on my account and gird Thyself for my sake and pour water into a basin and wash the feet of Thy servants and cleanse away the filth of Thy sons and of Thy daughters. Wash Thou the Feet of our mind, that we, imitating and following Thee, may put off from us our old garments and may say, 'By night I have put off my coat; how shall I put it on? I have washed my feet; how shall I defile them?' For as soon as Thou shalt have washed my feet, make me to recline with Thee, that I may hear Thy words, 'Ye call me Master and Lord; and ye say well; for so I am. If I then your Lord and Master, have washed your feet, ye also ought to wash one another's feet'. I too, therefore, am willing to wash the feet of my brethren, to wash the feet of my fellow disciples. And therefore, I take water, and I draw from the fountains of Israel that which I wring out of the Israelitish fleece. For at one time I wring water out of the fleece of the Book of Judges, and at another time water from the fleece of Kingdoms, and water from the fleece of Isaiah or Jeremiah, and I pour it into the basin of my mind, conceiving the sense in my heart; and I take the feet of those who offer themselves and prepare themselves for supper; and, in so far as the power lies in me, I desire to wash the feet of my brethren, and to fulfill the commandment of the Lord, that through the word of teaching the hearers may be purged from the contamination of their sins, and may cast away from themselves all the uncleanness of their vices, and may have clean feet wherewith they may mightily walk towards the preparation of the gospel of peace; so that all of us purified together in Christ Jesus by the Word, may not be rejected from the Bridegroom's chambers, because of our unclean garments, but that with shining vesture and washed feet and clean heart, we may recline at the banquet of the Bridegroom, our Lord Himself, Jesus Christ, to whom be glory and dominion for ever and ever. Amen.[1]

The Syrian leader, Ephraem (c. 306–73), also identifies the footwashing rendered by Jesus as signifying cleansing for the disciples. In the *Hymns of the Nativity* 18.7 Ephraem notes:

---

1.   Cited according to the translation of F.E. Warren, *The Liturgy and Ritual of the Ante-Nicene Church* (London: SPCK, 1912), pp. 161-62.

[see] how he (himself) on earth served, washing feet, purifying souls. Glory be to his submission.[1]

Here the emphasis seems to be upon his earthly ministry in which he accomplished spiritual cleansing. Yet, such actions are not limited to the disciples but also have implications for Ephraem's audience (*Hymns of the Church* 4.14-15):

has he (Christ whom we serve in the foreign land) not taken a guilt and placed it upon you which is greater than this! Water he drew and sanctified it; your sins he washed away from you. His body he broke before you, and his blood he mingled and gave it to you.[2]

Not only does Ephraem connect Jesus' footwashing with forgiveness of sins, but he also relates footwashing to the passion itself.

In discussing the Song of Songs, Gregory of Nyssa (*Comm. in Canticum Canticorum* 11.5.3) finds the true meaning of the beloved's words in the actions of Jesus. The significance of Christ's action is that sins are forgiven in the process:

So therefore, in this way the Bride came, in which [way] the Lord washes with water the feet of those who walk through her [the Bride] and wipes [them] with a towel which he wore (and the girdle of the Lord is power for cleansing of sins, the Scripture says; For the Lord was clothed in and wore power); because of this cleansing she guards the feet upon the royal way herself, not turning to the right or to the left, that lest leading either [foot] outside the way, the footstep might defile the foot with mire. . . This one [Jesus] washed the feet removing all earthly uncleanness [or *dirt*, ῥύπον] from the sandals.[3]

As has already been indicated, footwashing in connection with forgiveness of sin finds an extraordinary advocate in Ambrose of Milan. In one text (*Commentary on Luke's Gospel* 6.67), Ambrose seems to interpret the footwashing of the disciples by Jesus as cleansing from sins in general. Ambrose, who reads his view of John 13 into his commentary on Luke 9, offers a brief discussion of Jesus washing the disciples' feet:

1. Richter, *Die Fusswaschung*, p. 20.
2. Richter, *Die Fusswaschung*, p. 20.
3. *Gregorii Nysseni in Canticum Canticorum* (ed. H. Langerbeck; Leiden: E.J. Brill, 1960), pp. 330-31.

> He had the custom of washing the feet of his guests, and from the moment he received them into his house, he would not allow them to stay with soiled feet, but, however dirty they had become from the past life, he condescended to clean them for the rest of the journey.[1]

In this allegorical note, it is unclear whether Ambrose is implying that Jesus cleansed the disciples of their post-conversion sin in this footwashing, or from their pre-conversion sin.

Cyril of Alexandria (d. 444) sees a very close connection between Jesus' footwashing and the forgiveness of sins. In a discussion of Jn 13.8 (*Homilies on John's Gospel* 11.723) Cyril makes this explicit:

> Unless one washes, through his grace, from sin and erring defilement, he will have no share of life with him, and he will remain without a taste of heavenly kingdoms.[2]

While Cyril does not perceive the footwashing in isolation from other salvific acts, he does acknowledge it as a part of the process. At the very least, footwashing signifies forgiveness of sin.

Another Alexandrian, Bishop Ammonius, makes a similar identification of forgiveness of sin with Jesus' footwashing. In commenting upon Jn 13.8 Ammonius observes:

> Unless you receive the lesson of humility, you have no part with me, truly, unless one washes clean the dirt of sin through grace, that one does not obtain life, nor enjoy (have benefit of) the heavenly kingdom.[3]

The Syrian poet Cyrillonas (c. 400) describes footwashing in terms of cleansing and preparation. After the footwashing, Jesus is depicted as addressing the disciples in the following manner:

> See how I have washed and cleansed you; therefore hurry joyfully into the church and step into her doors as heirs![4]

Both cleansing from sin and preparation for future ministry are exhibited in this verse. Protection from Satan is a major part of this preparation:

---

1.   Cited according to the text of *Ambrose de Milan: Traité sur l'Evangile de S. Luc* (ed. G. Tissot; Paris: Cerf, 1971), I, pp. 251-52.
2.   Migne, *Patrologia Graeca*, LXXIV, p. 117.
3.   Migne, *Patrologia Graeca*, LXXXV, pp. 1482-82.
4.   Lohse, I, p. 20.

Step upon the evil one fearless and on the head of the serpent without trembling.[1]

After the footwashing and this word of comfort the disciples are directed by Jesus to commence their ministry:

> Go your ways without fear and proclaim my word in your cities. Sow the Gospel in the countries and let your love sink into the hearts of men! Proclaim my Gospel before the kings and reveal my faith before the judges! Behold, I who am your God have humbled myself and served you. . .[2]

In thoughts similar to Clement, Origen and Jerome, Cyrillonas views the footwashing as preparation for ministry. He, too, sees a connection between footwashing and forgiveness of sin.

Eucherius (d. 449), Bishop of Lyons, continues the thought of Ambrose in his understanding of the significance of Jesus' footwashing (*Instructions* I):

> Question: What mystery is contained in that place where the Lord washes the feet of the disciples?
> Answer: In that place the curse of 'treading' is dissolved, [in] which the devil set fire our lives by attacking [our] paths (Gen. 3.15). First, the bite of that one [is removed] by removing the obstacle from [one's] path. Next, with the proclamation, 'Behold I give to you power to tread upon snakes and scorpions' (Lk. 10.19), that curse is abolished.[3]

Both removal of inherited sin and commissioning for service are present in Eucherius's view of footwashing.

c. *Conclusions*. If, as this study has argued, the Johannine community engaged in the practice of footwashing as a religious rite, then in all likelihood it was held to signify the cleansing of believers from post-conversion sin.

1. As shown in chapter four, this understanding is in line with the results of the literary and exegetical analysis of Jn 13.1-20.
2. Of those scholars who believe that the Johannine community engaged in footwashing as a religious rite, there is near unanimity that the act signified cleansing to one degree or an-

1. Lohse,.I, p. 20.
2. *Ibid.*
3. Migne, *Patrologia Latina*, L, p. 803.

other. Two of the four cited clearly identify footwashing as
signifying the forgiveness of post-conversion sin.

3. The community's concern with post-conversion sin, evi-
    denced in 1 John, is compatible with the suggestion that some
    rite accompanied the confession and subsequent forgiveness
    of sin. The role of fellow Christians in the reconciliation
    process (1 Jn 5.16) is quite consistent with the evidence from
    Jn 13.1-20 (especially vv. 14-17) about the significance of
    the disciples carrying out Jesus' command.

4. Several of those writers in the early church who advocate the
    practice of footwashing understood it to signify the forgive-
    ness of post-conversion sin. One writer, Augustine, even
    makes the connection between the believers' role in the re-
    moval of a fellow believer's sin (Jn 20.23; 1 Jn 5.16) and the
    disciples' commission to wash one another's feet (Jn 13.14-
    17).

5. From the very earliest extant interpretations of Jn 13.1-20
    onwards, a penitential understanding of the pericope has fre-
    quently been given. Not only are there statements about the
    footwashing of John 13 and forgiveness of sin generally, but
    several writers understand this forgiveness as having refer-
    ence to post-conversion sin.

In the light of these considerations, if the Johannine community
practiced footwashing as a religious rite, the most plausible interpretation of the meaning they assigned to it is that footwashing signified
the forgiveness of post-conversion sin in the Johannine community.

2. *Was Footwashing a Sacrament for the Johannine Community?*

If footwashing was practiced as a religious rite signifying forgiveness
of post-conversion sin, the question which naturally arises is, was
footwashing considered to be a sacrament in the Johannine community? Of course, this question is related to the more fundamental one
concerning the place of any sacraments in the life of the community as
evidenced in the Fourth Gospel. Therefore, a discussion about the
classification of footwashing as a sacrament must wait until attention
has been given to the more basic inquiry.

a. *The Fourth Gospel and Sacramentalism.* The question of sacramen-

talism and the Fourth Gospel is a highly debated issue.[1] Since neither
Jesus' baptism nor the institution of the Eucharist are described in the
Fourth Gospel, several scholars have concluded that John is non- or
anti-sacramental.[2] The absence of these events may be interpreted in
another way, however. It has been proposed that, while John is not
anti-sacramental, he purposefully withholds the sacraments in certain
expected contexts in order to reinterpret or correct the current view
about them.[3] On the basis of (a) the eucharistic overtones of John 6,
(b) the Fourth Gospel's obvious assumption of the practice of baptism
(3.22; 4.1-2), (c) the implication that Jesus was baptized (1.32-34), (d)
the possible allusion to baptism in Jesus' words to Nicodemus (3.5), as
well as numerous other passages, many are convinced that John is not
anti-sacramental. This response is enunciated in a variety of forms.
Some scholars have argued that John is intentionally sacramental,
pointing to sacramental teaching throughout the book.[4] Another posi-

1. For an introduction and overview cf. the following works: R. Schnackenburg, 'Die Sakramente im Johannesevangelium', *Sacra Pagina: Miscellanea Biblica
Congressus Internationalis Catholici Re Biblica* (ed. J. Coppens, A. Descamps, E.
Massaux; Paris–Gembloux, 1959), II, pp. 235-54; R.E. Brown, 'The Johannine
Sacramentary', in *New Testament Essays* (New York: Paulist Press, 1965), pp. 51-
76; H. Klos, *Die Sakramente im Johannesevangelium: Vorkommen und Busse im
vierten Evangelium* (Stuttgarter Bibelstudien, 46; Stuttgart: Katholisches Bibelwerk,
1970); and R. Kysar, *The Fourth Evangelist and his Gospel* (Minneapolis:
Augsburg, 1975), pp. 249-59.

2. Bultmann, pp. 11, 138 n. 3, 677-79; E. Schweizer, 'Das Johanneische
Zeugnis vom Herrenmahl', *EvT* 12 (1952–53), pp. 341-63; H. Koester,
'Geschichte und Kultus im Johannesevangelium und bei Ignatius und Sacrament im
Johannesevangelium', *NTS* 7 (1960–61), pp. 110-25; G. Bornkamm, 'Die
eucharistische Rede im Johannes-Evangelium', *ZNW* 47 (1956), pp. 161-69;
Kysar, p. 259.

3. M. Barth, *Die Taufe—ein Sakrament? Ein exegetischer Beitrag zum
Gespräch über die kirchliche Taufe* (Zürich: Evangelischer Verlag, 1951); G.H.C.
MacGregor, 'The Eucharist in the Fourth Gospel', *NTS* 9 (1963), pp. 111-19; E.F.
Scott, *The Fourth Gospel, its Purpose and Theology* (Edinburgh: T. & T. Clark,
1920), pp. 122-32; K. Matsunaga, 'Is John's Gospel Anti-Sacramental?—A New
Solution in the Light of the Evangelist's Milieu', *NTS* 27 (1981), pp. 516-24; and
G.M. Burge, *The Anointed Community: The Holy Spirit in the Johannine Tradition*
(Grand Rapids: Eerdmans, 1987), pp. 150-97.

4. A. Schweitzer, *The Mysticism of Paul the Apostle* (trans. W. Montgomery;
New York: Holt, 1931), pp. 352-69; C.T. Craig, 'Sacrament in the Fourth Gospel',
JBL 58 (1939), pp. 31-41; Cullmann, *Early Christian Worship*, pp. 116-19; B.

tion is that John's teaching about the sacraments is quite symbolic and often is just under the surface in contexts which are not primarily sacramental.[1] Often this understanding is maintained in the midst of rigorous critical analysis of sacramental claims.[2] Despite his reservations about the abuses of reading in too much sacramentalism, C.K. Barrett notes, 'Yet it is true that there is more sacramental teaching in John than in the other gospels'.[3]

In the light of such a lack of consensus on sacramentalism and the Fourth Gospel, perhaps it is best simply to identify those religious rites which the community practised, without determining, in advance, their collective significance.

b. *Baptism and Eucharist in the Johannine Community.* While a well-developed sacramentalism is certainly not found in the New Testament, it appears that by the time the Fourth Gospel took final form, several actions came to hold a special place in the worship of the community.

It has already been suggested that baptism was an important practice of the Johannine community.[4] The following survey, which enumerates the prominent features of baptism in the Fourth Gospel, should provide adequate documentation for this suggestion.

1. In passages where the term βαπτίζω occurs, John the Baptist is never far away. Even when Jesus is the subject of the verse(s), John is mentioned. Although the Baptist is known

Vawter, 'The Johannine Sacramentary', *TS* 17 (1956), pp. 151-66; A. Corell, *Eschatology and Church in the Gospel of St John* (London: SPCK, 1958); and W. Wilkens, *Die Entstehungsgeschichte des vierten Evangeliums* (Zollikon: Evangelischer Verlag, 1958).

1. Hoskyns, *The Fourth Gospel*; J. Danielou, *The Bible and the Liturgy* (Notre Dame, IN: Notre Dame Press, 1956), pp. 208-10; R.H. Lightfoot, *St John's Gospel* (London: Oxford University Press, 1960); P. Niewalda, *Sakramentssymbolik im Johannesevangelium* (Limburg: Lahn, 1958); Brown, *The Gospel according to John*, I, pp. cx-cxiv; and S.S. Smalley, *John: Evangelist and Interpreter* (Nashville: Nelson, 1984), pp. 204-10.

2. Dodd, *The Interpretation of the Fourth Gospel*, pp. 133-43; Schnackenburg, 'Die Sakramente im Johannesevangelium'; G. Beasley-Murray, *Baptism in the New Testament* (Grand Rapids: Eerdmans, 1973), pp. 216-32.

3. Barrett, *The Gospel According to John*, p. 69.

4. Cf. especially the discussion of Jn 13.10 in Chapter 4, section C.2.c, above.

primarily as a witness in the Fourth Gospel, his work as a baptizer is significant.

2. Nowhere is the baptism of Jesus by John described. This exceptional omission is frequently explained as part of a polemic against John the Baptist sectarians.

3. Though a description of the baptism of Jesus is missing, this event is assumed in 1.29-34. Here, reference is made to the descent of the Spirit as a dove upon Jesus, information identical with that given in the Synoptic account of Jesus' baptism. The Fourth Evangelist appears to presume his audience's knowledge of the event.

4. The divine origin of John's baptism is clearly asserted in 1.33. The one who informed John of Jesus' identify is the same one who sent John to baptize.

5. In addition to knowledge of water baptism, the Fourth Evangelist makes reference to the promise of Spirit-Baptism (1.33).

6. The Fourth Gospel alone ascribes baptism to Jesus himself (3.22; 4.1). Not only does Jesus baptize, but he is more successful in his work than is John.

7. In an editorial aside (4.2), the Evangelist (or redactor?) clarifies Jesus' role in the baptisms. It was the disciples, not Jesus, who actually performed them.

8. Despite the absence of βαπτίζω, Jn 3.5 figures prominently in any discussion of baptism in the Fourth Gospel. In this passage Nicodemus is informed that unless he is born ἐξ ὕδατος καὶ πνεύματος he will not enter the Kingdom. The major issue concerns the term ὕδατος. Does it have reference to baptism? In this regard scholars are divided.[1] Those who discount Johannine sacramentalism reject any baptismal allusions here.[2] Others, who see an extensive sacramentalism in John, insist upon an identification between water and baptism.[3] Both positions appear to go beyond the evidence. Closer to the mark are scholars who take the baptismal motif

---

1. Cf. the discussion in Kysar, pp. 250-51, and Z. Hodges, 'Water and Spirit—John 3.5', *BSac* 135 (1978), pp. 206-20.
2. Bultmann (p. 138 n. 3), for example.
3. Cullmann, *Early Christian Worship*, pp. 75-78.

as secondary,[1] for it is difficult to believe that John's readers would not have made some sort of connection between ὕδα- τος and baptism.

Even if Jn 3.5 is discounted, a definite picture of baptism in the Fourth Gospel emerges. On the one hand, baptism is described without a great deal of fanfare. There is no description of Jesus' baptism nor is there a discourse on the significance of baptism (unless this explanation comes in ch. 3). Yet, Jesus' baptism is assumed, John's baptism is assigned divine origin, and both Jesus and his disciples are said to have baptized others. Whenever baptism is mentioned, it is always in a positive context. Therefore, while baptism in the Fourth Gospel is not overwhelmingly prominent, it appears to be a significant and positive practice in the Johannine community.

At least two dimensions of baptism's significance may be deduced from the Fourth Gospel. First, because of its obvious relationship with John's baptism, in all probability the practice signified forgiveness of sin. If the traditions about John are at all similar to those present in the Synoptics, forgiveness of sin is at the heart of this baptism. That Jesus himself is said to have baptized emphasizes the continuity between the views of baptism. Second, if there is a baptismal motif present in Jn 3.5, then another aspect of baptism's meaning is discernible. Baptism signifies entrance into the Kingdom of God. Both dimensions of baptism present in the Fourth Gospel, forgiveness of sin and entrance into the Kingdom of God, are also aspects prominent in other early Christian circles (cf. 1 Cor. 12.13; Gal. 3.27; Acts 2.38; 13.24; 19.4; 22.16; 1 Pet. 3.21; Tit. 3.5).

Although the evidence is not as explicit as with baptism, there are strong indications that the eucharist was also observed in the Johannine community. Not only does John 13 assume the meal as background (cf. the comments on Jn 13.2-4 in Chapter 4, section C, above) but John 6 contains numerous eucharistic overtones. In 6.53-59, Jesus says that those who eat his flesh and drink his blood have eternal life; this is language not unlike other early descriptions of the eucharistic elements: 'This is my body given for you', and 'This cup is the new covenant in my blood, which is poured out for you' (Lk. 22.19-20; cf. also Mk 14.22-24 and 1 Cor. 11.24-25). This eternal life, including

---

1. Brown, *The Gospel according to John*, I, p. 143.

resurrection at the last day, is based upon the fact that his flesh is real food and his blood is real drink. It is difficult to imagine the Johannine community reading this section of the Fourth Gospel without thinking of the eucharist. ·

In the light of these data, it may safely be assumed that both baptism and eucharist had their place in the Johannine community.

It should be noted that the primary objective of this section has not been to argue for a particular theological view of the sacraments in John. Rather, it has been to identify those rites that for all practical purposes may be identified as sacraments for the Johannine community.

c. *Footwashing as a Sacrament.* In the first-century church, baptism and eucharist were regarded as having been established by Jesus himself, as being directly related to his atoning death, and as continuing in the worshiping community. In view of these attitudes, several reasons may be offered in support of the classification of footwashing as a sacrament for the Johannine community. When John's account of the footwashing is examined, each of the above characteristics are present: (1) There is no doubt that, as portrayed in the Fourth Gospel, the footwashing is instituted by Jesus. (2) It is clear from a number of literary allusions in John's Gospel that the Footwashing is viewed as rooted and grounded in Jesus' atoning death. (3) On the basis of Jn 13.14-17 it has been demonstrated that footwashing is to be continued in the Johannine community. (4) Verses 14-17, taken as words of institution, are as explicit in terms of perpetuation of the practice as the eucharistic words of institution. If readers in the Johannine community were familiar with the synoptic traditions, the comparison between the two sets of words of institution could hardly be missed. (5) Finally, by taking the traditional place of the eucharist in the passion narrative, the footwashing appears in a sacramental context.[1]

There are even some writers in the early church that use sacramental language in describing the footwashing.[2] Origen's description

---

1. Several scholars are so impressed by this placement that they seek to understand the footwashing as a symbol of the eucharist. Cf. Chapter 1, section A.2, above.

2. J.N.D. Kelly observes, 'We should note that, while the technical terms for sacrament were to be μυστήριον in Greek and *sacramentum* in Latin, there are no

(*Genesis Homily* 4.2) of Abraham's example in receiving guests is cloaked in language which draws attention to the mysterious nature of footwashing:

> Nevertheless, even this is said mysteriously. For he knew that the mysteries of the Lord were not to be completed except in washing the feet.[1]

It appears that Origen here connects footwashing with 'sacramental language'. No more than this can be said.

If Origen's comments are ambiguous, Ambrose (*The Sacraments* 3.5) makes it quite clear that he regards footwashing as a mystery on the same level as baptism:

> (5) We are not unaware of the fact that the Church in Rome does not have this custom, whose character and form we follow in all things. Yet it does not have the custom of washing the feet. So note: perhaps on account of the multitude this practice declined. Yet there are some who say and try to allege in excuse that this is not to be done in the mystery, nor in baptism, nor in regeneration, but the feet are to be washed as for a guest. But one belongs to humility, the other to sanctification: 'If I wash not thy feet, thou shalt have no part with me'. So I say this, not that I may rebuke others, but that I may commend my own ceremonies. In all things I desire to follow the Church in Rome, yet we, too, have human feelings; what is preserved more rightly elsewhere we, too, preserve more rightly.[2]

It is obvious that Ambrose is so convinced of footwashing's sacramental character that if he must part company with Rome to preserve the rite he is willing to do just that. In a related passage (*Mysteries* 6.31) Ambrose refers to the fact that footwashing is a mystery:

> You went up from the font; remember the Gospel lesson. For our Lord Jesus Christ in the Gospel washed the feet of His disciples. When He came to Simon Peter, Peter said: 'Thou shalt never wash my feet'. He did not perceive the mystery, and therefore he refused the service, for he thought that the humility of the servant would be injured, if he patiently allowed the Lord to minister to him. And the Lord answered him: 'If I wash not thy feet, thou wilt have no part with Me'. Peter, hearing this, replies: 'Lord, not my feet only, but also my hands and head'. The Lord

absolutely certain instances of their use before the Alexandrian fathers and Tertullian respectively' (*Early Christian Doctrines* [London: A. & C. Black, 1977], p. 193).

1.   Cited according to the translation of Heine, *Origen: Homilies on Genesis and Exodus*, p. 105.

2.   Cited according to the translation of Deferrari, *Saint Ambrose: Theological and Dogmatic Works*, pp. 291-92.

answered: 'He that is washed needeth not save to wash the feet but is clean every whit'.[1]

Augustine himself (*Homilies on John* 58.5) uses sacramental language in describing the relationship of footwashing to the forgiveness of sins:

> And if He forgives us, when we have nothing to forgive; how much more ought we, who are unable to live here without sin, to forgive one another! For what else does the Lord apparently intimate in the profound significance of this sacramental sign, when He says, 'For I have given you an example, that ye should do as I have done to you'; but what the apostle declares in the plainest terms, 'Forgiving one another, if any man have a quarrel against any: even as Christ forgave you, so also do ye'.[2]

Although Augustine does not share Ambrose's exalted view of footwashing, he none the less feels comfortable with using the terminology 'sacramental sign' in describing the practice.[3]

In the light of footwashing's place in the Fourth Gospel and the limited relevant evidence from the early church, it may be concluded that footwashing functioned, alongside baptism and eucharist, as a 'sacrament' for the Johannine community. To put it another way, whatever one calls the rites of baptism and eucharist, one must say the same about footwashing in the Johannine community.

One question remains from this discussion on sacramentalism. Why

1. Cited according to the translation of Schaff and Wace, *Nicene and Post-Nicene Fathers*, X, p. 321.

2. Cited according to the translation of Schaff, *Nicene and Post-Nicene Fathers*, VIII, p. 307.

3. This Augustinian text leads P.G. Maness ('Feet Washing', Dissertation, Southern Baptist Seminary [1898]) to believe that Augustine refers to footwashing as a sacramental 'sign' on still another occasion. Maness observes that in the *Reply to Faustus* (19.14), Augustine compares the 'sacraments' of the Old Testament with those of the New Testament. He argues that if praiseworthy figures of the past preferred to suffer rather than to defile the 'sacraments' of the Old Testament, '. . . how much more should a Christian in our day be ready to suffer all things for Christ's baptism, for Christ's eucharist, for Christ's sacred sign. . .' (cited according to the edition of P. Schaff, *Nicene and Post-Nicene Fathers*, IV [Grand Rapids: Eerdmans, 1956], p. 244). Although Maness is quite certain that this text has reference to footwashing, Augustine may have in mind the sign of the cross which was used in baptism and the eucharist. Augustine (*Expositions on the Book of Psalms* 92.3) can also explain the footwashing exclusively in terms of humility.

does John replace the account of the eucharist with that of the foot-washing? Several factors may be involved. First, it is quite likely that the footwashing account has displaced that of the eucharist for literary purposes. It was noted in Chapter 4 that the literary genre of John 13–17 is that of a farewell discourse. By nature, farewell discourses prepare followers/children for the departure of the leader/father. Because of the preparatory nature of footwashing generally, the account of Jesus washing the disciples' feet was a natural way to begin the farewell materials. In as much as the footwashing pericope includes words of institution and fits the farewell genre so well, the account of the eucharist was omitted, with emphasis upon its character and meaning coming at the end of ch. 6.

Second, it is also possible that the footwashing has replaced the institution of the eucharist in John 13 owing to John's dating of the Last Supper on Passover eve, in distinction from the synoptics which place the Last Supper on Passover itself.

Third, since, as this investigation has suggested, footwashing was likely to have been accorded sacramental status in the Johannine community, an additional reason for this placement of the footwashing may be that, by displacing the account of the eucharist, sacramental emphasis is transferred to the footwashing.

Fourth, a related, but equally important, reason concerns John's view of the sacraments in general. In an extended note devoted to this issue, Schnackenburg makes several pertinent observations:

> In the first place, it is important to bear in mind that John passes over a great deal or else silently presupposes what is narrated in the synoptics. . . It is clear, however, that John expresses what is important to him even if the synoptics have already presented it with sufficient clarity. . . Why, then, does John leave so much out and yet include other material, in even greater detail? It is obviously because he is concerned with an interpretation and indeed with his own interpretation with its deep Christological insight.[1]

Schnackenburg rightly concludes that, while John is not anti-sacramental, he is critical of the sacraments and he intends '. . . to lead the community to a deeper understanding in its sacramental practice'.[2] By putting the footwashing narrative in the place of the institution of the

---

1.   Schnackenburg, *The Gospel according to John*, III, p. 45.
2.   *Ibid.*, p. 46.

eucharist, the Evangelist wishes to reveal as the real meaning of the eucharist 'the lasting revelation of Jesus' love for his own, the commemoration of his death and a share in his life'.[1] What necessitates such a corrective emphasis? While Schnackenburg speculates that docetism is the reason for this situation,[2] the answer may be found in an over—realistic view of the sacraments which appears to have emerged as early as the mid-fifties, and which perhaps made an impact upon the later 'orthodox' thought of the church. Evidently, the church at Corinth had developed a quasi-magical view of the sacraments, to the point that Paul had to address the problem (1 Cor. 10.1-11).[3] It appears that some in the church were claiming that, due to the presence of the sacraments in the community, no harm could come to them.[4] Gordon Fee observes:

> The nature of this argument strongly suggests that those who 'think they stand' (vs. 12) do so on the basis of a somewhat magical view of the sacraments. Otherwise one can scarcely make sense of the present paragraph (10.1-5). Therefore, their argument with Paul most likely included

1. Schnackenburg, *The Gospel according to John*, III, p. 46.
2. *Ibid.*
3. Clearly, the eucharistic problems at Corinth were complex. Recent analyses by G. Theissen and W. Meeks have offered insightful sociological discussions of 1 Cor. 11.17-34. However, Paul's sacramental emphasis in 1 Cor. 10.1-22 has largely been ignored. Cf. G. Theissen, *The Social Setting of Pauline Christianity* (Philadelphia: Fortress Press, 1982), pp. 145-74, and W. Meeks, *The First Urban Christians* (New Haven, CT: Yale University Press, 1983), pp. 157-62. Even Meeks's study devoted to 1 Cor. 10.1-22 gives surprisingly little attention to Paul's pointed argument about the 'sacramental provisions'. Cf. W. Meeks, 'And Rose Up to Play: Midrash and Paraenesis in 1 Corinthians 10.1-22', *JSNT* 16 (1982), pp. 64-78.
4. Barrett notes: 'Some Christians believed that their participation in the Christian sacraments guaranteed them against any possible loss of future salvation. They might commit idolatry (verse 6), and fornication (verse 7), they might tempt God (verse 9), and complain against him (verse 10), with impunity because they had been baptized and received the eucharist' (*The First Epistle to the Corinthians* [New York: Harper & Row, 1968], pp. 220-29; cf. also E. Käsemann, *Essays on the New Testament* (Philadelphia: Fortress Press, 1982), pp. 108-35; Opeke, 'βάπτω', *TDNT*, I, p. 542; H. Conzelmann, *1 Corinthians* (Philadelphia: Fortress Press, 1975), p. 167; Beasley-Murray, *Baptism in the New Testament*, pp. 181-85. C. Perrot questions this interpretation of 10.1-5 ('Les examples du désert [1 Cor. 10.6-11]', *NTS* 29 [1983], pp. 437-52, especially pp. 445-46). However, he fails to explain Paul's emphasis on the eucharistic elements.

some reference to their own security through the sacraments, which so identified them as Christians that attendance at the idol temples was immaterial since those 'gods' did not exist (8.4-6).[1]

Paul warned the community that the Israelites had been the recipients of 'baptism into Moses' and had partaken of 'spiritual food and drink', and yet their sacramentally washed and full bodies were scattered in the wilderness because God was not pleased with them. This problem at Corinth suggests that from an early period the sacraments were capable of a quasi-magical interpretation.

Ignatius seems to express a view of the sacraments which has moved some distance beyond that of the Fourth Gospel. William R. Schoedel, who defends Ignatius against charges that he held a magical view of the eucharist, concludes that the eucharist functions as 'the bearer of a sacred power...that confers immortality'.[2] Whether Ignatius manifests a magical view of the sacraments or not,[3] it seems that the function of the eucharist is quasi-magical. Ignatius incorporates into his letter to the Ephesians (20.2) a description of the eucharistic elements as 'the medicine of immortality' (φάρμακον ἀθανασίας), which allows one never to die but to live with Jesus forever. This descriptive phrase, along with other passages where Ignatius seems to understand the elements as literally the body and blood of Jesus (*Smyrneans* 6.2; *Romans* 7.3), points to an environment where a more mechanical view of the sacraments was held.[4] Both the Corinthian and Ignatian passages suggest that such conceptions concerning the sacraments were 'in the air' when John's Gospel was written.[5]

Perhaps the conclusions of C.K. Barrett are close to the truth:

> Consider the supper. The farewell meal of Jesus with his disciples is narrated at great length, but it is not a Passover meal, and no reference is made to the eating and drinking of bread and wine or to any words connected with them. We cannot say that John had no interest in Paschal themes; he represents Jesus as the true Paschal lamb who died at the very

1. G.D. Fee, *The First Epistle to the Corinthians* (Grand Rapids: Eerdmans, 1987), p. 443.

2. W.R. Schoedel, *Ignatius of Antioch* (Philadelphia: Fortress Press, 1985), p. 21.

3. A possibility suggested by Schnackenburg, *The Gospel according to John*, II, p. 62.

4. J.N.D. Kelly is in basic agreement with this reading of Ignatius (*Early Christian Doctrines*, pp. 197-98).

5. For a similar conclusion, cf. Barrett, *Essays on John*, pp. 84-85.

time that the animal sacrifices were being slaughtered in the Temple, fulfilling all that they foreshadowed. Nor can we say (though some would contradict me here) that John was not interested in, or even wished to depreciate, the Christian supper. I do not look upon John 6.51-58 as an interpolation by an ecclesiastical redactor, not least because it seems to me that to treat the passage as a piece of quasi-magical sacramentarianism is exegetically mistaken. In fact John offers a critique of such exaggerated and unguarded sacramental theology as appeared a few years later in the epistles of Ignatius (who writes of the eucharist as a medicine conferring immortality, an antidote against death; *Ephesians* 20.2) and no doubt was already current when John wrote. That he was unaware of the Christian practice of meeting, perhaps weekly, for supper is highly improbable; that he wished to bring this practice to an end is hardly less so. That he was critical of what his contemporaries were making of a practice in itself innocent and indeed desirable is, on the one hand, probable—Paul had been similarly critical in the preceding generation. . .John wrote at a time when the Christian rite was in danger of becoming a mechanical repetition of the Last Supper, which was believed to secure, *ex opere operato*, eternal life for the recipient. Thus John, first, focused Paschal significance not on a meal but on Jesus crucified himself—*he* was the lamb of God in his own action; secondly, detached what he had to say about eating the flesh and drinking the blood of the Son of Man from the Last Supper; and, thirdly, embedded these references to eating and drinking in a discourse which made it clear that receiving Christ, the bread of life, by faith belonged to a wider setting than a cult act, even though the cult act (which is clearly in mind in John 6) might be a particularly clear focusing of this receiving.[1]

Barrett goes on to note that this, then, leaves the Last Supper narrative open for the footwashing, which he views as an acted parable.

By putting the account of the footwashing in the place which the Last Supper normally occupies, John seeks to stress the true nature of the sacraments. It is here suggested that John corrects a quasi-magical view of the sacraments. Far from being magical rites, they are signs of God's gracious action based upon the death of Jesus. Such rites do not stand alone but must be accompanied by faith. Because of its self-effacing nature the footwashing could never be perceived apart from its roots in the humiliating death of Jesus. Consequently, the footwashing might be construed as the model sacrament for the Fourth Evangelist. Therefore, John both emphasizes the sacramental nature of footwashing and deepens the community's understanding of the

---

1. C.K. Barrett, *Church, Ministry, and Sacraments in the New Testament* (Exeter: Paternoster Press, 1985), pp. 73-74.

sacraments by placing the footwashing account at this strategic point in the narrative.

C. Conclusion and Proposal

This chapter has argued that, in all probability, footwashing was practiced as a religious rite by the Johannine community. It has been further suggested that the footwashing signified the cleansing of believers from post-conversion sin. If these conclusions are accurate, is it possible to go beyond these results to ascertain anything about the actual practice itself? In other words, is it possible to discern the frequency, location, or mode of the footwashing as observed by the Johannine community?

Unfortunately, the evidence from which to address such questions is extremely limited, so much so that any suggestions offered must be acknowledged to be guesswork.

Nevertheless, three things may be deduced about the community's practice. (1) In view of its placement in the Fourth Gospel, the footwashing was probably observed in conjunction with the eucharist. If so, it is possible that the footwashing took place in the context of a meal (perhaps the Agape?) together with the eucharist. It cannot be determined whether every eucharistic celebration would involve the footwashing.

(2) If the footwashing was observed in connection with the eucharist, then in all probability it preceded the Lord's Supper. John 13.1-30 is certainly open to such an interpretation. Of particular relevance are v.12, which describes Jesus as rejoining the meal, and v. 27, which records that the meal had been completed. According to the *Didache* (14), in some early Christian circles a period of confession of sin preceded the eucharist:

> 1. On the Lord's Day of the Lord come together, break bread and hold Eucharist, after confessing your transgressions that your offering may be pure; 2. but let none who has a quarrel with his fellow join in your meeting until they be reconciled, that your sacrifice be not defiled. 3. For this is that which was spoken by the Lord, 'In every place and time offer me a pure sacrifice, for I am a great King, 'saith the Lord, 'and my name is wonderful among the heathen'.[1]

---

1.   Cited according to the translation of Lake, *The Apostolic Fathers*, I, p. 331.

If the Johannine community's eucharistic celebration was anything like that described in the Didache, the footwashing would most easily fit at this point, serving as the sign that confessed sin was forgiven. The believer would then be able to sit at the Lord's table with a clear conscience.

(3) It is more than likely that the footwashing itself was carried out by all members of the community. Such participation would accord well with the commands of Jn 13.14-17 and also with the emphasis upon mutual intercession in 1 John. Since the confession of sin may have been a public one before the community,[1] the brotherly intercession could well have been quite specific in its petitions.[2]

It is not too difficult to envisage a footwashing of this sort in the context of the house church of the late first century.[3] The environment of the home, as well as the small number of people involved, would be conducive to such mutual confession and intercession.

---

1. Cf. Brown, *The Epistles of John*, p. 208.

2. If so, then perhaps the directive of 1 Jn 5.16-17, concerning sins for which believers should offer intercession and sins for which they should not, have to do with confessed (μὴ πρὸς θάνατον) and unconfessed (πρὸς θάνατον) sin. The confessed sin, which would be brought into the sight of the community, would not result in death owing to the prayers of the believers, while unconfessed sin would remain hidden and would result in death.

3. For information on the house church in the Johannine community cf. J. Lieu, *The Second and Third Epistles of John* (Edinburgh: T. & T. Clark, 1986), pp. 132-34.

Chapter 6

CONCLUSIONS AND IMPLICATIONS

This investigation has produced several results which make a contribution to scholarship on the footwashing pericope. The following enumeration of these points roughly follows the developmental order of the study.

First, the survey of prominent interpretations of footwashing offered in Chapter 1 serves to update the reviews of scholarship given by Richter and Lohse. This survey not only examines much of the materials cited by Richter and Lohse, but supplements their work by including most of the relevant literature since 1967.

Second, the textual problem in Jn 13.10 has received more attention here than in any previous study. Often, scholars have decided to exclude the phrase, εἰ μὴ τοὺς πόδας, for interpretative—rather than text critical—reasons. As a result, the meaning of the passage has been skewed. Instead of determining the sense of the passage first and allowing that meaning to determine the textual decision, this study has argued for the inclusion of εἰ μὴ τοὺς πόδας, on the basis of superior external evidence, as well as internal probability. Not only does this result force a reconsideration of the meaning of Jn 13.10 on the basis of the longer reading, but it is also essential for a more accurate reading of the footwashing pericope.

Third, in order to understand the meaning of footwashing in Jn 13.1-20, an extensive body of evidence on the function and meaning of footwashing in antiquity has been brought together. Although several scholars have admitted the need for such a collection, few have done more than cite a few examples of footwashing in antiquity when interpreting John 13. This study has compiled one of the most extensive catalogues of citations about footwashing in antiquity, and at the same time, has given the texts themselves in English translation. Such a compilation is available nowhere else. The endeavor is not without reward, for this survey informs a reading of Jn 13.1-20 at almost every point. One of the most significant of its findings is the discovery that footwashing in its many uses always denotes preparation of one kind or another. Not only does this finding help to unravel the significance of the footwashing in John 13, but it also explains why footwashing stands first in the farewell materials. By utilizing an act which signifies preparation, the author makes a smooth transition to the farewell discourses, which themselves prepare the disciples for Jesus' departure. In addition, this survey has located examples of individuals who without obligation wash the feet of another. In most of these cases, love is the motive for such action. Yet, despite the similarity to other footwashing motivated by love, Jesus' action as described in John 13 has been shown by this investigation to exhibit a unique nature, for this account of a superior voluntarily washing the feet of an inferior is without parallel in antiquity. Peter's mistaking the footwashing for an act of hospitality is understandable in the light of the fact that footwashing was a most common part of hospitality in antiquity.

Fourth, the place and function of the footwashing pericope in the narrative of the Fourth Gospel has been established. While the place of the pericope in the Book of Signs has been recognized by many scholars, the significance of its placement and its relationship to the farewell discourses proper has rarely been explored. This study has shown that the footwashing pericope is a strategic part of the farewell materials, for as an act of preparation it epitomizes the farewell discourses as a whole. It is the first part of the disciples' preparation for Jesus' departure, bringing cleansing to them. One of the implications of this study is that scholars must reassess the prevailing trend to examine the footwashing pericope in isolation from the farewell discourses and vice versa.

Fifth, the reading of John 13 offered in this study has demonstrated that the pericope need not be divided into two parts, but makes good sense as it stands. This result calls for a paradigm shift concerning assumptions about the literary unity of John 13, for many scholars feel obliged to find two contradictory interpretations of the footwashing in the pericope. This reading of the passage indicates that scholars must now take seriously the text as it stands rather than playing vv. 6-10 off against vv. 12-20. When the pericope is unnecessarily divided, the meaning of the footwashing for the community is inevitably distorted.

Sixth, reading Jn 13.1-20 as a literary unit has revealed that the footwashing is not an option for the disciples but a necessity if they are to maintain a share in Jesus' destiny. More particularly, footwashing conveys a cleansing that supplements the bath (baptism) that has earlier produced a more fundamental cleansing. The footwashing at Jesus' hands serves as a sign of continued fellowship with him and as an additional cleansing in the disciples' lives. When the commands to wash feet (13.14-17) are read in the light of vv. 6-10, it becomes clear that Jesus, as here portrayed, intends his followers to continue the practice of footwashing and for this practice to have a significance related to that of his own action.

Seventh, through use of the concept of implied readers in the Fourth Gospel, through exploration of actual readers of the Fourth Gospel in the early church, and through evidence of the practice of footwashing in early Christianity, this investigation has demonstrated the strong probability that the Johannine community engaged in the practice of footwashing as a religious rite. Despite the lack of scholarly reflection about this possibility, there is every reason to believe that footwashing was part of the community's life and practice. One of the major implications of this conclusion is that future scholarship must take the likelihood of this practice seriously, no longer ignoring the issue nor dismissing it as an unimportant aspect of the pericope. In fact, it would appear that future discussion of the Johannine community's distinctive beliefs and practice in general must make footwashing one of its prominent features.

Eighth, utilizing evidence similar to that used to establish the likelihood of the practice, this study has also shown that the most probable meaning of footwashing for the community has to do with the issue of post-conversion sin. Not only is this interpretation supported by the literary and exegetical analysis, by the interpretation of the pericope in the early church, and by the interpretations of those scholars who believe that the community engaged in such a rite, but it also dovetails neatly with the Johannine community's preoccupation with post-conversion sin, as evidenced in 1 John. This finding reveals that, at the very least, scholars have not taken a major interpretive option seriously enough, often mentioning a possible penitential interpretation of Jn 13.1-20 in a single sentence.

If, then, these are the major contributions of this investigation, what areas may be identified as fruitful topics for future research? Several questions present themselves for further consideration.

1. Since it appears that the footwashing tradition is at least as old as the Johannine community, one logical question is, does the footwashing tradition go back to the historical Jesus?

2. If the footwashing tradition is an ancient one, what accounts for its absence from the synoptic accounts?

3. What accounts for the differing responses to footwashing in the early church? Why, despite its prominent supporters, did it not come to be acknowledged by all as a necessary part of Christian worship?

4. If the footwashing did serve as a sacrament in the Johannine community, practiced by all (including women), what are the implications for the study of the roles of women in this community and more generally in the early church?

5. What would be revealed from a comparison between the Johannine community's response to post-conversion sin and the responses of other early Christian groups?

6. As this investigation has shown, literary criticism can bring a valuable balance to source criticism of the Fourth Gospel. Perhaps such a balance is needed not only in the case of Jn 13.1-20, but in other passages in the Fourth Gospel that may have been inadequately interpreted by critics too eager to identify sources.

7. A final question remains for those concerned with applying the results of biblical research to the life of the contemporary church. What is the theological relevance of the Johannine community's view of footwashing for contemporary Christian worship? Such a question is particularly important, for on the one hand, it would be wrong to dismiss footwashing as one would dismiss baptism for the dead, a practice based on one quite enigmatic verse (1 Cor. 15.29). On the other hand, there is clearly more direct biblical support for the practice of footwashing than for several later practices of the church, for example, the choice of Sunday rather than the Sabbath as the special day of worship. In any event, in the light of the evidence here presented, the issue of the relevance of footwashing for the contemporary church may well need reassessment.

SELECT BIBLIOGRAPHY

1. *Texts and Translations*

Ambrose, *Ambroise de Milan: Traité sur l'évangile de S. Luc*, I (ed. G. Tissot; Paris: Cerf, 1971).

—*Of the Holy Spirit*, trans. P. Schaff and H. Wace, in *Nicene and Post-Nicene Fathers*. X (Grand Rapids: Eerdmans, 1955).

—*The Sacraments*, trans. R.J. Deferrari, in *Saint Ambrose: Theological and Dogmatic Works* (Washington, DC: Catholic University Press of America, 1963).

Ammonius, *Fragmenta in S. Joannem*, in *Patrologia Graeca*, LXXXV (ed. J.P. Migne; Paris, 1858).

Apollonius Citiensis, *In Hippocratio De Articulis Commentarius* (ed. F. Kudlien; Berlin: Akademie Verlag, 1965).

Apostolic Constitutions, trans. A. Roberts and J. Donaldson, in *Ante-Nicene Fathers*, VII (Grand Rapids: Eerdmans, 1956).

Apuleius, *Apology*, trans. H.E. Butler, in *The Apology and Florida of Apuleius of Madaura* (Oxford: Clarendon Press, 1909).

Aristophanes, *Wasps*, trans. B.B. Rogers, in *Aeschylus, Sophocles, Euripides, and Aristophanes* (Chicago: Encyclopedia Britannica, 1952).

Athenaeus, *Deipnosophistes*, trans. C.B. Gulick, in *Athenaeus: The Deipnosophists*, IV, VI (London: Heinemann, 1969, 1937).

Augustine, *Homilies on John*, trans. P. Schaff, in *Nicene and Post-Nicene Fathers*, VII (Grand Rapids: Eerdmans, 1956).

—*Letters*, trans. P. Schaff, in *Nicene and Post-Nicene Fathers*, I (Grand Rapids: Eerdmans, 1952).

Basil, *Homilia Dicta Tempore Famis et Siccitatis*, in *Patrologia Graeca*, XXXI (ed. J.P. Migne; Paris, 1857).

Benedict of Nursia, *The Rule of Saint Benedict* (trans. J. McCann; London: Burns, Oates, and Washbourne, 1921).

Caesarius of Arles, *Saint Caesarius of Arles: Sermons* (trans. M.M. Mueller; 3 vols.; New York: Fathers of the Church, 1956–73).

The Canons of Athanasius of Alexandria (trans. W. Riedeland, W.E. Crum; London: Williams and Norgate, 1904).

Canons of the Synod of Elvira, in *The Synod of Elvira and Christian Life in the Fourth Century* (trans. A.S.S. Dale; London: Macmillan, 1882).

Catullus, *The Poems of Gaius Valerius Catullus* (trans. F.W. Cornish; Cambridge, MA: Harvard University Press, 1912).

Charlesworth, J.H. (ed.), *The Old Testament Pseudepigrapha* (2 vols.; Garden City, NY: Doubleday, 1983).

Clement of Alexandria, *Clement of Alexandria: Christ the Educator* (trans. S.P. Wood; New York: Fathers of the Church, 1954).

Cyprian, *Epistles*, trans. A. Roberts and J. Donaldson, in *Ante-Nicene Fathers*, V (Grand Rapids: Eerdmans, 1951).

Cyril of Alexandria, *Homilies on John's Gospel*, in *Patrologia Graeca*, LXXIV (ed. J.P. Migne; Paris, 1864).

Didache, trans. K. Lake, in *The Apostolic Fathers*, I (Cambridge, MA: Harvard University Press, 1912).

Epictetus, *The Discourses of Epictetus* (trans. G. Long; New York: A.L. Burt, 1897).

Eucherius, *Instructions*, in *Patrologia Latina*, L (ed. J.P. Migne; Paris, 1846).

Eusebius, *Eusebius: Ecclesiastical History* (trans. K. Lake, J.E.L. Oulton; 2 vols.; Cambridge, MA: Heinemann, 1923–25).

Fabius Pictor, *De Iure Sacerdotis*, in *Historicorum Romanorum Reliquiae*, I (ed. H. Peter; Stuttgart: Teubner, 1967).

Gregory the Great, *Saint Gregory the Great: Morals on the Book of Job* (trans. anon.; 2 vols.; London: Oxford University Press, 1845).

Gregory of Nyssa, *Gregorii Nysseni in Canticum Canticorum* (ed. H. Langerbeck; Leiden: Brill, 1960).

Herodotus, *History* in *Herodotus*, I, III (trans. A.D. Godley; Cambridge, MA: Harvard University Press, 1963–64).

Homer, *Homer: The Iliad* (trans. A.T. Murray; 2 vols.; Cambridge, MA: Harvard University Press, 1946).

—*Homer: The Odyssey* (trans. A.T. Murray; 2 vols.; London: Heinemann, 1919).

Ignatius, *Epistles to the Ephesians, Smyrneans, and Romans*, trans. K. Lake, in *The Apostolic Fathers*, I (Cambridge, MA: Harvard University Press, 1912).

Irenaeus, *Against Heresies*, trans. A. Roberts, J. Donaldson, in *Ante-Nicene Fathers*, I (Grand Rapids: Eerdmans, 1953).

Jerome, *The Letters of St Jerome.* I (trans. C.C. Mierow; New York: Newman Press, 1963).

John Cassian, *Institute of the Coenobia*, in *Nicene and Post-Nicene Fathers*, 2nd ser. (Grand Rapids: Eerdmans, 1964).

John Chrysostom, *Genesis Homily*, in *Patrologia Graeca*, LIII (ed. J.P. Migne; Paris, 1862).

—*Saint John Chrysostom: Commentary on Saint John the Apostle and Evangelist, Homilies 44-88* (trans. T.A. Goggin; New York: Fathers of the Church, 1960).

Josephus, *Josephus: Jewish Antiquities*, V (trans. H. St J.Thackeray, R. Marcus; Cambridge, MA: Harvard University Press, 1966).

Juvenal, *Juvenal: Satires* (trans. J. Mazzaro; Ann Arbor: University of Michigan Press, 1965).

Lucian, *Lucian: Demonax* (trans. A.M. Harmon; London: Heinemann, 1913).

Martial, *Martial: Epigrams*, I (trans. W.C.A. Ker; London: Heinemann, 1930).

Martyrdom of Polycarp, trans. C.C. Richardson, in *Early Christian Fathers* (New York: Macmillan, 1970).

Meleager, *Palatine Anthology*, in *The Greek Anthology*, IV (trans. W.R. Paton; Cambridge, MA: Harvard University Press, 1968).

The Mishnah (trans. H. Danby; London: Oxford University Press, 1974).

Origen, *Origenes Werke: Der Johanneskommentar* (ed. E. Preuschen; Leipzig: Hinrichs, 1903).

—*Origen: Homilies on Genesis and Exodus* (trans. R.E. Heine; Washington: Catholic University of America Press, 1982).

—*Origenes Werke*, VII (ed. W.A. Baehrens; Leipzig: Hinrichs, 1921).

—*In Librum Judicum*, trans. F.E. Warren, in *The Liturgy and Ritual of the Ante-Nicene Church* (London: SPCK, 1912).

Pachomias, *Pachomian Koinonia* (trans. A. Veilleux; Kalamazoo, MI: Cistercian Publications, 1981).

Paulinus of Nola, *Letters of Paulinus of Nola* (trans. P.G. Walks; New York: Newman, 1967).

Petronius, *Petronius: Satyricon* (trans. M. Heseltine; London: Heinemann, 1930).

Philo, *De Specialibus Legibus*, in *Philo*, VII (trans. F.H. Colson; London: Heinemann, 1968).

—*De Vita Mosis*, in *Philo*, VI (trans. F.H. Colson; London: Heinemann, 1966).

—*Philo: Questions and Answers on Genesis*, Supplement I (trans. R. Marcus; Cambridge, MA: Harvard University Press, 1971).

—*Philo: Questions and Answers on Exodus*, Supplement II (trans. R. Marcus; Cambridge, MA: Harvard University Press, 1970).

Plato, *Symposium*, in *Plato: Lysis, Symposium, Gorgias* (trans. W.R.M. Lamb; London: Heinemann, 1925).

Pliny, *Pliny: Natural History*, VII (trans. W.H.S. Jones, Cambridge, MA: Harvard University Press, 1956).

Plutarch, *Moralia, Bravery of Women*, in *Plutarch's Moralia*, III (trans. F.C. Babbitt; Cambridge, MA: Harvard University Press, 1968).

—*Plutarch's Lives*, I, V, VIII (trans. B. Perrin; New York: G.P. Putnam's Sons, 1914–19).

Polycarp, *Epistles to the Philippians*, in *Apostolic Fathers*, II (trans. K. Lake; London: Heinemann, 1913).

Seneca, *Seneca ad Lucilium Epistulae Morales*, II (trans. R.M. Gummerie; London: Heinemann, 1920).

Sozomen, *Ecclesiastical History*, trans. P. Schaff and H. Wace, in *Nicene and Post-Nicene Fathers*, II (Grand Rapids: Eerdmans, 1957).

Sparks, H.F.D. (ed.), *The Apocryphal Old Testament* (Oxford: Clarendon Press, 1984).

Sulpicius Severus, *Life of St Martin*, trans. P. Schaff and H. Wace, in *Nicene and Post-Nicene Fathers*, II (Grand Rapids: Eerdmans, 1957).

Tertullian, *The Apology*, trans. A. Roberts and J. Donaldson, in *Ante-Nicene Fathers*, III (Grand Rapids: Eerdmans, 1951).

—*On Baptism*, trans. A. Roberts and J. Donaldson, in *Ante-Nicene Fathers*, III (Grand Rapids: Eerdmans, 1951).

—*De Corona*, trans. A. Roberts and J. Donaldson, in *Ante-Nicene Fathers*, III (Grand Rapids: Eerdmans, 1951).

—*To His Wife*, trans. A. Roberts and J. Donaldson, in *Ante-Nicene Fathers*, III (Grand Rapids: Eerdmans, 1951).

Theodore of Mopsuestia, *Theodori Mopsuesteni: Commentarius in Evangelium Iohannis Apostoli* (ed. J.M. Voste; Louvain: Versio, 1940).

2. General and Reference Works

Bauer, W., *A Greek–English Lexicon of the New Testament and Other Early Christian Literature* (ed. W.F. Arndt, F.W. Gingrich; Cambridge: Cambridge University Press, 1952).

Blass, F. and A. Debrunner, *A Greek Grammar of the New Testament and Other Early Christian Literature* (ed. R.W. Funk; Chicago: Chicago University Press, 1961).

Brown, C. (ed.), *New International Dictionary of New Testament Theology* (4 vols.; Grand Rapids: Zondervan, 1978).

Brown, F., S.R. Driver and C.A. Briggs, *A Hebrew and English Lexicon of the Old Testament* (Oxford: Clarendon Press, 1976).

Chamberlain, W.D., *An Exegetical Grammar of the Greek New Testament* (Grand Rapids: Baker, 1941).

Kittel, G. and G. Friedrich (eds.), *Theological Dictionary of the New Testament* (trans. G.W. Bromiley; 10 vols.; Grand Rapids: Eerdmans, 1964–74).

Liddell, H.G. and R. Scott, *A Greek–English Lexicon* (Oxford: Clarendon Press, 1966).

3. Commentaries on the Fourth Gospel

Barrett, C.K., *The Gospel according to St John* (Philadelphia: Westminster Press, 1978).

Bauer, W., *Das Johannesevangelium* (Tübingen: Mohr, 1912).

Beeckman, P., *L'Evangile selon Saint Jean* (Paris: Beyaert–Bruges, 1951).

Bernard, H., *A Critical and Exegetical Commentary on the Gospel according to John* (2 vols.; Edinburgh: T. & T. Clark, 1928).

Brown, R.E., *The Gospel according to John* (2 vols.; Garden City, NY: Doubleday, 1966–70).

Bruce, F.F., *The Gospel of John* (Grand Rapids: Eerdmans, 1983).

Büchsel, F., *Das Evangelium nach Johannes* (Göttingen: Vandenhoeck & Ruprecht, 1946).

Bultmann, R., *The Gospel of John* (trans. G. Beasley-Murray; Philadelphia: Westminster Press, 1971).

Bussche, H. van den, *L'Evangile du Verbe* (2 vols.; Brussels: Pensée Catholique, 1961).

Carson, D.A., *The Gospel according to John* (Grand Rapids: Eerdmans, 1990).

Countryman, L.W., *The Mystical Way in the Fourth Gospel* (Philadelphia: Fortress Press, 1987).

Durand, A., *Evangile selon Saint Jean* (Paris: Beauchesne, 1927).

Godet, F., *Commentary on the Gospel of John*, III (trans. T. Dwight; New York: Funk & Wagnalls, 1888).

Goetmann, J., *Saint Jean* (Paris: Cerf, 1982).

Haenchen, E., *John*, II (trans. R.W. Funk; ed. R.W. Funk, U. Busse; Philadelphia: Fortress Press, 1984).

Hengstenberg, E.W., *The Gospel of St John*, II (Edinburgh: T. & T. Clark, 1865).

Hirsch, E., *Das vierte Evangelium* (Tübingen: Mohr–Siebeck, 1936).

Hoskyns, E.C. and F.M. Davey, *The Fourth Gospel* (London: Faber & Faber, 1956).

Hunter, A.M., *According to John* (London: SCM Press, 1968).

Kreyenbuhl, J., *Das Evangelium der Wahrheit*, II (Berlin: C.A. Schwetschke und Sohn, 1905).

Lagrange, M.J., *Evangile selon Saint Jean* (Paris: Gabalda, 1936).

Lightfoot, R.H., *St John's Gospel* (Oxford: Oxford University Press, 1960).

Lindars, B., *The Gospel of John* (London: Oliphants, 1972).
MacGregor, G.H.C., *The Gospel of John* (London: Harper, 1959).
Marsh, J., *The Gospel of St John* (London: Penguin Books, 1968).
Michaels, J.R., *John* (New York: Harper & Row, 1984).
Mollat, D. *L'Evangile de Saint Jean* (Paris: Cerf, 1960).
Morris, L., *The Gospel according to John* (Grand Rapids: Eerdmans, 1971).
Sanders, J.N., *A Commentary on the Gospel according to St John* (ed. B.A. Mastin; London: A. & C. Black, 1968).
Schick, E., *Das Evangelium nach Johannes* (Würzburg: Echter, 1967).
Schnackenburg, R., *The Gospel according to St John* (trans. D. Smith, G.A. Kon; 3 vols.; New York: Crossroad, 1987).
Strachan, R.H., *The Fourth Gospel* (London: SCM Press, 1960).
Strathmann, H., *Das Evangelium nach Johannes* (Göttingen: Vandenhoeck & Ruprecht, 1959).
Tasker, R.V.G., *The Gospel according to St John* (Grand Rapids: Eerdmans, 1965).
Tillmann, F., *Das Johannesevangelium* (Bonn: Hanstein, 1931).
Westcott, B.F., *The Gospel according to St John* (Grand Rapids: Eerdmans, 1975).
Wikenhauser, A., *Das Evangelium nach Johannes* (Regensburg: Pustet, 1957).
Zahn, T., *Das Evangelium des Johannes* (Leipzig: Deichert, 1921).

4. *Commentaries on Other Biblical Books*

Ackroyd, P.R., *The Second Book of Samuel* (Cambridge: Cambridge University Press, 1977).
Anderson, A.A., *Psalms*, I (London: Oliphants, 1975).
Barrett, C.K., *The First Epistle to the Corinthians* (New York: Harper & Row, 1968).
—*The Pastoral Epistles* (Oxford: Clarendon Press, 1963).
Borse, U., *1. und 2. Timotheusbrief, Titusbrief* (Stuttgart: Katholisches Bibelwerk, 1986).
Briggs, C.A. and E.G. Briggs, *The Book of Psalms*, II (Edinburgh: T. & T. Clark, 1907).
Brown, R.E., *The Epistles of John* (Garden City, NY: Doubleday, 1982).
Brox, N., *Die Pastoralbriefe* (Regensburg: Pustet, 1969).
Bürki, H., *Der erste Brief des Paulus an Timotheus* (Wuppertal: Brockhaus, 1974).
Carr, G.L., *The Song of Solomon* (Downers Grove, IL: InterVarsity, 1984).
Conzelmann, H., *1 Corinthians* (Philadelphia: Fortress Press, 1975).
Dibelius, M. and H. Conzelmann, *The Pastoral Epistles* (Philadelphia: Fortress Press, 1972).
Donier, P., *Les Epîtres Pastorales* (Paris: Gabalda, 1969).
Eaton, J.H., *Psalms* (London: SCM Press, 1967).
Fee, G.D., *1 and 2 Timothy, Titus* (San Francisco: Harper & Row, 1984).
Ginsburg, C.D., *The Song of Songs* (New York: Ktav, 1970).
Guthrie, D., *The Pastoral Epistles* (Grand Rapids: Eerdmans, 1957).
Hertzberg, H.W., *1 and 2 Samuel* (trans. J.S. Bowden; Philadelphia: Westminster Press, 1964).
Holtz, G., *Die Pastoralbriefe* (Berlin: Evangelische Verlagsanstalt, 1972).
Hyatt, J.P., *Exodus* (Grand Rapids: Eerdmans, 1980).
Keil, C.F. and F. Delitzsch, *Commentary on the Old Testament in Ten Volumes* (trans J. Martin; Grand Rapids: Eerdmans, 1975).

Kent, H.A., Jr, *The Pastoral Epistles* (Chicago: Moody, 1982).

Kidner, D., *Psalms 1–72* (Downers Grove, IL: InterVarsity, 1978).

Kelly, J.N.D., *A Commentary on the Pastoral Epistles* (New York: Harper & Row, 1963).

Lieu, J., *The Second and Third Epistles of John* (Edinburgh: T. & T. Clark, 1989).

Marshall, I.H., *The Epistles of John* (Grand Rapids: Eerdmans, 1978).

Mauchline, J., *1 and 2 Samuel* (London: Oliphants, 1967).

McCarter, P.K., Jr, *2 Samuel* (Garden City, NY: Doubleday, 1984).

Noth, M., *Exodus* (trans. J.S. Bowden; Philadelphia: Westminster Press, 1962).

Pope, M.H., *The Song of Songs* (Garden City, NY: Doubleday, 1977).

Ridderbos, H., *De Pastorale Brieven* (Kampen: Kok, 1967).

Roloff, J., *Der erste Brief an Timotheus* (Zurich: Benzinger Verlag, 1988).

Schnackenburg, R., *Die Johannesbriefe* (Freiburg: Herder, 1975).

Smalley, S.S., *1, 2, 3 John* (Waco, TX: Word, 1984).

Smith, H.P., *A Critical and Exegetical Commentary on the Books of Samuel* (Edinburgh: T. & T. Clark, 1899).

Spicq, C., *Les Epîtres Pastorales* (Paris: Gabalda, 1947).

Stott, J.R.W., *The Letters of John* (Grand Rapids: Eerdmans, 1988).

Wenham, G.J., *The Book of Leviticus* (Grand Rapids: Eerdmans, 1979).

Westermann, C., *Genesis 12–36: A Commentary* (trans. J.J. Scullion; Minneapolis: Augsburg, 1985).

White, N.J.D., *The First and Second Epistles to Timothy and the Epistle to Titus* (Grand Rapids: Eerdmans, 1910).

5. Special Studies

Ahr, P.G., 'He Loved Them to Completion?: The Theology of John 13–14', in *Standing Before God: Studies on Prayer in Scripture and in Tradition* (ed. A. Finkel, L. Frizzell; New York: Ktav, 1981), pp. 73-89.

Barrett, C.K., *Church, Ministry, and Sacraments in the New Testament* (Exeter: Paternoster Press, 1985).

—*Essay on John* (Philadelphia: Westminster Press, 1982).

Barth, M., *Die Taufe—ein Sakrament? Ein exegetischer Beitrag zum Gespräch über die kirchliche Taufe* (Zürich: Evangelischer Verlag, 1951).

Beasley-Murray, G., *Baptism in the New Testament* (Grand Rapids: Eerdmans, 1973).

Behler, G.-M., *Les paroles d'adieux du Seigneur* (Paris: Cerf, 1960).

Benoit, P., 'Die eucharistischen Einsetzungsberichte und ihre Bedeutung', in *Exegese und Theologie: Gesammelte Aufsätze* (Düsseldorf: Patmos, 1965).

Bornhäuser, K., *Das Johannesevangelium eine Missionschrift für Israel* (Gütersloh: Bertelsmann, 1928).

Brown, R.E., *The Community of the Beloved Disciple* (New York: Paulist Press, 1979).

—*New Testament Essays* (New York: Paulist Press, 1965).

Brown, R.E., K.P. Donfried, and J. Reumann, *Peter in the New Testament* (Minneapolis: Augsburg, 1973).

Burge, G.M., *The Anointed Community: The Holy Spirit in the Johannine Tradition* (Grand Rapids: Eerdmans, 1987).

Corell, A., *Consummatum est: Eschatology and Church in the Gospel of St John* (London: SPCK, 1958).

Crowfoot, J.W., G.M. Crowfoot, and K.M. Kenyon, *The Objects from Samaria* (London: Palestine Exploration Fund, 1957).

Cullmann, O., *Early Christian Worship* (ed. A.S. Todd, J.B. Torrance; London: SCM Press, 1953).

Culpepper, R.A., *Anatomy of the Fourth Gospel* (Philadelphia: Fortress Press, 1983).

Daniélou, J., *The Bible and the Liturgy* (Notre Dame: Notre Dame Press, 1956).

Daube, D., *The New Testament and Rabbinic Judaism* (New York: Arbo, 1973).

Dodd, C.H., *Historical Tradition in the Fourth Gospel* (Cambridge: Cambridge University Press, 1963).

—*The Interpretation of the Fourth Gospel* (Cambridge: Cambridge University Press, 1970).

Douglas, M., *Purity and Danger* (London: Routledge & Kegan Paul, 1966).

Edwards, R.A., *The Gospel according to John: Its Criticism and Interpretation* (London: Eyre & Spottiswoode, 1954).

Ellis, E.E., *Paul and his Recent Interpreters* (Grand Rapids: Eerdmans, 1961).

Farag, W., 'Religious Footwashing in Doctrine and Practice with Special Reference to Christianity' (Dissertation, Dropsie University, 1970).

Fenton, J.C., *The Passion according to John* (London: SPCK, 1961).

Feuillet, A., *Johannine Studies* (trans. T.E. Crane; New York: Alba House, 1965).

Fiorenza, E. Schüssler, *In Memory of Her* (New York: Crossroad, 1983).

Fortna, R.T., *The Fourth Gospel and its Predecessor* (Edinburgh: T. & T. Clark, 1989).

Gärtner, B., *Iscariot* (Philadelphia: Fortress Press, 1971).

Godwin, J., *Mystery Religions in the Ancient World* (San Francisco: Harper & Row, 1981).

Goppelt, L., *Theology of the New Testament*, I (ed. J. Roloff; trans. J. Alsup; Grand Rapids: Eerdmans, 1981).

Grant, M., *The Art and Life of Pompeii and Herculaneum* (New York: Newsweek, 1979).

Grelot, P., 'L'interprétation penitentielle du lavement des pieds', in *L'homme devant Dieu. I. Mélanges offerts au père Henri Lubac* (Paris: Aubier, 1963), pp. 75-91.

Grill, J., *Untersuchungen über die Entstehung des vierten Evangeliums*, II (Tübingen: Mohr–Siebeck, 1923).

Grundmann, W., *Zeugnis und Gestalt des Johannesevangelium* (Stuttgart: Calwer, 1961).

Guthrie, D., *New Testament Introduction* (Downers Grove, IL: InterVarsity, 1970).

Harrison, P.N., *The Problem of the Pastoral Epistles* (London: Oxford University Press, 1921).

Hengel, M., *Crucifixion* (trans. J. Bowden; Philadelphia: Fortress Press, 1977).

Higgins, A.J.B., *The Lord's Supper in the New Testament* (London: SCM Press, 1952).

Howard, W.F., *Christianity according to St John* (London: Duckworth, 1958).

—*The Fourth Gospel in Recent Criticism and Interpretation* (London: Epworth, 1955).

Huby, J., *Le discours de Jésus après la cêne suivi d'une étude sur la connaissance de foi dans saint Jean* (Paris: Beauchesne, 1951).

Jeremias, J., *The Unknown Sayings of Jesus* (trans. R. Fuller; London: SPCK, 1964).

Jonge, M.de, *Jesus: Stranger from Heaven and Son of God* (trans. and ed. J.E. Stecley; Missoula, MT: Scholars Press, 1977).

Joüon, P., *L'évangile de notre Seigneur Jésus-Christ* (Paris: Gabalda, 1930).

Käsemann, E., *Essays on the New Testament* (Philadelphia: Fortress Press, 1982).

Kelly, J.N.D., *Early Christian Doctrine* (London: A. & C. Black, 1977).

Klos, H., *Die Sakramente im Johannesevangelium: Vorkommen und Busse im vierten Evangelium* (Stuttgarter Bibelstudien, 46; Stuttgart: Katholisches Bibelwerk, 1970).

Kötting, B., 'Fusswaschung', in *Reallexicon für Antike und Christentum*, VIII (ed. T. Klauser; Stuttgart: Hierseman, 1950–), pp. 743-59.

Kysar, R., *The Fourth Evangelist and his Gospel* (Minneapolis: Augsburg, 1975).

Lohse, W., 'Die Fusswaschung (Joh 13.1-20); Eine Geschichte ihrer Deutung' (Dissertation, Friedrich-Alexander-Universitat zu Erlangen–Nurnberg, 1967).

Martin, R.P., *New Testament Foundations*, I (Exeter: Paternoster Press, 1975).

Maynard, A., 'The Function of Apparent Synonyms and Ambiguous Words in the Fourth Gospel' (Dissertation, University of Southern California, 1950).

Meeks, W.A., *The First Urban Christians* (New York: Yale University Press, 1983).

Menoud, P.H., *L'Evangile de Jean d'après les recherches récentes* (Paris: Delachaux et Niestlé, 1943).

Metzger, B.M., *The Text of the New Testament* (Oxford: Oxford University Press, 1968).

—*A Textual Commentary on the Greek New Testament* (London: United Bible Societies, 1971).

Michaelis, W., *Die Sakramente in Johannesevangelium* (Bern: BEG, 1946).

Mlakuzhyil, G., *The Christocentric Literary Structure of the Fourth Gospel* (Rome: Pontifical Biblical Institute, 1987).

Moule, C.F.D., 'The Judgment Theme in the Sacraments', in *The Background of the New Testament and its Eschatology* (ed. W.D. Davies, D. Daube; Cambridge: Cambridge University Press, 1964).

Munck, J., 'Discours d'adieu dans le Nouveau Testament et dans la littérature biblique', in *Aux sources de la tradition chrétienne* (ed. O. Cullmann, P.H. Menoud; Neuchâtel: Delachaux et Niestlé, 1950).

Neufeld, E., 'Hygiene Conditions in Ancient Israel (Iron Age)', in *Biblical Archaeologist Reader*, IV (ed. E.F. Campbell, Jr, D.N. Freedman; Sheffield: Almond Press, 1983).

Neusner, J., *A History of the Mishnaic Law of Purities: Part Twenty-two: The Mishnaic System of Uncleanness* (Leiden: Brill, 1977).

—*Judaism: The Evidence of Mishnah* (Chicago: University of Chicago Press, 1981).

Niewalda, P., *Sakramentssymbolik im Johannesevangelium* (Limburg: Lahn, 1958).

Owanga-Welo, J., 'The Function and Meaning of the Johannine Passion Narrative: A Structural Approach' (Dissertation, Emory University, 1980).

Rad, G. von, *Der heilige Krieg im alten Israel* (Göttingen: Vandenhoeck & Ruprecht, 1958).

Reim, G., *Studien zum alttestamentlichen Hintergrund des Johannesevangeliums* (Cambridge: Cambridge University Press, 1974).

Richter, G., *Die Fusswaschung im Johannesevangelium* (Regensburg: Pustet, 1967).

Robinson, J.A.T., 'The Significance of the Foot-Washing', *Neotestamentica et Patristica* (ed. A.N. Wilder, *et al.*; Leiden: Brill, 1962), pp. 144-47.

Schnackenburg, R., 'Die Sakramente im Johannesevangelium', in *Sacra Pagina: Miscellanea Biblica Congressus Internationalis Catholici de Re Biblica*, II (ed. J. Coppens, E. Massaux; Paris–Gembloux, 1959), pp. 235-54.

Schoedel, W.R., *Ignatius of Antioch* (Philadelphia: Fortress Press, 1985).

Scholer, D.M., 'Sins Within and Sins Without: An Interpretation of 1 John 5.16-17', in *Current Issues in Biblical and Patristic Interpretation* (ed. G. Hawthorne; Grand Rapids: Eerdmans, 1975), pp. 230-46.

Schultz, J., *The Soul of the Symbols* (Grand Rapids: Eerdmans, 1966).

Schulz, A., *Nachfolgen und Nachahmen* (Munich: Kösel, 1962).

Schweitzer, A., *The Mysticism of Paul the Apostle* (trans. W. Montgomery; New York: Holt, 1931).

Scott, E.F., *The Fourth Gospel, its Purpose and Theology* (Edinburgh: T. & T. Clark, 1920).

Segovia, F.F., 'Discipleship in the Fourth Gospel', in *Discipleship in the New Testament* (ed. F.F. Segovia; Philadelphia: Fortress Press, 1985), pp. 76-102.

—*Love Relationships in the Johannine Tradition* (Chico; CA: Scholars Press, 1982).

Sickenberger, J., *Leben Jesu nach den vier Evangelien* (Kurzgefasste Erklärung, 6; Münster: Aschendorff, 1932).

Smalley, S.S., *John: Evangelist and Interpreter* (Nashville: Nelson, 1984).

Solages, B. de, *Jean et les Synoptiques* (Leiden: Brill, 1979).

Spitta, F., *Das Johannes-Evàngelium als Quelle der Geschichte Jesu* (Göttingen: Vandenhoeck & Ruprecht, 1910).

Stählin, W., *Das johanneische Denken: Eine Einführung in die Eigenart das vierten Evangeliums* (Witten: Luther-Verlag, 1954).

Staley, J.L., *The Print's First Kiss* (Atlanta: Scholars Press, 1988).

Stauffer, E., *New Testament Theology* (trans. J. Marsh; London: SCM Press, 1955).

Streeter, B.H., *The Four Gospels: A Study of Origins* (London: Macmillan, 1961).

Sudhoff, K., *Aus dem antiken Badewesen. Medizinisch-kulturgeschichtliche Studien an Vasenbildern* (Berlin: Allgemeine Medizinische Verlagsanstalt, 1910).

Taylor, V., *Jesus and his Sacrifice* (London: Macmillan, 1959).

Theissen, G., *The Social Setting of Pauline Christianity* (Philadelphia: Fortress Press, 1982).

Thurston, B.B., *The Widows: A Women's Ministry in the Early Church* (Philadelphia: Fortress Press, 1989).

Thüsing, W., *Die Erhöhung und Verherrlichung Jesu im Johannesevangelium* (Münster: Aschendorff, 1960).

Verner, D.C., *The Household of God: The Social World of the Pastoral Epistles* (Chico, CA: Scholars Press, 1983).

Volger, W., *Judas Iskarioth* (Berlin: Evangelische Verlagsanstalt, 1983).

Warnach, V., *Agape: Die Liebe als Grundmotiv der neutestamentlichen Theologie* (Düsseldorf: Patmos, 1951).

Werner, M., *The Formation of Christian Dogma* (trans. S.G.F. Brandon; London: A. & C. Black, 1957).

Whitacre, R.A., *Johannine Polemic: The Role of Tradition and Theology* (Chico, CA: Scholars Press, 1982).

Wilkens, W., *Die Entstehungsgeschichte des vierten Evangeliums* (Zollikon: Evangelischer Verlag, 1958).

Windisch, H., *Johannes und die Synoptiker* (Leipzig: Hinrichs, 1926).

—*Taufe und Sunde im ältesten Christentum bis auf Origenes* (Tübingen: Mohr–Siebeck, 1908).

Zweifel, B., 'Jésus lave les pieds de ses disciples' (Thesis, Lausanne University, 1965).

6. Periodical Literature

Bacon, B.W., 'The Sacrament of Footwashing', *ExpT* 43 (1931–32), pp. 218-21.

Bangerter, O., 'Les veuves des épîtres pastorales, modèle d'un ministère féminin dans l'église ancienne', *Foi et Vie* 83 (1984), pp. 27-45.

Betz, O., 'Die Proselytentaufe der Qumransekte und die Taufe im NT', *RQ* 1 (1958), pp. 213-324.

Bishop, E.F., ' "He that eateth bread with me hath lifted up his heel against me"—Jn xiii. 18 (Ps xli. 9)', *ExpT* 70 (1958–59), pp. 331-33.

Boismard, M.-E., 'Le lavement des pieds (Jn, XIII, 1-17)', *RB* 71 (1964), pp. 5-24.

Bornkamm, G., 'Die eucharistische Rede im Johannes-Evangelium', *ZNW* 47 (1956), pp. 161-69.

Braun, F.M., 'Le lavement des pieds et la réponse de Jésus à saint Pierre (Jean XIII, 4-10)', *RB* 44 (1935), pp. 22-33.

Brooks, O.S., 'The Johannine Eucharist: Another Interpretation', *JBL* 82 (1963), pp. 298-99.

Campenhausen, H. von, 'Zur Auslegung von Joh 13, 6-10', *ZNW* 33 (1934), pp. 259-71.

Craig, C.T., 'Sacramental Interest in the Fourth Gospel', *JBL* 58 (1939), pp. 36-39.

Dobschütz, E. von, 'Zum Charakter des 4. Evangeliums', *ZNW* 28 (1929), pp. 161-77.

Dreyfus, P., 'Le thème de l'héritage dans l'Ancien Testament', *RSPT* 42 (1958), pp. 3-49.

Dunn, J.D.G., 'The Washing of the Disciples' Feet in John 13.1-20', *ZNW* 61 (1970), pp. 247-52.

Fiebig, P., 'Die Fusswaschung', *Angelos* 3 (1930), pp. 121-28.

Fridrichsen, A., 'Bemerkungen zur Fusswaschung', *ZNW* 38 (1939), pp. 94-96.

Grossouw, W.K., 'A Note on John XIII 1-3', *NovT* 8 (1966), pp. 124-31.

Hein, K., 'Judas Iscariot: Key to the Last Supper Narratives?', *NTS* 17 (1970–71), pp. 227-32.

Hodges, Z., 'Water and Spirit—John 3.5', *BibSac* 135 (1978), pp. 206-20.

Hultgren, A.J., 'The Johannine Footwashing (13.1-11) as Symbol of Eschatological Hospitality', *NTS* 28 (1982), pp. 539-46.

Jimenez, R.M., 'El discípulo de Jesucristo, según el evangelio de S. Juan', *EstBíb* 30 (1971), pp. 269-311.

Kaefer, J. P., 'Les discourses d'adieu en Jean 13.31–17.26: rédaction et théologie', *NovT* 26 (1984), pp. 253-82.

Knox, W.L., 'John 13.1-30', *HTR* 43 (1950), pp. 161-63.

Koch, W., 'Zur Einsetzung des Busssakraments', *ThQ* 130 (1950), pp. 296-310.

Koester, H., 'Geschichte und Kultus im Johannesevangelium und bei Ignatius und Sacrament im Johannesevangelium', *NTS* 7 (1960–61), pp. 110-25.

Kundsin, K., 'Die Wiederkunft Jesu in den Abschiedsreden des Johannesevangeliums', *ZNW* 33 (1934), pp. 210-15.

Lohmeyer, E., 'Die Fusswaschung', *ZNW* 38 (1939), pp. 74-94.

MacGregor, G.H.C., 'The Eucharist in the Fourth Gospel', *NTS* 9 (1963), pp. 111-19.

Manns, F. 'Le lavement de pieds. Essai sur la structure et la signification de Jean 13', *RSR* 55 (1981), pp. 149-69.

Matasunaga, K., 'Is John's Gospel Anti-Sacramental?—A New Solution in the Light of the Evangelist's Milieu', *NTS* 27 (1981), pp. 516-24.

Maynard, A., 'The Role of Peter in the Fourth Gospel', *NTS* 30 (1984), pp. 531-48.

Meeks, W.A., 'And Rose Up to Play: Midrash and Paraenesis in 1 Corinthians 10.1-22', *JSNT* 16 (1982), pp. 64-78.

Metzger, B.M.,'A Reconsideration of Certain Arguments against the Pauline Authorship of the Pastoral Epistles', *ExpT* 70 (1958), pp. 91-101.

Michaels, J.R., 'John 12.1-22', *Int* 43 (1989), pp. 287-91.

Michl, J., 'Der Sinn der Fusswaschung', *Bib* 40 (1959), pp. 697-708.

Miline, M.J., 'A Greek Footbath in the Metropolitan Museum of Art', *AJA* 48 (1944), pp. 26-63.

Moore, W.E., 'One Baptism', *NTS* 10 (1964), pp. 504-16.

Mussner, F., 'Die Fusswaschung (John 13.1-17): Versuch einer Deutung', *Geist und Leben* 31 (1958), pp. 25-30.

Painter, J., 'The Farewell Discourses and the History of Johannine Christianity', *NTS* 27 (1980-81), pp. 525-43.

Perrot, C., 'Les examples du désert (1 Co. 10.6-11)', *NTS* 29 (1983), pp. 437-52.

Richter, G., 'Die Fusswaschung Joh 13.1-20', *MTZ* 16 (1965), pp. 13-26.

—'The Washing of Feet in John 13.1-20', *TD* 14 (1966), pp. 200-205.

Schneiders, S.M., 'The Foot Washing (John 13.1-20): An Experiment in Hermeneutics', *CBQ* 43 (1981), pp. 76-92.

Schweizer, E., 'Das johanneische Zeugnis von Herrenmahl', *EvT* 12 (1952-53), pp. 341-63.

Segovia, F.F., 'John 13.1-20, The Footwashing in the Johannine Tradition', *ZNW* 73 (1982), pp. 31-51.

Simon, U., 'The Poor Man's Ewe-Lamb. An Example of a Juridical Parable', *Bib* 48 (1967), pp. 207-42.

Suggit, J.N., 'John 13.1-30: The mystery of the Incarnation and of the Eucharist', *Neot* 19 (1985), pp. 64-70.

Swetnam, J., 'A Review of Georg Richter, *Die Fusswaschung im Johannesevangelium. Geschichte ihrer Deutung*', *Bib* 49 (1968), pp. 439-46.

Vawter, B., 'The Johannine Sacramentary', *TS* 17 (1956), pp. 151-66.

Weiser, A., 'Joh 13, 12-20: Zufügung eines späteren Herausgebers?', *BZ* 12 (1968), pp. 252-57.

Weiss, H., 'Footwashing in the Johannine Community', *NovT* 21 (1979), pp. 298-325.

Wojciechowski, M., 'La source de Jean 13.1-20', *NTS* 34 (1988), pp. 135-41.

7. *Other Works on Footwashing*

Clevinger, D., 'The Role of Footwashing in John' (ThM Thesis, Dallas Theological Seminary, 1984).

Derrett, J.D.M., 'Domine, tu mihi lavas pedes (Studio su Giovanni 13.1-30)', *BO* 21 (1979), pp. 12-42.

Eisler, R., 'Zur Fusswaschung am Tage vor den Passah', *ZNW* 14 (1913), pp. 268-71.

Genuyt, F., 'Les deux bains: analyse sémiotique de Jean 13', *SB* 25 (1982), pp. 1-21.

Giess, H., *Die Darstellung der Fusswaschung Christi in den Kunstwerken des 4–12 Jahrhunderts* (Rome: Herder, 1962).

Haring, N.M., 'Historical Notes on the Interpretation of John 13.10', *CBQ* 13 (1951), pp. 355-80.

Jaubert, A., 'Une lecture du lavement des pieds', *Muséon* 79 (1966), pp. 257-86.

Kassing, P. and M. Laach, 'Das Evangelium der Fusswaschung', *Erbe und Auftrag* 36 (1960), pp. 83-93.

Lazure, N., 'Le lavement des pieds. Jn 13.1-15', *AsSeign* 20 (1973), pp. 53-64.

Linzey, A., 'The Significance of Feet Washing in John' (MDiv Thesis, Grace Theological Seminary, 1985).

Maness, P.G., 'Essays on Feetwashing' (Southern Baptist Theological Seminary, 1989).

—'Feet Washing' (Dissertation, Southern Baptist Theological Seminary, 1989).

Nicol, G.G., 'Jesus' Washing the Feet of the Disciples: A Model for Johannine Christology?', *ExpT* 91 (1979), pp. 20-21.

Rhodes, D.R., 'The Service of the Washing of Feet on Holy Thursday' (MDiv Thesis, St Vladimir's Seminary, 1977).

INDEXES

INDEX OF REFERENCES

OLD TESTAMENT

INDEX OF AUTHORS